mary
kennedy
Paper Tigers

mary
kennedy
Paper Tigers

MERLIN
PUBLISHING

First published in 2003 by
Merlin Publishing
16 Upper Pembroke Street
Dublin 2, Ireland
Tel: + 353 1 6764373
Fax: + 353 1 6764368
publishing@merlin.ie
www.merlin-publishing.com

ISBN 1–903582–55–5

A CIP catalogue record for this book is available
from the British Library.

10 9 8 7 6 5 4 3 2

Typeset by Carrigboy Typesetting Services
Cover design by Graham Thew Design
Cover Image courtesy of Colm Henry Photography
Printed and bound in Denmark, by Nørhaven Paperback A/S

'For my mother whose love
is all around us still.'

Contents

Setting the Scene

During the summer, I recorded an interview for TG4 and one of the questions I was asked sparked a trail of thought that forced me to view my life from the outside, looking in. I was shown a photograph of myself at about eight years of age and asked; 'What would that girl think of the woman sitting here today?' It was a good question. I answered that I hoped she would feel that the woman had lived an interesting, fulfilling life; had availed of all the opportunities presented to her along the way and had overcome obstacles rather than let them get the better of her. Driving home after the interview, my thoughts drifted back to the time that photograph of me and my grandmother in the sitting room in Brigid's Road in Clondalkin, where I grew up, was taken. I found it hard to fully understand that that little girl was actually me. We tend to think of ourselves as the way we are in the present day so for me the young person in the photograph seemed like somebody else altogether. Little did she know what destiny had in store for her: the good times, the bad times; happiness, sadness; success, failure; new life and death. In fact if my memory of the time that photo was taken serves me correctly, my major preoccupation revolved around the pain of having to sleep with hairclips digging into my head as my mother tried to get curls into my straight pudding bowl hairstyle for the photo. I also hated having to wear those dresses with puff sleeves, which I now think are very sweet. And I'm sure I was chomping at the bit to get back out to play with the other kids on the road. Having photos taken wasn't a spontaneous or stress free interlude in those days. For a start, very few people had cameras, so the session was planned in advance and because there were two families of us, living side by side, the duration was at least doubled.

Let me tell you about my family's set up. My mother and her sister Eilish had had a double wedding and bought houses beside each other out in Clondalkin when it was a tiny village on the outskirts of Dublin. They had grown up in the city, near the cattle markets on the North Circular Road and so moving out to Clondalkin was like moving to the country for them. But they had a wonderful life there and so did we children. The first thing the two couples did when they got back from their honeymoons (they did have separate honeymoons!) was to knock down some of the low back wall between the two houses to make a stile so that we could walk easily from one house to the other.

A year after my parents were married, I was born and three months later, Auntie Eilish had her first baby, William. Two years later, Auntie Eilish had Brian and two months later, Mam had John. Three years after that, Auntie Eilish had Barry and one year later again, Mam gave birth to Deirdre. Then 18 months later, Tony was born. It seemed perfectly normal to all of us to have cousins next door who were really like brothers who lived in a different house.

I'm glad now though that my mother and my aunt organised those photo sessions because there's nothing like a photograph to bring back memories of occasions and special moments. It's ironic, given the long suffering expression on my face in a lot of the photos taken in those early years that I developed a huge interest in taking photographs. I have albums going back to 1969, when I was given a present of my first instamatic camera. There are a lot of memories in those years of photos that are now catalogued and displayed and that give me great pleasure when I sit down and just pick out an album at random.

There's been a lot of living done and documented in those photo albums and although life has its ups and downs and can be very difficult at times it's made me what I am today, who I am today.

We're a bit like sponges progressing through life soaking up different information, experience and qualities along the way. Did that eight-year-old girl have any notion what experiences lay ahead of her? Did she ever think that she would go to the gaeltacht at twelve and be homesick for the first time in her life, or that she'd go to university and become a teacher of Irish and French? Did she dream that she'd spend a year in France? Could she have guessed that her father would die suddenly while she was there? Did she ever imagine that she'd marry and have four children and that marriage would end in separation? Or that she'd get a part-time job in RTÉ and would end up working there full-time? Did that girl ever picture herself visiting interesting places, did she have any idea that she'd know immense happiness and great sadness and meet some amazing people? No of course she didn't, how could she?

And does this woman look back at that photo of herself and wish she'd done things differently or that she'd grasped certain opportunities and allowed others to pass her by? No, because then I wouldn't be me. I'd be a different person if I had charted a different course through life. I cannot see the point in agonising over what might have been. As Saint Joan of Arc says in George Bernard

Shaw's play, 'If ifs and ands were pots and pans there'd be no need of tinkers'. My life has been rich at times, it's been difficult at times but the way we deal with what life places in our path is what makes us the people we are. At the moment my life is busy, fulfilling, interesting, challenging; not without difficulties. And those difficulties get me down at times. For the most part though I enjoy life. I make the most of it. I keep myself fit and I keep in touch with friends. Those are two essentials for me. I also remind myself that things can change very suddenly. What's a problem today can be solved tomorrow. Equally, some tragedy may befall us without any prior notice so it's important to live every moment of every day. Isn't it ironic and sadly prophetic that it was James Dean, who died so tragically and so young who said, 'Dream as if you'll live forever; live as if you'll die tomorrow.'

Lights, Camera, Action . . .

I have no doubt whatsoever that if that eight-year-old-girl in the photograph had been told that she would one day work in television she would have said in absolute disbelief 'Yeah, sure and pigs might fly'. You might just as well be trying to convince her that she would go to the moon one day. When I was growing up television was something that happened in Hollywood in my head. I remember watching programmes like *Mr Ed* and *Tammy* and drooling over the clothes and the lovely houses but it was a different world. One that I would never have aspired to although I did try unsuccessfully to do my hair like Tammy's. I don't have much recollection of early Irish television programmes but I do remember enjoying listening to Maureen Potter on the radio as we were having our Sunday lunch. For goodness sake, how could you have any notions of working in television when they wouldn't even read out your name on Santa's list on the radio on Christmas Eve. Every year I got whatever chores I had to do finished by lunchtime on Christmas Eve so that I could sit on a stool in the pantry and listen to see if my letter or even just my name would be read out. I sat there for hours every year and waited in vain. And every year my mother would say 'maybe next year'. It never happened. I guess this was a territory that was outside our ken as a family. I think that must be why, if I'm given a birthday request or special occasion to mention on TV I always try to include it because I know how thrilled I would have been to have heard my name read out all those years ago.

I suppose the Irish dancing classes, the elocution and the public speaking and debating were sewing the seeds and preparing the way for this kind of work in a way, although that wasn't the intention at all. I was sent to Irish dancing because I used to turn my toes in as I walked and to elocution because I was painfully shy. It's strange but true. The other two happened through school but all of them together gave me a confidence and got me used to performing in public, in front of an audience, up on a stage which can be a very scary place to be. I actually started off though in RTÉ quite by accident and without planning it at all. I saw an ad for part-time continuity announcers in the newspaper and decided I'd give it a go.

I'd just come back from France where I'd been teaching English for a year and was about to start a full-time job as a teacher of French and Irish at my alma mater Coláiste Bríde in Clondalkin. And I was looking for something else to do because I'd always worked while I was a student and I thought I'd have a lot of time on my hands if I only had one job. Then I saw the ad and I answered it. I wasn't hopeful because everybody said you had to know some-body who was somebody to get into RTÉ. Well, take it from me, that's not the case. I knew nobody. I couldn't even manage to get my name read out by Santa on Christmas Eve.

The selection process was rigorous and nerve wracking; each stage whittled down the numbers. The initial inter-view was okay. Then there was a camera test. I'd never stood in front of a camera in my life before. I nearly died of fright. I was over that hurdle and then I had another interview that made the camera test seem like a day out with friends. It was tough and I felt really out of my depth, coming from Clondalkin to those lofty environs of

Montrose in Dublin 4. I was on my own too. A bit of moral support would have helped but I had told nobody about this little adventure so that I wouldn't have to tell them when I was rejected, because I was so sure that I hadn't a hope. You could have knocked me over with a feather when the letter arrived to say that I'd been accepted for a two-week training course at the end of which there would be further auditions. Was there no end to this torture?

Six of us turned up on the first day and we worked hard for the two weeks. I learned so much on that course which is not surprising really when you consider that I knew absolutely nothing at the start of it. I was the equivalent of an artist's blank canvas. We were taught how to sit, stand, write scripts, get a message across in maybe ten seconds, and of course how to talk to camera. That was the hard part. To look into that black hole and perform as if you were talking to someone in the same room as you, having a chat, without all that technology and wires and flexes and power hopping off satellites or whatever it does and landing in the back of a television set in that person's home. We were taught strategies to help achieve this one-to-one type scenario. The course was run by Una Sheehy and Brigid Kilfeather, two women who were formidable presences in the beginning but who warmed up as we seemed to be making a bit of progress in the second week. They had very high standards of presentation and even after I got the job they were extremely vigilant because I'd often get little memos from Brigid Kilfeather after I'd done a continuity duty pointing out a mistake I'd made. I used to wonder if she ever went out at night. How come she always seemed to be watching TV when I was on? Such was my naïveté that I didn't realise this was all part of the follow up on the training course and that she'd be given a tape of my early performances to watch in her office so that she could keep an eye on me. She was after all Head of Speech Standards and although I used to hate to see her handwriting on an envelope addressed to me in the office I'm very glad she was so attentive. It kept me on my toes and made me very aware of getting the message across in an accessible and correct way. Her philosophy was that it was a mark of respect to the viewer and their right to expect that.

I enjoyed those early days of continuity announcing, after I got over my beginner's nerves. The very first shift I did was a momentous occasion for the whole family. I made my first announcement on a Saturday evening. It lasted 20 seconds and when it was over and the camera was off me I let out a big sigh and threw my eyes up to heaven in utter relief. Only the camera wasn't off me. There was a fade down of a second or two after I finished speaking so that sigh and my expression were captured on screen and on my Uncle Tom's cine camera. He had filmed it off the telly. Well you learn something new every day and every time you go on camera. There was great excitement in the family and one of my big regrets in life is that my Dad wasn't alive to enjoy it. He had died the year before and he would have been so proud. He was always encouraging me with debating and particularly public speaking and used to buy me books on the subject and books of essays and speeches to read. There was a bit of a performer in him too of course. He loved the amateur dramatics. There was also a part of him that would have taken satisfaction in the fact that a daughter of his had gone to college, had lived abroad and was now working part-time for RTÉ. He had left school after his Inter Cert and felt that every opportunity should be grasped and exploited fully. My mother was a totally different kettle of fish. She was probably more nervous than I was on that first day and she was certainly more nervous than I was in the years that followed. I feel nervous myself now when I'm sitting in the audience watching one of my children doing the Feis.

I used to look on a shift in continuity as a night out. I'd be teaching all day and then go in to start at six o'clock. I'd go to make-up and then get the script which would outline the programmes for the evening and the time to be filled between each one: 10 seconds, sometimes 20 and always a precise 30 seconds over the station clock coming up to the nine o'clock news. The atmosphere was very convivial. As well as the announcer there was the director, the sound engineer and the presentation assistant, who kept the time and logged everything during the evening, and in the studio there were two slide readers. Those were the days when at the end of each commercial break there were a few advertising slides and the accompanying script was read live in studio. Also in the presentation area was Master Control, which as the name suggests, steered the ship and kept it on course. Now the presentation situation is automated to the extent that there are two people working together, the announcer and the director. We had lots of laughs and endless cups of tea back then. The number of shifts increased when the staff announcers took time off for holidays. I got three months full-time work when Thelma Mansfield was on maternity leave. That was tough going, doing two full-time jobs for that length of time but I survived and the experience was invaluable. I also covered for Thelma when she had her second son and once for Máire deBarra's maternity leave.

Marian Finucane was there at the time too. She was the one who proposed me for membership of Equity.

As the flying hours increased, so too did the opportunities to present programmes. In 1981, I was Doireann Ni Bhriain's understudy when she presented the second ever Eurovision Song Contest to come from Ireland. That's part of a long Eurovision saga and needs a chapter to itself.

In the autumn of that year, RTÉ began making a monthly package of its output for transmission on cable television in the States. I was chosen to link these packages along with Seán Duignan and Brendan O'Reilly. The package would be made in the Montrose studios on the first Tuesday of every month. It was a great opportunity, certainly but how would I manage it with a full-time teaching job? I had resigned myself to turning the offer down when a friend suggested I just ask the school principal for the time off anyway. I wasn't hopeful and I also felt I was being a bit cheeky even asking. But as it happened the school principal, Sr Paul, also thought it was a great opportunity and bent over backwards to rearrange the timetable. I ended up teaching the first class on Tuesday mornings, racing out to RTÉ for ten o'clock and then back to school for the last class. I got to visit New York for that programme which was a great thrill. And to think I almost threw it away without trying. It was a lesson to me which I've often reminded myself of. If something is worth having, it's worth fighting for.

The following year I presented a summer bi-lingual chat show called *An Crúiscín Lán* which came from some lovely venues around the country, places like Kilkenny Castle and the Crawford College of Art and Design in Cork. One of the highlights for me was the opportunity to interview the actress Siobhán McKenna 'as Gaeilge'. She had beautiful Irish and wonderful stories to tell and I was so impressed by the way she carried herself. She glided into the room with her neck stretched and her head held high, like a swan. She was beautiful and theatrical and very warm and encouraging to me. That series provided my first insight into how the other half lives and boy did they live differently to me. I remember getting changed in Lady Pakenham's bedroom in Tullynally Castle, outside Castlepollard. I nearly fell out of my standing when I walked in. It was about the size of the whole of our house. I've gotten quite used to being in houses now that would easily accommodate a small village but that was my introduction to an existence that was as different to my own as if it were part of another planet. A number of years later when I was presenting another summer time programme called *A Stretch in the Evening*, the crew and I were being shown around the residence of Sheikh Muhammad in Kildangan Stud. My eyes were out on stalks as we went from one beautifully decorated room to the next. The camera man was getting a bit fed up with my oohs and aahs and when we got to the Sheikh's bedroom, complete with a four poster bed the size of a small football pitch, he turned to me and said, 'I'm sure you're relieved Mary, to know that he sleeps lying down, like the rest of us!' You can't beat an RTÉ crew for keeping you grounded.

Other opportunities that presented themselves to me in those early years included a stint at the Dublin Horse Show in '84. The whole of the Sports Department were off at the Los Angeles Olympics and they needed some-body at the RDS for the week. I learnt a lot about show jumping and about style that week. (I'll be talking about that further on in this book. Most of all though I learnt about 'winging it' as they say when an event finished sooner than expected for example and the time had to be filled. I was exhausted when the week was over. It was more great experience though. *Give Us a Chance* was a programme on subject choices for secondary school students. That was right up my alley because I was still teaching at the time. There were lots of music programmes over the years too and I enjoyed every one of them. From the *Listowel Fleadh Cheoil* to the *GPA Piano Competition*, to the *Opening Night Concert for Lyric FM* and many programmes of Christmas Carols from different parts of the country. The Fleadh in Listowel was a learning experience for me. I learnt that crews are a crowd of jokers and you've got to have your wits about you. The programme closed with me doing a piece to camera from the centre of Listowel at night. I was to say my piece and then turn around and walk away from the camera. So I did what I was told and I walked and I walked and I walked. I could have made it from Kerry to Cork if the director hadn't finally taken pity on me and told me to stop. I felt like a right eejit and the crew and the locals who had gathered in the street had a great laugh at my expense.

I took a career break from teaching when my third child, Eoin, was born in 1989. A while after his birth, I began to do a little bit more continuity, to keep the finger in and also because I genuinely enjoyed being in RTÉ and keeping in touch with everybody. In 1992, the newsroom advertised for part-time newscasters and I decided to give it a try. I was really delighted when I made the cut and what started out as an occasional shift in the newsroom soon became more and more frequent. I was in awe of the place. To an outsider passing by on the way to the coffee bar there always seemed to be an air of urgency about the newsroom. It was serious and important stuff that was happening behind those partitions. It's no wonder then that I was nervous as a kitten when I first ventured into the place. The shyness didn't last long though because you couldn't meet a nicer bunch of people. They were warm and welcoming and went out of their way to explain things to the newcomer. I had never used a word processor nor had I extracted news from the wires and I had never edited news packages. In fact the only thing I'd done before was the studio bit. The newsroom staff were helpful, patient and always checking to see that I was okay. Because of that, I've always been conscious of people coming into a situation for the first time and try to treat them in the same way I was treated when I started in the newsroom.

The work of the newsroom is undoubtedly serious and important stuff. There are frequent set deadlines and there can certainly be an air of urgency about the place at times but that doesn't mean there's no fun there. The people were great craic and I enjoyed every minute of my five years there. There was always a laugh to be had and some great nights out too. Workwise, I particularly liked editing packages for television news, where you'd sit with an editor and match the reporter's words with pictures, some of which the reporter would have sent back and others you'd get from the library. It was like making a patchwork quilt and I got a great sense of satisfaction when everything would fall into place and the words and the pictures would tell the story. I still love to watch those packages on the TV news and see the different ways they're edited.

The years I've spent in RTÉ have afforded me opportunities way beyond anything that eight-year-old would have aspired to in a million years. And yet they happened to that eight-year-old girl which makes me realise that anything is possible if you've got a fairly positive outlook on life, if you're prepared to take risks and if you're prepared to keep trying, even in the wake of defeat and failure.

'Only a man who knows what it is like to be defeated can reach down to the bottom of his soul and come up with the extra ounce of power it takes to win when the match is even.' Those are the words of Muhammad Ali, a hero to many when I was growing up. A fighter in every sense of the word, a flamboyant character in his day, and still held in great regard as witnessed by the welcome he received at the Opening Ceremony of the Special Olympics in Croke Park last June. I suppose the biggest risk I've taken was giving up a permanent and pensionable job for this fickle business. And I have a fairly positive attitude to life. I don't believe in worrying about things that might happen. Time enough for that when and if they do.

I'm glad I took some risks though because if I hadn't I'd have missed out on so many interesting once in a lifetime experiences. Like crash landing on the flight deck of the JFK, the American aircraft carrier, which visited our shores in 1996 as part of their Independence Day celebrations. I was presenting *A Stretch in the Evening* and that week the programme came from the JFK. It was a stomach churning experience. The plane seemed to fall out of the sky and was caught by a giant hook on the deck which made it stop dead almost immediately. I was given a certificate at the end of the week to say that I was an honorary 'tailhooker' of the US navy. Leaving the ship was just as thrilling. I travelled in a COD, carrier onboard Delivery. You board it from the back and sit in seats that face the back of the plane. There are no windows and it's like being inside a long tube lined with sacking. Everybody wears a cranial (a crash helmet), earplugs, goggles and a life jacket with a tube of sea dye so that you can be spotted in the event of falling in the water. Before take off an officer briefs all the passengers. There's no way he'd be heard at all once the engines are fired up. He told us his signal to us would be his two arms waving above his head, at which point we would grip the straps of our safety belts, put our heads in our chest and our feet up on the seat in front. This procedure is to counterbalance the effect of the G force which was so powerful that I thought my eyes had literally gone around the side of my face. Take off was momentous. The engines roared and the plane was attached to a catapult which was drawn back and then released so we were shot off at high speed and when the plane reached the end of the flight deck it felt as if we dropping into the sea before we soared into the sky. It was a scary moment but I took consolation from the fact that there were marines leaving for shore leave on the same flight and they seemed quite calm. Until I took my seat beside one of them and he told me it was only his second such flight and he was scared stiff.

There were five thousand US Navy personnel on the JFK, 300 of them were women. They had their separate wing of the ship and when we went to film their quarters a female marine had to walk ahead of us shouting 'Male on deck, male on deck'. We visited the mess decks where food was being served all the time. With that many people on board working different shifts it was always somebody's lunchtime. There was a library on board but the hum of the engines was audible even there. The whole place was a maze of narrow corridors and flights of stairs.

I met a lot of the marines and fighter pilots during that couple of days on board. Some of them were part of the Top Hatters Squadron, the oldest in the American navy. They were flying F14 Tom Cat fighters. One of the pilots, his nickname was Matt the Cat, had seen 60 or 70 hours of combat during operation Desert Storm and said during our interview 'Ye know, war is not a pretty thing'. During the Iraqi war, this year I thought of them and wondered about their circumstances. They were all some mothers' sons.

I met the one time England rugby captain, Will Carling while I was doing a summer chat show to replace *Kenny Live*. It was July '97; little did anybody know that a few weeks later his former lover, Princess Diana would be dead. It was a great coup for us on the programme to get him into studio. He was in the country to promote a sporting event. You could see why Diana fell for him. He's a very handsome and charming man. At the production meeting on the Friday, we debated whether or not it would be okay to ask him 'the Diana question'. We knew if we asked his PR people they'd probably say no so we decided to say nothing and see if they told us it was a no-go area. If they did we'd respect that. That's the ethics of broad-casting as far as I'm concerned. If you agree not to talk about something with your guest, you don't. Nobody said anything to us so we asked the question. Will was a bit taken aback but he was gracious in his reply. As he left the studio though, he was overheard saying to his minders 'I told you they'd ask me that'. They should have embargoed the subject. Thank God they didn't though because it would have seemed ridiculous, from the viewers' point of view not to ask about Diana. I remember I asked him how he coped with the scandal and the media attention at the time. He actually blushed and said 'You learn an awful lot about yourself when you go through something like that. It's not very pleasant and I wouldn't really like it to happen again'. At that point he gave a nervous laugh and made a face which left us in no doubt that this was the biggest understatement ever as far as he was concerned. He was living with his new partner at that stage and they were expecting a child the following October.

Sophie Dahl was a guest that summer; she's a real beauty in my eyes. And Frank McCourt was a real flirt! He was a very funny guest. He'd come from dinner in the American Ambassador's residence and invited me back there after the show. He invited me on air, during the interview though so it doesn't count. It was just harmless fun. We celebrated the 75th anniversary of the formation of An Garda Síochána one night and of the Aer Corps another night. The opening of that show involved me being winched into an Aer Corps helicopter, flying over Dublin Bay and then lowered onto the front lawn of RTÉ. I enjoyed that and the views were spectacular. The week before the Horse Show, I arrived into RTÉ on horseback. I didn't enjoy that. The horse was as big as a house, a beautiful creature, part of the Irish Nations Cup team but I was scared stiff. I have had a fear of horses since the day of my first Communion, when like every other child in Dublin we visited Dublin Zoo. I had a lovely time until the end of the pony ride when the minder let go of the reins so that he wouldn't be in the photograph of me in my finery atop this little pony. The photo was taken, the flash went off and so did the pony with me screaming on his back, my Communion veil billowing behind me and my mother trying to grab hold of it in a valiant but ill conceived rescue attempt. She was left holding a veil and

I continued on the pony until he decided the crisis was over and he stopped under a tree. I was shaken and stirred and needed a choc ice to calm my nerves.

A highlight of that summer show was the tribute to John Giles for which six of his former teammates from Leeds United travelled from England. It was a mark of the regard in which they held him that they all made a huge effort to be there. These were legendary figures in soccer terms, Norman Hunter, Alan Clarke, Mick Bates, Eddie Gray, Bobby Collins and the late Billy Bremner, and they were besieged in the canteen by eager not so young fans who remembered the entertaining games they'd provided during their heyday. They were good humored and obliging from the moment they entered the complex. And we tried their patience. The format we had decided on, to get maximum wow factor, was to have them lined up behind the set. I would call them on, and one by one they'd make an entrance to tumultuous applause. Their rehearsal was scheduled for 5.30, half an hour before the tea break and they duly presented themselves at the appointed time. Unfortunately, as is often the case, rehearsals were running behind schedule and just as the conquering heroes were lined up behind the scenery, it was time for tea. This meant that they would have to come back in an hour for rehearsal. No problem, they said. And it was no problem. They came back in the same good humour, entered in to the spirit of the occasion and the show was a great success. The studio audience went wild when they appeared one by one, from the back of the set and walked down the steps to the strains of the signature tune for *Match of the Day*. They also stayed around afterwards and had their photos taken with members of the audience. A true measure of the men. And a measure also of John Giles because they did it for him. Nobby Stiles was in the audience that night as well. He and John played together in Manchester United in the late fifties and early sixties. In fact in the summer of '58, John invited Nobby over to Dublin for a visit, introduced him to his sister Kay who went on to become Mrs Nobby Stiles in 1963, the year John and his wife Anne were married also.

There have been other great opportunities afforded to me by my work in RTÉ that I treasure and that I'll deal with in separate chapters. I love working on *Open House*. *Up for the Match* lends itself to all sorts of texting fun during the championships and *The People of the Year* awards give us all an opportunity to recognise people to whom we all owe a debt of gratitude for the difference they make in this world. All of these experiences I have had during my time in RTÉ have coloured my perception of the world and I'm glad about that. They've made me realise that there are so many strands to this rich tapestry of life.

Open House

You couldn't get a better example of the rich tapestry of life than a programme like *Open House*. It embraces everything from gardening and cookery, to music, fashion, health, sad stories and happy stories, all of them to do with real people who are going about their daily lives. I love the fact that people can tune into the programme and get information, consolation, motivation and entertainment. They may receive information that's useful to them or consolation that other people have similar difficulties to their own or motivation to change something in their life that is causing them sadness or stress. Most of all *Open House* provides entertainment. We get a lot of feedback from the viewers and it's nice when people say they found a particular item useful or that they got a laugh when they were feeling a bit low. My life is very satisfying and very busy during the *Open House* season. People are often surprised when they realise that Marty and I don't just rush into RTÉ after lunch and present the programme. I wish it could be that simple. *Open House* is more akin to a well oiled machine that starts up at the end of the summer and continues to gather momentum until the following Easter, during which time we will have made 130 programmes of an hour and a quarter duration. When I say we, I'm not just talking about Marty and me. The *Open House* production team consists of about 24 people, from executive and series producers to directors, broadcast co-ordinators, researchers, administration, and presenters. Then of course there's the wardrobe, make-up, the studio team, the call centre team where viewers phone calls are taken and hospitality, which is an essential part of the *Open House* experience. Ask any of the guests, for whom the programme is their first time on TV and they'll tell you they calmed their nerves before going on with a cup of tea or coffee and a chat and realised that it's not as scary as they thought and that they didn't feel the need to run out of the building anymore.

It's hard to believe we've just begun our sixth season of the programme. The time has flown by since Marty and I presented the very first programme in September 1998. Before that the afternoon audience had been well served for many years by *Live at Three* with Thelma Mansfield and Derek Davis. *PM Live* replaced it in September '97 and that programme had five presenters: Thelma, Ciana Campbell, Alf McCarthy, Marty and me. I moved from the newsroom to be a part of that programme and wondered about the wisdom of so doing when it was announced during the course of that year that *PM Live* would not continue into a second year and that the afternoon programme would be advertised in the independent sector. That was a scary time and made me wonder where to now? I crossed my fingers and hoped for the best. It was a time when the insecurity of this business was brought home to me but I have to say I'm quite philosophical in situations like that. I do believe that there's no point in worrying about things before they happen and I also believe that when one door closes, another opens somewhere.

Many independent production companies applied for the slot, among them Tyrone Productions who proposed Marty and me as their presenters if they were successful. Thankfully they won the competition and I've thoroughly enjoyed working on the programme from the beginning.

Our day begins at 9.30 a.m. with a production meeting in the office. We grab a coffee; sit at the round table, with Larry Masterson our series producer and all the team, and go through the day's running order. There are two producers, Dolores Comerford and Kate Shanahan and they work a day in the office with the researchers putting the following day's programme together and the next day they're in studio producing that programme. Whichever of them is in studio that day will go through the running order, from opening animation, through all of the items: interviews, music, competitions, fashion, cookery, even commercial breaks right through to the closing animation and credits. The researchers involved with the different items explain how they will work. If it's an interview situation, we'll find out at the meeting how many people are involved; if there's some video footage, some photos; a helpline may need to go on screen; anything that will add to the impact of the item and make it more interesting for the viewer. If there are problems with any item they'll be discussed at the meeting although sometimes things don't become obvious until we get to the rehearsal stage on the studio floor. The researcher will have spoken in depth with the guests involved in any item and provided a typed document, a brief, with all of the relevant information for Marty and myself. Although we do different items, depending on the day, we always study each other's briefs because the nature of a live show is such that things can go wrong and the running order may have to change while we're on air and I might end up doing an interview that Marty was due to do or vice versa. So you've got to be prepared for all eventualities. 'Bí ullamh' is the motto, like the Boy Scouts.

After the production meeting, there's a chance to deal with a bit of post or make a few phone calls before going over to studio 1 for camera rehearsal at 10.30. We walk through the programme then with the whole studio crew, floor manager, cameras, lighting, sound, and the director and crew in the control room. Then there's a bit of sitting around. The craic is good though and it's a great opportunity for a bit of wit and repartee. It's not just about having a laugh though. We use that time to study briefs and as we say ourselves to 'get our heads around' the items we're doing. The way it works for me is I read the brief and highlight the important bits. I write words or thoughts that strike me as I'm reading it in the margins and then I sit back and let the story sink in. I decide what the most important points in the story are and then I ask myself what questions I would want an interviewer to ask on my behalf if I was the viewer sitting at home on the couch. I think it's essential to envisage what the viewer would want asked because I look on the role of the interviewer or presenter as facilitator, a conduit of information. There can be nothing more frustrating than watching or listening to an interviewer and saying to yourself at the end of it, 'I wish she'd asked . . .' I realise the situation is different if the interviewer is Graham Norton or Ruby Wax, maybe. In that situation, the guest is there almost as an accessory to the presenter's act. Graham or Ruby is the star. On *Open House*, we're aware of the fact that we're there so that the viewer can engage with the guest who has a story to tell perhaps, or a point to put across, or a piece of information to share that may benefit others. We also make that point to the guests, some of whom will be appearing on television for the first time. They're understandably nervous and over that cup of tea in our hospitality room, we point out to them that the story they have to tell will strike a chord with some viewers who may be feeling they're the only one with a particular problem. Maybe a viewer will learn how to improve their own situation by listening and watching. A nervous guest can feel differently about going on TV when they realise they are actually helping others and as I say the urge to run out of the building disappears.

The camera rehearsal takes us up to 12.30, lunchtime, which is a sandwich at the desk and again a chance to go through the finer details of the day's programme. At 1.30 we go back over to the studio building, go to wardrobe and decide, with the help of the experts, what to wear. Eileen Chalmers is the person in the wardrobe department assigned to look after me. She lays out clothes for me on a weekly basis, complete with jewellery and shoes to match. If I wear a dark outfit one day, I'll go for something light in colour the next, and so on. It's wonderful to have that help with clothes because there are so many bits of information vying for position in the old head at that point that it's difficult to organise your outfit as well. Eileen has a great eye and is a big help and I know Marty feels exactly the same about Brigette Horan, the woman who looks after his clothes in the wardrobe department.

After the clothes decisions are made, it's up to the make-up department for what I refer to as the chill out time of the day. It's the closest thing you'll get to a relaxing massage without any massaging going on. I regularly fall asleep while Antoinette Forbes Curham, the head of the make-up department, is doing my make-up and the great thing about it is you can sit into that chair looking like the wreck of the Hesperus and get out of it half an hour later looking and feeling a hell of a lot better. Isn't it lovely to have a job like that where everybody you come in contact with is improved by your intervention?

By this stage, it's getting close to on airtime and it's time to go to the hospitality room and meet the guests. This is an important part of the programme for us because as I say a lot of the people that appear on *Open House* are members of the public who have some experience to talk about which might hopefully benefit somebody who's watching. We appreciate their participation and this is an opportunity to let them know that, to thank them for taking the time off work maybe, to help others. It makes a big difference to a nervous guest as I've already said and it breaks the ice. Everybody who comes on *Open House* loves the hospitality room. There's a lovely calm atmosphere there, low lights and candles, comfy couches and a big welcome. It's nice too for the contributors because they have a chance to meet the other guests on that day's programme and there's a feeling of 'we're all in this together'. Sometimes, of course, it's just not possible to meet everybody. There are days when Marty or I just don't make it to the hospitality room because some item needs an extra talk through with the researcher or the producer and there are times when the guest can't make it to studio before the programme starts. Where possible though, we have that time in the hospitality room and it's a nice interlude before going into studio and getting onto the roller coaster.

The time flies during the programme. The hour and a quarter seems like a couple of seconds. Once the signature tune is played and the opening animation is on screen, there's no stopping until the end. I like it like that though. There's an energy associated with live television that keeps everybody motivated and busy. The duration of the items is important. They've got to be long enough to get the message across but not so long that people might lose interest. There are of course times when I feel I'd have loved to have had more time with some guest but that's a good sign. It means there was lots of good material there and sometimes it happens that a guest might come back again to elaborate on some area of their experience which needs a few more minutes. There's a flexibility about the programme which allows that and it helps to keep things interesting and up there for the viewers.

On the other hand there are the familiar items that are a feature of the programme which people like also. Fashion is one. Folk just can't get enough of it. For a lot of people, it's a great way of finding out what's in the shops and what the trends are. It's a bit of a preview for them and saves them a bit of footwork too. If they see something they like on *Open House*, they know where they can go and get it. They've got to be quick though. Such is the power of television that featured clothes tend to fly out of the shops very quickly. The same is true of books. When a book is reviewed and strikes a chord, go for it quickly because it won't be in the bookshop for long. Again, it's nice to be given a recommendation and that's what happens on the day of the book review. They fly off the shelves. Gardening is very popular as well and every Thursday, the phone lines hop with viewers' queries. Dermot O'Neill has all the answers although we don't get through a fraction of the calls in the time available.

Another great favourite is cookery and the *Open House* chef has become a big star in this country. Not surprising at all because Neven Maguire is a great cook and a really warm, generous and friendly young man to boot. He never gets flustered. I suppose years of rushing around a restaurant kitchen is a good way of learning to cope with pressure. He's calm always and I imagine he's the same in his own restaurant kitchen. I can't imagine him screaming and roaring and throwing pots and pans all around the place. He got a real baptism of fire here. I remember his very first appearance on *Open House*, five years ago. It was also his very first time on television and it was not a trouble free experience. At the back of the studio, there is a big hydraulic steel door separating the studio from the scene dock, the place where all the props and scenery are kept. One of those sets is the kitchen one which is on wheels and is brought into the studio when it's needed. The staging crew will activate the steel door that will slide back and the workspace complete with hob and sink will be wheeled into position for the chef to use. That's the theory anyway and that's always been the case, except for one day in the first season when Neven was making his TV debut. On that occasion, the door stuck, or the hydraulic mechanism stuck or something else happened. The bottom line was that the door didn't open and the kitchen set remained in the scene dock. It was going nowhere. What to do? There was a fair amount of panic as the minutes were ticking away and it was obvious the door was not going to open. A decision had to be made. A hand held camera was taken from the studio to the scene dock and Neven hurriedly laid out his ingredients and did the cooking in the less than salubrious surroundings of the scene dock. It's not a pretty place. It's a big grey warehouse really with a fair through flow of people. It's not brightly lit either and the concrete walls never look inviting. And it was in those grey, dimly lit and quite grotty surroundings, with people passing by that Neven Maguire made his first appearance on TV and it didn't knock a feather out of him. It was funny to see him, smartly dressed in his white chef's jacket creating an elaborate and exotic dessert that was topped with spun sugar in the scene dock. He just got on with it as if he were working in the kitchens of the Ritz. He was as unflappable then as he is now. Everything has gone quite smoothly in the kitchen since that day though; only the odd minor incident to report. Like the day I was standing beside Neven as he was squeezing lemon juice onto a pan. The juice went in all directions, including into my left eye. I gave a little jump backwards and we had a laugh but the thing about lemon juice is that it's very tart and it caused my eye to water. The more I tried to pretend nothing was wrong, the more it looked as if I was crying. By the end of the item, my eyes were streaming and I handed over to the very quick-witted Marty Whelan who didn't waste the opportunity and certainly wasn't lost for words. I think he said he was sorry Neven was having that effect on me, that things were never as bad as they seemed. He was sorry for my trouble. All the while the camera is jumping from his face to my streaming eyes and I'm doubled up in fits of laughter, unable to explain what had actually happened.

These things happen on live television and add to the fun. I remember another occasion when Marty and Ted Courtney were talking opera. There was a bottle of champagne on the table which would be opened at the end of the ten-minute chat to celebrate some particular moment. That was the plan anyway. Unfortunately, about half way through the item, the heat of the studio got to the bottle of champagne and it just popped its cork. It made a great sound. It was a hilarious moment as champagne sprayed everywhere, all over Ted and Marty and even the lens of the camera. Then there was the winner of one of our competitions on the programme. The prize was a very nice rowing boat, with lots of polished wood and brass fittings. It was won by a woman in the south west who kind of dissipated our moment of glory and generosity by asking if she could have the money instead. What can you say?

We have a lot of fun making *Open House*, both behind the scenes and while we're on air and I realise it's a great privilege to have a job that's interesting and different every day and which brings me into contact with so many people from so many walks of life, each with a story to tell or a talent to display. It's demanding and challenging but it's stimulating and a real eye-opener at times. One of the qualities that I have come to admire greatly is the resilience of the human spirit. So many of the guests that join us on *Open House* are inspirational in their capacity to care for others, to overcome huge obstacles, to embrace life and move on from painful situations, to accept what life has asked them to endure, and most of all they're inspirational in their capacity for love. I never cease to be amazed at how some people have worked so successfully and against many odds at opening their hearts and confronting that fearful habit of closing to pain. These are people who acknowledge the painful parts of life, realise that pain, sorrow anguish and trouble are part of life. They accept them and seem to make them safe and manageable therefore. They acknowledge their presence in life and place them in proper perspective. It's when they're left unattended that the painful parts of life tend to overtake us and overwhelm us. By sharing their stories of pain and how they coped, they really do offer hope and consolation to others who take great comfort from seeing people who've overcome situations similar to their own. We have phone calls and letters from viewers telling us that they took the first step to dealing with a problem after seeing someone on *Open House*. I know I speak for the whole programme team when I say that it's a great thrill when we hear that. We're all human. We all know what it's like to be ill or sad or depressed and if we can improve the lot of even one person by what we're doing, we're delighted.

A programme like *Open House* makes you realise that people are the most important thing in life. Bonding and communication are the two activities of the mind and heart that give meaning to our lives. Without them, life is empty, no matter how busy or how active or how wealthy someone is. It's heartening to realise that mainly what motivates people is that desire to communicate. For the most part, people want to laugh every day, to seek peace, to show compassion, to be kind and forgiving. Look at Anne Frank as an example of that disposition. 'In spite of everything', she said, 'I believe that people are good at heart'. On *Open House*, we find that people are always willing to help if they can.

Another aspect of the programme that viewers love and that we enjoy are the specials that we do from time to time. A celebration of some well-known person who has made a major contribution to the world of entertainment perhaps. You mention the person you're celebrating and ask people to participate and they all respond so positively. When we did a special on Jimmy Magee for instance, Barry McGuigan was in England but he insisted on flying over for the afternoon. A measure of the high regard he had for Jimmy. The same can be said of the other people whose lives have been celebrated on *Open House* specials, people like Daniel O'Donnell, Paddy Cole, Ciaran MacMathuna, to mention but a few. Everybody is very willing to be a part of those programmes because they value the contribution the special guest has made in their chosen field. It's nice to know that in this world of show business and celebrity, the basic values of friendship and support are highly prized by Irish people, no matter what their standing.

I love the job I do. I love meeting people from those different walks of life, hearing their stories and passing them onto the people who tune into *Open House* for entertainment, information, support and consolation. It's nice to feel a part of that process of interaction between people. So that's a bit of an insight into my working life at the moment. There are other aspects of my life that we'll have a peep at in the following chapters, some very ordinary, some a bit unusual, all of them part of what lay in store for that eight-year-old girl photographed in Clondalkin one sunny day with her grandmother.

What's Another Year!

There can't be a primary school teacher in the country who hasn't told the story of King Bruce in his cell watching the spider climb and fall back down and climb again and again until he reaches his goal. And there can't be an adult in the country who hasn't been reminded of hearing that parable from their school days when disappointment strikes and something we want and have been striving for is denied us. The next step is crucial. Do we collapse in a heap of disappointment, do we become bitter, or do we take a deep breath and follow the spider up that wall again?

My Eurovision journey began in 1981. The contest was coming from the RDS because Johnny Logan had won the previous year with Shay Healy's song *What's Another Year*. Doireann Ni Bhriain was the presenter and there was great excitement all over the country. This was after all, only the second time that Ireland had hosted the event. We hadn't yet got used to the idea that we were in a league of our own when it came to striking the winning formula for Eurovision. With a couple of weeks to go to the Song Contest, there was talk of an NUJ strike, in the event of which, there might be a difficulty for Eurovision, given that Doireann was a member of the NUJ. So, just in case, it was decided that she should have an understudy. To say that I was surprised to be phoned and told that understudy was me is a huge understatement. I was only a wet week in the organisation, working as a part-time continuity announcer, while at the same time, working full-time as a teacher. To go from continuity announcing to shadowing Doireann in rehearsal for Eurovision was a quantum leap for me and a leap of faith for RTÉ. I loved it though and it gave me great insight into the amount of work that goes into a television production. I said in the previous chapter that people are often surprised to hear that Marty and I are at work from early morning to present a programme that goes on air mid afternoon. I was very surprised to see the amount of work that went into the Eurovision production. It was a question of all hands on deck and everybody seemed to get a great thrill and satisfaction out of the work and the fact that they do it so well in RTÉ.

The week was stimulating, exciting and great fun. Richard Lewis designed a dress for me for the occasion. I went to all the parties hosted by the different embassies during Eurovision week – this social whirl was new to me. And I spent the week in the RDS soaking up the atmosphere, meeting people from so many different countries and learning a lot about presenting from Doireann Ni Bhriain.

She was a great role model and mentor. Her script, which I too had to learn off by heart (there was no autocue), was warm and welcoming to all contestants and included a major celebration of our Irish culture. Her demeanour all week was calm and professional. I think it was from her I got my utter conviction that the presenter should be a conduit, a facilitator of the flow of information between the viewer and the material to be transmitted. She was also friendly and helpful to me (a novice) and I'm sure she needed that extra bit like a hole in the head. I learnt so much from sitting in the auditorium, watching her and listening to her. Doireann put a lot of emphasis on the inter-cultural exchange and greeted each jury in their own language. It took a bit of work getting those greetings and then writing them out phonetically and learning them all but it was worth it. Our language, even if we don't use it regularly, is so much a part of what we are as Irish people. I think it's important to acknowledge that such is the case for other peoples as well, especially in the case of emerging states, like those from the former Yugoslavia like Bosnia Herzegovina, Croatia and Slovenia for whom it was significant to hear their languages being spoken on the international stage so soon after the trauma of the war.

Fast forward to 1988 and Eurovision is back in the RDS in Dublin, thanks once again to Johnny Logan winning in '87, this time with his own composition *Hold Me Now*. Presenter auditions were held in RTÉ and there was massive speculation as to who would be chosen. I had been rightly bitten by the Eurovision bug by now and desperately wanted to host the contest. I've tried to remember how I felt going into the audition and I just can't dredge up the feeling but I must have been a bit confident of my chances. I had the languages, I had a lot more flying hours on live television in the intervening seven years and let's face it I'd been there and learned the ropes. Sure you'd be forgiven for thinking it'd be a shoe-in, a formality. But no. It most certainly was not. I don't remember how I felt before the audition, but I do remember how I felt during it. 'Rattlin' describes it well I think. And I didn't get the gig. Pat Kenny and Michelle Rocca presented Eurovision that year and I sat in the audience as an invited guest. It was a great show. That was the year Celine Dion won for Switzerland with *Ne Partez Pas Sans Moi*. That was a good move for her, to put it mildly. I was well over the disappointment of not getting the gig by that stage but when I think back to that time now I realise I just had to pick up the pieces and get on with life. It's easy to philosophise now with the benefit of hindsight and having got the job eventually and say that 'what's for you won't pass you' but at the time I didn't know when, if ever, Eurovision would be back in Ireland and I did know that with every passing year there would be a new crop of potential presenters.

Which is what happened actually. In 1993, Eurovision was back in Ireland thanks to Linda Martin's fine win in Sweden with *Why Me*, a song penned by Johnny Logan (he just seemed to hit the nail on the head, every time). So the race was on again. Who would get the job of presenting this most prestigious and highly regarded TV production which had the added advantage of being expertly done by RTÉ? Let's face it, we had a fair bit of practice at it and also RTÉ personnel took great pride in the high standards that had been set in previous years and in the fact that delegates from other countries would be hoping and praying for an Irish victory because they knew it would be a very professional and trouble-free production and also they knew they'd have a ball.

There was no shortage of people who were ready, willing and able to present themselves for audition. It's a procedure that is not for the faint hearted, I can assure you. You've got to prepare and present a three-minute opening to the show, using Irish, English and French. Then you introduce a few of the pieces of films from the competing country (they're known affectionately as post-cards) followed by a few of the songs. Then the fun of the audition begins: the voting. The scoreboard goes up. You explain the voting procedure in both English and French, and what will happen if you can't make contact with any jury. There is a spokesperson for the country who delivers the votes sometimes in French and sometimes in English. You repeat them in both languages and believe me, in that mock-up situation designed to test the auditionee's grace under pressure, everything that can possibly go wrong, does. The phone line will go down, the spokesperson will mumble, the votes will be given in the wrong order, the same country will be voted for twice, two countries will receive the same votes, the scoreboard won't be updated correctly, the scrutineer will interject and ask for something to be repeated or clarified, and all of this has to be sorted in both English and French. You've got to have your wits about you. It's like stepping onto a roller coaster and hanging on for dear life until it comes to a stop. Then you emerge, drained and glad it's over. And you hope for the best with fingers and toes crossed while the tapes are assessed and the press speculation mounts. Those weeks were endless. I really wanted to get this gig. I had been told I'd done a good audition. Let's face it, I'd had enough practice at it by this stage. After the disappointment of 1988 though I was being very cautious and not responding to any of the speculation that I had a good chance. I was afraid to hope and afraid to feel confident. And I was right on both counts because I didn't get the call. I was working in the newsroom at the time and I was in on an early Saturday morning radio shift, when I opened the news-paper and read that my newsroom colleague, Fionnuala Sweeney, was to present the contest from Millstreet. I was gutted and ill prepared for reading it in the paper. King Bruce's spider was well and truly on the ground and knocked out. The disappointment was enormous; a physical stomach-churning occasion wouldn't even come close to describing that morning. I was close to tears all day, but I had to keep going and remind myself that nobody died and that it was a fair contest which someone else won. It was as simple as that.

I went down to the newsagent's in the Merrion Centre between the 10.00 a.m. and 11.00 a.m. bulletins and bought a congratulations card which I wrote back in the newsroom and left in Fionnuala's pigeonhole because I knew that she would be in on the early radio shift on the Sunday morning. She phoned me from work the next day to say mine was her first card, she was thrilled to get it and appreciated that under the circumstances it must have been difficult for me to send it. Not in the slightest; I genuinely had no difficulty in putting myself beyond my own misery to wish her well. It's not as if she had done something to hurt me. She won, I lost. I told her I was delighted that she was chosen above all the other people, because she worked in the newsroom and we could all share in the excitement of her getting the gig. And there was great excitement. Joe Mulholland was Director of News at the time and he was a great man for marking celebratory occasions, so we had a bit of a do to celebrate Fionnuala being chosen and one hell of a do when she returned to the newsroom, having done a great job in Millstreet.

So 1993 was Fionnuala's year. It was also Ireland's year again because Niamh Kavanagh won with that gorgeous ballad, *In Your Eyes*. The closing moments of the voting were hugely exciting because everything hinged on the last vote given by the last country to vote, which was Malta but only because it had been impossible to make contact with Malta earlier on. Now, if Malta was incommunicado again, victory would go to Ireland because we had 175 points at that stage. The United Kingdom, with 164 points was in second place. They were represented by Sonia, who

sang *Better the Devil You Know*. If Malta did give their votes
and if they gave us even two votes then we'd win. But if
they gave us no points and gave 12 to the UK, then they'd
win by one vote. You can imagine the tension in the arena
in Millstreet as the votes were delivered. Un point, deux
points and so on to dix points which went to Luxembourg.
There was a gasp in the arena because up to this,
Luxembourg had the grand total of one point, 'un point'
and here was Malta giving them ten of the precious things.
It was time for the spokesperson to say where the 'douze
points' were going. Everything now hung in the balance.
Malta hadn't given any votes at all to either Ireland or the
United Kingdom. If they gave their top score to us or to
any other country except the UK, we'd win but if they
gave 12 points to the UK, they'd beat us by a point. You
could hear a pin drop. It was magic and when the
spokesperson said 'Et l'Irlande . . .' that was enough. You
couldn't actually hear her say 'douze points' because the
place erupted. It was great to be present for such an
exciting finale and one which went in favour of the home
crowd. The party afterwards was amazing. It was such a
tight finish and two in a row for Ireland.

I had resolved after the auditions in 1993 that I
wouldn't audition again. My resolution wasn't tested the
following year because there were no auditions. Moya
Doherty was the producer and she chose her presenters
without audition. They, of course were Gerry Ryan and
Cynthia Ní Mhurchú and that of course was the year
of Riverdance and of another Irish victory with the
Brendan Graham song, *Rock 'n' Roll Kids* sung by Charlie
McGettigan and Paul Harrington. It was a most memorable contest and I know that for me, the realisation that
this was something out of the ordinary happened when

Michael Flatley jumped onto the stage. I felt a shiver run down my spine and I, like everybody else who was watching Eurovision that night, was spellbound.

It was three in a row for Ireland and Eurovision was back in the Point in 1995. I wasn't asked to audition and I didn't apply I wasn't being defeatist. I was actually quite happy to accept that it just mustn't be for me. I remember when I was auditioning back in '88, asking a senior producer if he had any advice he could give me. I'll never forget what he said and I still believe it's the only way to proceed in this business. 'Be fully prepared for that audition and when you go into it, be yourself. That way, if you have what they want, you'll get the gig. If you try to be something you're not and you get it, you'll be found out eventually, because if there's one thing that's impossible to fake, it's sincerity.' That's what happened each time. I did the homework and then, in audition, I didn't try to be hip or cool. I suppose you could say I did it my way. And my way wasn't what was wanted up to this point.

To say I was surprised to get a phone call from John McHugh doesn't quite hit the spot! I knew him to see as the producer of *Kenny Live* and I realised he was producing the Eurovision that year, so when I answered the phone one Monday evening in March and this voice said, 'Hi Mary, this is John McHugh', I honestly didn't know what to expect. And he didn't enlighten me either. He quite simply asked me to meet him for coffee the following morning. I was afraid to allow myself to hope because I couldn't bear the thought of another disappointment. I convinced myself that he was going to ask me to maybe have some chats in French or Irish with the person he'd chosen. After all I hadn't even done an audition. I thought he might want me to do courtesy work with the visiting delegates, or make the tea or hand out party passes. Anything except present the damn thing. I don't think I slept much that night, surprise, surprise. And when I met John the following morning and I asked him what it was about, he assumed I'd realised but he just didn't want to say it to me over the phone. He said he'd taken out my audition from '93 and liked it and that I was his choice to present the Eurovision this year. I wanted to throw my arms around him and hug him to death and jump up and down and run around the canteen like an eejit telling people my news but I couldn't. I had to sit quietly and calmly opposite him and listen to him telling me that it was very important that nobody find out about this until it was announced on *Kenny Live* the following Saturday night. That scared me. Now I wanted to jump up from the table and leave him in case anybody might put two and two together seeing us having coffee. And as the week went on and the press speculation mounted, it became increasingly difficult to field the questions and give nothing away. Remember I was working in the newsroom at the time and my colleagues were people who had a nose for a story and were highly skilled at eliciting information. But I gave nothing away. I was almost paranoid about the secrecy at this stage. I even felt that if it leaked out, they might change their minds altogether and give the gig to somebody else. My name featured in the newspaper stories but so did other people's and we managed to get to the Saturday without anyone knowing for sure.

Kenny Live was fun. Eva's nineteen now, she was eleven at the time and she was much more impressed by the fact that a young up-and-coming boyband, in braces and cloth caps were on the show. These were the early days of Boyzone and she was a big fan. I remember feeling nervous before going out to be interviewed by Pat, but I said to myself in the wings, Mary, you've wanted this for a long time. Make the most of it. Enjoy the moment. I gave myself the same talking to on a number of occasions between that night and the 13th of May, when the enormity of the undertaking would hit me. My jaw hit the floor, for instance, when I went into the Point for the first time and saw how big the place was. I watched the set being built and realised I would be up there in the middle of that stage with three and a half thousand people in the audience. I had another wake up call when I saw the row of commentary boxes going in at the back of the auditorium and realised that these would be filled by commentators talking to hundreds of millions of people in many different countries. I had many nervous moments during the weeks before the contest but I never wanted out. It was a dream come true. The spider had finally scaled the wall and the whole experience was the sweeter for having had to wait for it.

I appreciated every minute, starting with that appearance on *Kenny Live*. After the show, we were all back in the green room and among the people who phoned through was Fionnuala Sweeney. People often ask me what it was like presenting Eurovision and I tell them it was a magical time. It was like being in Disneyland; hard work, mind and scary at times but thoroughly enjoyable. There were lovely moments during the run up to the big night. I was thrilled to meet President Mary Robinson when she hosted a party in Áras an Uachtaráin. The school where I'd been teaching (I was on career break at the time) invited me to visit and the teachers and pupils (all 750 of them) were very warm and welcoming. I was really pampered and I took to that like a duck to water.

There were some funny incidents as well. On the night before the contest, after the dress rehearsal, the audience left and we did a mock voting with the juries in the different locations around Europe. One of them had been waiting too long in situ apparently for this to happen and by the time I called on the spokesperson to deliver his country's votes, he was absolutely plastered. He made no sense whatever. In fact, there were times when he was, as they say nowadays, vertically challenged. He kept falling off his chair! His votes were all over the place. It brought me back to the audition stage where everything that could go wrong, did. He gave votes in the wrong order. He voted for one country twice. He voted for his own country. It was a baptism of fire for me and it wasn't helped by the fact that the crew in the control room were laughing so loudly that I could hear them through the floor manager's headset. Needless to say, he was replaced the following night and everything went very smoothly.

Eurovision '95 was a spectacular and beautiful production. The set was amazing. The crew joked that the arrival of the Queen of Sheba hadn't a patch on my entrance onto that stage. After the Eurovision theme music (Charpentier's *Te Deum*) was played and the lights went up I was standing at the top of 13 steps, which were covered in black silks. As I walked into the light, the silks were pulled away, one step at a time, to reveal metallic silver steps with fluorescent lights under each one. When I got to the last one and emerged onto the stage, all the steps were lifted into the air amid a pyrotechnic extravaganza. The audience gasped. There are a couple of logistical considerations though with an entrance like that. One cannot come onstage for Eurovision and be picking one's way down this amazing staircase in an effort to avoid standing on the silks and to know when one has reached the last step. I had to look cool, calm and collected and more importantly I had to look out into the auditorium. So, I had to count the steps as I was walking and make sure I started counting on the very first one. And I had to maintain a pace that allowed the people at the bottom of the staircase to remove the silks and reveal the staircase without me stepping on them. The press were at the dress rehearsal on the Friday night and on Saturday morning there was a very funny cartoon in one of the papers, showing yours truly her gorgeous Richard Lewis gown all over the place, tumbling head over heels down the staircase with a piece of black silk caught in the heel of her shoe. The production team saw it and tried to ensure that I didn't, in case it might make me nervous of that happening. I saw it by lunchtime though and we all had a good laugh.

Richard Lewis is renowned for his classy slinky silk jersey evening dresses and they're not shown at their best when there are three battery packs sticking out from the small of the woman's back who's wearing them. This problem presented itself at the dress rehearsal when it looked a bit like a waist-high bustle. What to do about that little problem? The three battery packs had to stay. One was for the mic, the second the standby mic and the third for my earpiece. The solution worked really well. It was decided that I would wear a pair of cycling shorts under the two dresses and there would be one pack on my back and one on the back of both my legs. It might not have been glamorous, but it worked. The long, elegant line of the dresses was preserved and nobody knew that underneath those glamorous gowns, I was wearing very unglamorous, black cycling shorts. Until the morning after

Eurovision that is, when there was an article in the newspaper to that effect. Again, we all had a good laugh.

I have to say my memory of that time is one of hard work, great laughs and great satisfaction. A spectacular production. I was glad I greeted all the contestants in their different languages and I have Doireann to thank for making me aware of the value of that. Norway won with *Secret Garden*. They had Irish help though. The violinist Fionnuala Sherry performed with Rolf Lufland that night and *Secret Garden* has gone from success to success since that win. The interval act was super too, although, coming in the year after Riverdance it didn't get its due recognition. John McHugh commissioned Mícheál Ó Súilleabháin to write a hauntingly beautiful piece called *Lumen*, which began with the monks of Glenstal performing Gregorian chant. They were then joined by Mícheál playing piano and by Brian Kennedy, Máire Brennan and Clannad, Nóirín Ní Riain and na Casaidigh. *Lumen* is a celebration of the very best of Irish traditional and Celtic spiritual music and when I listen to it now it brings me peace and tranquillity and very dear memories of those rehearsals for the interval act when I sat in the auditorium and listened to all of those wonderful Irish musicians blending their voices and amalgamating their talents.

The satisfaction element comes undoubtedly from the fact that this was the culmination of 14 years of striving towards this goal. The analogy of King Bruce and the spider describes it well for me and I hope that people reading this will be encouraged to continue striving for what they want in life. We set ourselves targets and we work towards them and when we encounter obstacles along the way, as we do, we must pick ourselves up, dust ourselves down and start all over again. This is not easy unless you've got access to a crystal ball and can see that in the future, things will go your way. You've got to be positive about something that is proving elusive and strive for it without knowing the eventual outcome. In 1988, having understudied for Doireann seven years previously, I thought I'd be picked to present Eurovision and I wasn't. I had to accept that. In 1993, I tried again, hopeful but cautious. Again I was unsuccessful. And again I was disappointed. In 1994, there were no auditions but I remember clearly sitting at home watching Gerry and Cynthia being announced as presenters and interviewed on *Kenny Live* and wanting desperately to be put through my paces by Pat. The odds against Ireland winning three Eurovisions in a row were huge so I wasn't feeling hopeful that night. And yet, 12 months later, it was my turn to sit on that couch and talk to Pat about how it felt to be chosen to present the contest. It felt really good. Life has a funny way of sorting itself out, that's for sure!

More of the nice memories I have of that time are coming to me as I write. I mentioned Joe Mulholland earlier. He was the Director of News at the time, my boss. His wife Annie is French and she has always been associated with Eurovision presenters. One meets her first at the audition stage. She's the person who makes your life hell by ensuring that everything that can go wrong will go wrong with the voting. It must break her heart to make things difficult for the hopeful candidate because she's a gentle, warm, friendly woman who would bend over backwards to help anyone out. After the auditions are completed, Annie's Cruella de Ville role evaporates and she becomes the French language coach for the presenter, French and English being the official languages of the European

Broadcasting Union. I looked forward to our language sessions. It was time out for me and a great opportunity to speak French again. Annie and I met once or twice a week, at about 11.00 a.m. (coffee time!), in her house, and because my French was okay, having lived in France and taught English there after I finished my degree, we'd sit and chat, en francais, about anything and everything. I remember one day, drinking coffee and chatting about cats in her sunroom, with the smell of her spring flowers coming through the open window. She had wild garlic growing and the smell of that on the breeze was lovely. Another time, we talked about her family and upbringing in France. She told me about the organic market in Pearse Street. It was always relaxing, always animated and those meetings are as much a part of Eurovision for me as the actual contest on the night of the 13th of May. Annie was hugely supportive from the beginning right through that week in the Point and she was there, keeping a watchful eye on pronunciation and affiliated matters during all rehearsals. We shared a taxi home from the Point on the night before the contest. We had endured two dress rehearsals that day with two different audiences and then the ordeal of the mock voting, which I mentioned earlier, the highlight of course being the entertainment value of our inebriated friend in foreign parts. We were both absolutely exhausted and could barely speak, but as I was getting out of the taxi, Annie touched my arm and said the most encouraging thing possible on the eve of this huge event. In spite of my tiredness, I was walking on air as I made my way up my driveway to the front door. It made me realise how important it is to say words of encouragement to people around us. Don't just think positive things or tell others how great so and so is. It's crucial to let the person know you think they're good at what they do. I know that for me it meant a lot to have her vote of confidence. I went to bed that night with affirmation ringing in my ears.

And I needed it. I know what nerves are. I feel them often when I go in front of a camera to do something new to me or something I haven't done for a while. I feel nerves always when I go out onstage in front of a live audience. I'm familiar with the butterflies doing somersaults in my tummy. What I learnt for the first time, the night before Eurovision is that these butterflies can kick in while you're actually sleeping. I fell into the bed that night, totally exhausted and I fell asleep almost immediately. I slept well for a few hours but I woke at about 4.00 a.m. and to my absolute horror, I had a swarm of butterflies in my stomach. The nerves had obviously kicked in while I was sleeping and that was what woke me so early on that Saturday morning, the day of the contest. I wouldn't have believed that those nerves could establish themselves during sleep. What incredible lively machines we humans are for that to happen. In rest and deep sleep, my nervous system was gearing itself up for the day ahead, which would be one of anticipation, attempts at relaxation, not a lot of food. I tried to eat but I was just too nervous. Those butterflies fluttered inside me all day.

I was collected from home at 8.30 a.m. in a shiny black limo and driven to the production office at the back of the Point. I spent some time at the desk looking over notes and those foreign greetings. Then it was time to get my hair done, the dress on and make-up done for the third and final dress rehearsal at noon. It went well for everybody: cameras, sound, lighting, orchestra, performers, stage crew, control room crew and juries. It takes a lot of people to make a Eurovision song contest. The organisation involved is incredible and the sense of teamwork is very uplifting.

When that dress rehearsal was over and the post mortem was complete, I went off in the limo, which had been placed at my disposal for the day, to try to get some rest in my room in the Berkley Court Hotel. Rest maybe, sleep no way. I spent the two hours going through the motions of closing my eyes, breathing deeply and willing sleep to come. But those butterflies made sure that wasn't going to happen. I presented that contest over and over in my head while I lay there and tried to anticipate the worst-case scenario so as to head it off at the pass. I reminded myself how important it would be to begin counting those steps on the very first one or else there'd be uncertainty and a potential jolt at the end. I practised those greetings to the different juries and tried to anticipate what they might say in reply. What if they said something else in their language which I wouldn't understand? I decided that I would smile, pause and just ask them for their votes please. I was well versed in the procedure should something go wrong with the voting. I knew that when the cameras would go to the green room during the voting to check on the excitement there, I'd be told through my earpiece in advance so that I could look at the right monitor. And I had a few lines ready in my head to cover the winner's walk from the green room to the stage. I hoped they would be brisk and dying to get onstage so that I wouldn't be left covering for too long. And the rest was in the lap of the gods. That's how I spent my two free hours that afternoon. It was nice to get away from the Point for a while and to have the absolute quiet of the hotel bedroom to get my head around those things.

And so back to the Point at about six o'clock. The excitement was palpable from the gates. The front courtyard was packed with press photographers, delegates, guests arriving, all chatting and laughing and looking forward to a great night. I almost had a panic attack. I thought I'd been nervous all day but it was nothing compared to the feelings that were coming my way then. What sort of a fool was that spider to try and try again to scale that wall? Why didn't he just make a life for himself on the floor of the cell and keep King Bruce company during his sojourn there. If an escape had presented itself to me at that moment I would have been very tempted to take it. None did and of course I'm glad the whole thing happened. But I know there have been less spectacular events over the years that were scary and difficult and instead of biting the bullet I took the escape route of compromise or avoidance. The problem there is that the difficult situation remained and continued to be a difficult situation. I know now that the contemplation of action in such a scenario is the hardest part. When we take the first step of dealing with the dilemma, which usually amounts to verbalising it to someone, there's a sense of relief first of all and support and a realisation that this problem can be solved.

I verbalised my state of nerves when I got back to the Point that evening to Kevin Linehan, who's the commissioning editor for entertainment and music at RTÉ now and who, in 1995, was the producer assigned to me, the presenter for the duration of Eurovision. He was a rock of support all the time and kept an eye on everything that concerned me. He decided if I was being asked to do too much, what interviews should be done and when, and he was by my side during all of the rehearsals and meetings. He was kind and considerate all the time and one very sweet touch, which I remember still, happened just after I came off stage, exhausted but elated at the end of the live transmission. Let me explain: it was a gruelling week and in order to be in top form it was a very abstemious week, in spite of all the functions and parties we attended throughout. It's no secret that I'm partial to a drop of champagne when it's presented to me and there was no shortage of it that week, but I said no every time. It was crucial that I felt clearheaded always, so I resisted the temptation.

And so the week continued and the day arrived and the contest went on air at eight o'clock and whenever I came off stage, Kevin was there to bring me to my dressing room or the green room or the hair and make-up room and to keep an eye on the clock so that I'd be standing by with plenty of time before the next bit on stage. Anyway, when the credits rolled and the programme finished amidst a hail of confetti and fireworks and a very happy Norwegian contingent celebrating onstage, I made my way off, and there was Kevin, standing in the wings with two glasses and a chilled bottle of champagne. What a kind and thoughtful soul. That was the start of the celebration that continued right through the night at the Point, the RDS and beyond. I don't think anybody wanted the night to end. In spite of the exhaustion of all the work and commitment for a period of weeks, everybody was in great form and there's nothing to compare with the feeling of satisfaction and fulfilment when the job has been well done and received well. RTÉ's reputation as the best producer of Eurovision both on screen and behind the scenes was intact and enhanced even, by this third in a row. RTÉ personnel were wondering what we would do for excitement the following year with no Eurovision. We'd got so used to having the contest come from Ireland that it felt strange and sad in a way to be handing it over to another country. All of the visiting delegates went home extremely happy, whether they did well in the contest or otherwise. Everybody had a great week. It was an occasion of cultural exchange, of networking and of many people renewing friendships that had begun at previous Eurovisions.

I took the next week off and enjoyed my time at home although there's always a bit of an anticlimax after the event. It can lead to gloomy days of wanting to turn the clock back and do it all over again but the gloomy feeling passes and normality returns.

When I went back to work in the newsroom there were celebrations. I already said that Joe Mulholland was good at recognising people's efforts and he threw a party that was a lot of fun. He also had an extra interest in Eurovision because of his wife, Annie's involvement with the presenters.

And so after three years in a row in Ireland, Eurovision left our shores . . . but not for long. In 1996, in Norway, Eimear Quinn singing another of Brendan Graham's songs, *The Voice*, represented us and of course, she won. So the following year, we're back in the Point. Ronan Keating and Carrie Crowley presented the contest and I was once again sitting in the audience, but this time, it felt wonderful to be sitting there watching other people onstage and wishing them well. Having finally scaled the wall, the spider was content. I sat there, enjoyed the show and relived some of the memories of two years previously.

Katrina and the Waves won for the Royaume Uni that year and Eurovision hasn't been back to Ireland since. There've been changes along the way that I think have diminished the contest somewhat. I regret the fact that the orchestra is no longer a part of the contest. Backing tracks will never fill that void for me. I'm also not a fan of televoting. I think these songs that have been composed by serious songwriters deserve to be considered by a jury who listen to the song over and over and make informed decisions as to its quality: lyrics, melody, general appeal. The way things are at the moment, the decision is made by fast diallers who make instant or political decisions. In this case also, countries with big populations will have more voting power. I don't think that's as it should be either.

One of the highlights of my broadcasting career was presenting the Eurovision Song Contest. It was a magical moment. Actually it was a magical six weeks, from the time the announcement was made, through all the preparations and on to the night of the 13th May 1995 at the Point Theatre in Dublin when a dream came true for me. It was also my King Bruce and the spider moment because I had wanted to do this job for a long time and had tried for it before without success. Professionally it was beneficial in that it increased my profile and thereby brought more and more work my way. And on a personal level, it introduced me to a woman who became a friend and whose enthusiasm for life is refreshing. A few months after Eurovision in 1995, I got a phone call from a softly spoken woman who introduced herself as Sylia and explained that she was part of a Jewish Women's group called the Dublin Ziona. They met in each other's houses from time to time and the next meeting would be in the house she shared with her daughter and son-in-law. She asked me if I'd come along and talk to them about the Eurovision song contest. I was immediately enthralled by this woman's vivacity and warmth and agreed to go along and bring whatever bits and pieces I could. It was a great night. We sat around in a circle in the sitting room, I reminisced and they asked questions. I brought along the two gowns and the jewellery and the specially covered shoes that I'd worn and they were passed around the group. Then Sylia's daughter, Frayeh and some other women produced this sumptuous supper of tea and sandwiches and cakes and chocolates. It was a lavish presentation, they'd gone to an awful lot of trouble and after supper, Sylia presented me with a certificate stating that a tree had been planted in my name in the Dublin Playground in Migdal Ha'Emek. I was really touched by that and would love some day to go to Israel to see it. That evening marked the beginning of my friendship with Sylia and her family, all of them warm, and friendly. Sylia is in her eighties, a diminutive and softly spoken woman but a live wire still, full of chat and a great, sometimes wicked, sense of humour. I enjoy visiting her although I'd like to have more free time to visit her more often. I'm glad she made that phone call and invited me to her Ziona meeting. I'm glad our paths have crossed and she introduced me to some of the riches of the Jewish culture in this country.

Eurovision is the reason I became friendly with Sylia and for that reason also it has a special place in my heart. It was demanding and necessitated a lot of juggling on the home front with four children to be considered. Lucy was four on the 12th of May, the day before Eurovision, the day of the dress rehearsals. I was in the Point all day. That was tough. Actually, I hated it. Her party had to be postponed till the following week. That's one of the realities of motherhood when mother works outside the home. Her party was lovely as it happened because I was relaxed and on a week's break and the weather was good and we were able to have the party in the back garden.

The photos tell the tale of a happy occasion, but on Friday, 12th, the day of her Birthday, I was not able to be there with her. I think any mother who has ever found herself in a similar situation will know how that felt. Giving birth to a child establishes a bond that will never ever be broken.

Taking account of that caveat and acknowledging that regret as part of my whole Eurovision experience, I have to say that it was a thrilling and gratifying part of my broadcasting career. Also, I had to wait 14 years for it and as I said earlier, things that we have to strive for without knowing if we will ever realise them are all the sweeter for that struggle. A bit like the spider in King Bruce's cell.

Mum's the Word

Working on *Open House* is demanding and stimulating. I enjoy the work and the fun involved in being part of a team. The season flies by and we emerge at the end of 130 programmes, exhausted and glad of the break. For me the first two months of that break are spent reclaiming the house, putting an order on things, clearing out cupboards and drawers that have had things thrown into them during the programme run for lack of another few hours in the day. Then at the end of June when the children are all on summer holidays, it's time to decamp to Wexford.

In fact, I'm sitting here in Rosslare, at the beginning of this year's two-week holiday that I take every year with my children, my brother and his wife and their two children. It's lashing rain. It has been since yesterday evening. And before that, during the afternoon, it was cold and windy. We left the beach after the two youngest, Dermot and Lucy, had their swim because it was freezing. It rained all through the night and looking out the window, I see no break in the grey sky which has me wondering what we'll do today because it's going to be wet, wet, wet. Don't get me wrong, I like Rosslare, but I need sunshine. So, you might ask, why am I here? I'm here because my children love their holidays in Rosslare and along with their cousins, won't tolerate holidays anywhere else. In fact, last year, we compromised and spent the first week in Antibes in the south of France, so that we'd be guaranteed a bit of sunshine. It was glorious but the children couldn't wait to get home and down to Rosslare. They wanted us to come home from the airport (around midnight) and head for Wexford immediately. This year, they didn't want to 'waste' a week of their holiday abroad. 'But you're paying, you should decide where the holidays and the money are spent. Why do you do it?' I've asked myself that question many times and I've come to the conclusion that part of the reason has to be because I'm a mother.

I will do anything and everything I can for my children. I will put myself and my own needs second to theirs always. And there isn't a hint of 'martyrdom' doing this. It's part of my make up and has been since the moment Eva, my eldest was born. I'm not unique in this. I imagine every mother reading this will recognise the trait as one she shares also.

My own mother was exactly the same. It's as an adult looking back that I realise all the sacrifices she made for her children. At the time, we just took it as our due I suppose. She sat on cold beaches, sometimes wrapped in a fur coat to keep the wind at bay, when we were young. She brought us to our dancing and elocution and swimming and music classes, sharing the delivery and collection with other mothers on the road. They say that a suburban mother's role is to deliver her children obstetrically once and by car for ever after. In those days it wasn't even that simple because nobody had a car. In the case of the Irish dancing for instance it was a matter of getting the 51 bus from Clondalkin to Aston's Quay at teatime on cold dark Friday evenings, walking up O'Connell Street and on to North Great George's Street to the Inis Ealga School of Dancing. She then waited while myself and two friends had our lesson. We three enjoyed ourselves immensely, not so much for the Irish dancing, because we never practised much and were always in trouble. Actually, we did practise

. . . at the bus stop, waiting for the 5.30 bus in to town, which was always late.

My mother needed those trips like a hole in the head, but she made them and continued to put herself at the disposal of the other three after me, because she wanted us to have every opportunity in life that she could manage. There wasn't any money to spare while we were growing up, but for activities that would enhance our lives, Mam's attitude was always, 'Sure, we'll find the money somewhere'. And she put as much time and energy into extra-curricular pursuits for Tony, the youngest, as she did for me, the eldest, even though she was that bit older and had been doing for so many years. I remember distinctly her saying often 'I did it for the others, I'll do it for them all'.I remember also, the way, at mealtimes, she'd serve out the food for all of us first and leave herself last in case there wouldn't be enough or somebody might want more. I remember that very clearly now, because I do it myself.

So what is it that makes us fools for our children and willing fools at that? When maternal instinct is mentioned, we think of the need to protect our children, to ease their way through life, to provide for them, to encourage them in their endeavours, to teach them right from wrong and to respect other people. We love them so very deeply and unconditionally from the moment they're born or even before that. I have a very distinct recollection of being overwhelmed by a feeling of love for Eva when I first felt her move in my womb about 19 weeks into my first pregnancy. The feeling was new to me and was a very powerful surge in my stomach that I didn't quite understand at the time but which I now know was a physical manifestation of that emotional phenomenon of motherly love. And it doesn't go away. Eva is nineteen now and an adult and I feel exactly the same protective instinct as I did when she was a baby. As I do for Tom, Eoin and Lucy as well. Although I worried terribly when I was pregnant for the second time that I wouldn't be able to love any baby as much as I loved Eva. I lay awake at night wondering how I would be able to make a place in my heart for another child because my heart was totally filled by Eva. I knew the theory that the heart expands to take in as many children as needs be but I genuinely couldn't appreciate how this would happen. I had to experience it to know that it's true. Think of the sleepless nights I could have saved myself, and the worry.

Worry is something I, as a mother, am very familiar with and it's a comfort to know that I'm not alone. Every mother I know shares those fears and the trait goes way way back. This letter dates back to Papyrus in Egypt around 2000 BC. 'Dear Mother, I'm fine. Stop worrying about me!'

When my children were small, I worried about their development, their health, would they be popular at school, would they have friends or would they be bullied, would they be happy? These concerns proved groundless and yet I still worry. I believe that coupled with the privilege of giving life, goes the responsibility of teaching how to live life. Am I teaching them to think, to feel, to imagine, and to believe? Am I teaching them kindness, fairness, compassion and consideration for others? Am I too soft, too strict? Am I giving them a good study and work ethic? Am I giving them every opportunity to sample different extra-curricular activities? Am I showing them the value of friendship and loyalty and honesty and spirituality? In a word, am I doing my best for them? I know it's been said that any mother could perform the jobs of several air traffic controllers with ease and there are times when I feel I'd make a good juggler but is this what's required? There isn't a day goes by that I'm not wondering and worrying how my children are right now; how they'll 'turn out' as they say, whether they'll be happy and fulfilled and whether I could fight their corner harder for them, give them more of my time and of myself.

When I'm thinking rationally, I know that I do my best, that I shouldn't judge myself too harshly and that we all need to forgive ourselves and be grateful for the good things and the bad things in our lives because they help us grow. And my goodness, forgiveness is something we mothers have in abundance when it comes to our children. The French novelist Honoré de Balzac, writing back in the nineteenth century summed that maternal trait up pretty well when he wrote: 'The heart of a mother is a deep abyss at the bottom of which you will always discover forgiveness'.

It's true we have no shortage of forgiveness for our children. It goes hand in hand with unconditional love. It's a different story when it comes to myself and the way I fulfill my role as mother. I wonder why? I think it has a certain amount to do with the fact that I am part of the early generations of Irish mothers to have the opportunity to work full-time outside the home. My experience of being mothered is totally different to my experience of mothering. My mother was subject to the marriage bar so she had to resign from her job in the civil service when she got married. She was a full-time home keeper and mother from then on and she never approved of mothers working outside the home and said so on many occasions. Mind you, her disapproval of my working first as a teacher and then in RTÉ didn't stop her from looking after my children for me. She was my childminder and I honestly believe that experience was a very valuable one for my children. They had a very close relationship with their grandmother which is part of their psyche now.

The fact that my mother was full-time in the home though has influenced the way I judge myself as a mother. She was always there when we came in from school. For seven months of the year, I'm not there when my children come in from school. I work outside the home and part of the legacy of being of this transitional generation of Irish mothers is a dose of guilt because I'm not doing it the way my mother did.

You see my generation of women has that one particular quality in common and in abundance. It's called guilt and it assaults us frequently, when we examine our lives, our relationships, and our careers. It's a legacy of our upbringing. We are a generation that was reared to be polite and respectful always and there's nothing wrong with that. But our sense of self, our confidence was not well nurtured or developed. We were taught not to have notions or to question authority. So is it any wonder that whenever the issue of work and mothers is raised it brings out the need in us to defend our choices? And choices they are. If I want to work outside the home why should I feel that my children are not getting the best upbringing that I can give them? Guilt. That's why. If I decide to be a stay at home mother why should I feel that I'm letting the sisters down or that I'm not pulling my economic weight? Guilt. That's why.

The challenge for us mothers therefore is to overcome this guilt. We get one swing on this merry-go-round called life and I am convinced that we have to be true to ourselves and live the life we want, that we feel will make us happy and fulfilled human beings. A satisfied mother, whether she's working inside or outside the home is going to have a better relationship with her children than one who is frustrated, overburdened and unhappy.

On the one hand, I love my children dearly and they know it. They are the greatest gift I have been given in life. I love these lines from *The Witless Mother*, by the Belfast poet Emily Orr. 'All that I knew of heaven, I saw in my baby's eyes.'

Children truly are a gift from God and from the time my first child was born, I have viewed life differently. I've seen beauty in every part of their beings, their smiles, their soft skin, their thoughts, their words, their concerns, their games, and their drawings. They really are heavenly creatures. I enjoy their happy times and I comfort them when they are troubled or sad. On the other hand, I work outside the home and I love my job. And I love to come home in the evenings and be with my children.

I value greatly having a good relationship with my children and I'm always asking them how things are, if there's any news, anything bothering them. They don't always open up, especially in those early teenage years. They do know however that when they want to, they can. I believe good relations are rooted in good communication. We're all aware of parent-child relationships breaking down. Parents working outside the home is not the issue; ground rules, discipline, respect and responsibility are. I believe we have a duty to nurture these qualities in our children from a very early age. Sadly, in these times when small children are quite often spoiled rotten, such qualities are underdeveloped and I pity any parent who tries to teach them to adolescent or teenage children because, quite frankly, it's too late.

I've been very lucky because the two careers I've had fitted in quite nicely with my children's schedules. When I was teaching, I was at home when they were and had the long summer holidays. And now that I'm presenting *Open House*, I also have the summer off and that's nice too. I like to be here when they come home from school, especially when they're preparing for exams, as was the case last year with Eva and Tom. But I also know that by the end of the summer, I'll be looking forward to combining work and home life for another while. It'll be exhausting but rewarding.

That's my choice and it fits in with what I tell my children about living life to the full and taking advantage of every opportunity, of embracing the ups and downs, the good times and the bad times that go to make up this rich tapestry of life. One thing is certain. My two daughters will have a different role model when it's their turn. They will enter motherhood having been mothered by a woman who worked inside and outside the home. I hope this will mean they can choose their lifestyle without the burden of guilt and feeling of being an inadequate mother.

There is no doubt that motherhood alters one's life totally and irrevocably. I view the world now through my children's eyes in a way. I was quite surprised by how suddenly this happened after Eva was born in January 1984. That was the year of the Ethiopian famine when the TV footage of starving people shocked the world and led to Bob Geldof's massive relief effort and also to the foundation of Self Help, the charity set up by members of the Irish Farmers Association to work toward famine prevention in Africa. They asked me to lead their annual trek to Africa last year. We travelled to Eritrea and it was a life changing experience. Like everybody else, I was shocked and saddened by those pictures of people dying of hunger in Ethiopia in 1984 but this time it was different. When I looked at a picture of a starving child I saw my darling baby daughter's face and I could feel the tug at my heartstrings as if it was my child on that television screen. I think that's what empathy must really mean: being able to feel what the mother and child were suffering. That was certainly a turning point for me and I will always do what I can to relieve that kind of suffering because we can make such a difference with very little effort.

If I take on a difficult challenge, I'm hoping my children will feel they can do that too. I want them to feel that the world is their oyster. I gave Eva a flying lesson for her eighteenth birthday. Not because she has ever mentioned flying as a career choice or even as a hobby she'd like to take up. I wanted to convey to her the message that the sky's the limit. My wish is for them to live happy, satisfying lives and that the world will be a better place for their presence in it. I'm happy when they're happy. It breaks my heart to see them sad. They are as much a part of me now as when they were growing inside me and we were joined by the umbilical chord. I feel drawn closer and closer to them as the years go by and they get bigger and begin to have their own lives. I don't think there will ever be a time when they are not the most important part of my life. They are the greatest gift that I have been given. They are all so different from each other. Eva is sensitive; my mother was always talking about the fact that she's 'a real softie'. Tom is comical and very easy-going and brings out the protective side in women, young and old. Eoin is very caring and aware of others' needs. I attribute that to the fact that he began life in the womb as a twin.

In May 1988, two years after Tom was born I was pregnant with my third child but had a miscarriage at 13 weeks. I was heartbroken at the loss of the baby and continued to write the date of the miscarriage into my diary for years afterwards. This gave me a sense of the baby existing; that it wasn't just over and done with and forgotten. I took great comfort from this because, at 13 weeks, I miscarried a fetus which for me was as much my baby as if it had continued to grow and thrive and be born on its due date. Needless to say I was delighted to be pregnant again some months later and when the bleeding started at about the three months stage, I was so disappointed and frightened. I thought God, please, not another miscarriage. The ultrasound scan told the story very plainly. I saw two sacs on the screen: one had a heartbeat, the other didn't. I was pregnant with twins and one had died. I miscarried one of those babies and just prayed and prayed that the other would hold on. He did and although I gave birth to one healthy baby at full term I always regard him as a twin. Eoin has an awareness of others that is remarkable and which I like to attribute to the fact that he began life in that way. I think it's a lovely quality and I remind him how special it is and how special he is.

Lucy is the youngest and I have yet to meet a more vibrant, articulate and energetic being. She's at that lovely stage of talking non-stop, telling me everything, being wonderfully affectionate. She sends me gorgeous good night texts just before she goes to sleep. I know that will change as she enters her teenage years, but I accept that these are the different stages children go through and that they're gathering life lessons along the way. There are times though that I feel I'd like to freeze the moment and just enjoy Lucy's open, smiling innocence and joy as they are right now. She finished primary school this summer and asked me if she could have a barbecue in the back garden on the last day of term for her school friends because they'd never all be together again. I said okay and when it got nearer to the date I asked her how many were coming. I got a bit of a shock when she replied in her chirpy fashion. 'All of them'. So, at the end of June, Lucy played host to 35 boys and girls from St Colmcille's Senior School. The sun shone. I don't even want to think about what I would have done if it had rained. It was a great occasion actually. Their teacher, Brian McGabhann dropped in and they were delighted. Lucy took it all in her stride. Like I said, she has an open, joyous attitude to life which is very precious. Life goes on though and children grow up and it's so important to enjoy all of those stages and not try to rush them on. When I was teaching Irish I loved *Subh Milis,* a little poem by Séamus O'Néill, which describes a situation familiar to all parents, the one where you go to open the door and the handle is sticky with jam because your youngster, oblivious to the niceties of domestic living, has passed that way before you. The temptation is to throw your hands up in the air in exasperation, but the poet here suppressed his anger.

> Mar smaoinigh mé ar an lá
> A bheas an baschrann glan,
> Agus an lámh bheag
> Ar iarraidh.

'I thought of the day the door handle would be clean but the little hand would be no more.' A reminder that children grow up all too quickly. It might not seem that way when we're getting up three and four times a night to one or other of them and when a trip in the car feels like a military campaign with all the paraphernalia that has to be organised. But it's true.

My children are my greatest joy and my greatest gift in life and I know one thing for sure. One gift that I can and will give them until the day I die is the certainty of my love and support. I will be there for them always. I want them to know that. I want them to realise that I'm content when they're happy, and that they are constantly in my thoughts and those thoughts are full of love, support and concern. I want them to realise I know them deeply, and for them to be comforted by that. As Patrick Kavanagh was comforted to know his mother sensed his every thought.

> You will know I am coming though I send no word
> For you were lover who could tell
> A man's thoughts – my thoughts – though I hid them –
> Through you I knew Woman and did not fear her spell.

(From In Memory of my Mother, Died, November 10th, 1945) I'd like my children to know the world and its people through me and to have no fears, as I knew the world through my mother. There were times when I was adamant that I would mother differently, more liberally and more openly but for the most part, the role models I was following in my mother and her mother before her were pretty hard to beat. They taught me fairness and compassion, kindness and love. And I'm grateful for that. I can't think of a nicer compliment to a mother.

Growing Years

My grandmother was a woman of great physical strength and great strength of character. She had a sharp wit, was staunchly nationalist and a pivotal force in our family. She was a matriarch; a powerful presence and we loved having her in our lives. Every Thursday Uncle Tom (next door) collected Granny during his lunch break and brought her out to Clondalkin for the afternoon and evening. She'd have dinner in one house and tea in the other and then play a few games of cards after tea. The two husbands, my Dad and Uncle Tom, would drive her home about ten o'clock. As children we looked forward to Thursdays because there was always something a bit special for tea and lots of cakes and apple tart. In the winter the fire would be lit in the sitting room as well as the kitchen and there was always a cosy sense of special occasion. Even when Granny got very old and was content to sit by the fire in the sitting room and just have a cup of tea and a slice of bread and butter on a tray while we were eating in the kitchen, I still loved her presence in the house. I hope my children have similar fond memories of their granny's latter days when she was ill and sat by the fire in our house.

Another aspect of my grandmother's presence in our lives was the Saturday night visit to her house. We stayed at home with the two fathers while my mother and Auntie Eilish would go to spend the evening with Granny and their sister Kathleen, who lived at home. I enjoyed those Saturday nights because it was a very relaxed regime when my father was in charge. We moved between the two houses and watched television in pyjamas and dressing gowns, after that institution of the Saturday night bath. Again, I have happy memories of those nights, sitting on the floor, by the fire, with my brothers, my sister and my cousins while my Dad and Uncle Tom would watch *Match of the Day* with John Dalgetty from across the road, who always joined them when the two wives had gone to Ellesmere. We might be given a bar of chocolate and a glass of orange and then again we might not.

Times were very simple then by comparison with these days when there always seems to be bottles of fizzy drinks in the fridge and sweets and biscuits in the cupboard to which my children help themselves. Those things were a rare luxury when I was growing up. I remember vividly that one of the highlights of Christmas was the six bottles of lemonade that were bought and that lasted right through the holiday season to be drunk at our parents' discretion. A glass of cream soda was something we relished at Christmas time and boy did we drink it sparingly because there wouldn't be a second one going. This is a far cry from my kitchen where a two-litre bottle can disappear at one sitting.

My grandmother lived to be a hundred and two and loved nothing better than to sit and chat, a trait my mother got from her and I think it must have passed down the female line because I'm partial to swapping stories with folk myself. Granny grew up in Newtown in Carlow. She was very bright and did well at school. When she came to the end of her primary school days she was about fourteen and stayed on to help the teacher. Whenever we got good marks in a school test, she'd always say by way of praise 'the sod of turf wasn't wasted on ye'. That was the way in her day. The children brought in a sod of turf for the school fire. She also told us that on cold days, her mother would give her two warm potatoes to hold in her pockets to keep her hands warm.

She was married from her aunt Mary Cooper's house on Stephen's Green in 1911. The wedding took place in Westland Row church. Her husband, Chris Dowdall, worked in Guinness until he died. They had seven children, five girls and two boys, one of whom, Billy died in 1939 of TB. He was twenty-six. She was a very resourceful woman and when she was pregnant with her first child, she noticed what she described as big, white, midwives' aprons on the clothes line of the house backing on to hers, so she got up on a chair one day, called over the wall to the woman, confirmed she was a midwife and 'engaged' her for the delivery! No visits to obstetricians and antenatal clinics for the likes of my grandmother in those days. You just got on with it.

She was also very politically aware and had very strong nationalist views. She attended all the rallies outside the GPO in the early years of the twentieth century. Some of her brothers were in the old IRA and she used to tell us stories of the goings on in the streets where she lived as a young wife and mother during the Troubles. A neighbour of hers was married to a well-known IRA activist and his wife used to hide guns under the mattress in the baby's pram. One day the Black and Tans came to the house looking for the man and when they couldn't find him, they took the family dog and slit him from the neck right down his body. As children we listened wide-eyed to these stories that were part of a very difficult time in Irish history. One of Granny's brothers, Peter, was shot dead by the Black and Tans on Ferrycarrig Bridge in Wexford. She told us that his comrades brought his body home to his mother's house in Carlow and laid him on two chairs in the kitchen. Can you imagine the heartbreak in that house at the time?

Not surprisingly, Granny maintained strong nationalist views always and wouldn't even watch British television in her old age. She was of her time, a strong woman physically and psychologically. She had a deep faith and devotion to the Catholic church and she just adored company. We loved hearing stories of the card games and sing songs that took place in her house in Ellesmere. They seemed to happen at the drop of a hat.

Another thing my grandmother loved was fine-bone china and she had a lovely collection in her china cabinet that I used to take out and look at when I was visiting her. For her part, Granny loved to tell the story of where she got a particular tea set, who gave it to her and she also enjoyed just feeling the fine china. There was one set that I truly loved for its delicacy and also for its tiny lilac flowers on the cups and saucers and for the lovely shape of the sugar bowl and jug. My mother bought it for Granny with her first week's wages when she started work. I have that set now and I wish I didn't because I got it when we were clearing out Mam's house after she died and dividing up her bits and pieces. Little did I realise during all those years of visiting Granny and asking her if I could open her china cabinet to hold that set, that it would be in my house one day having been given back to my mother when Granny died and given to me when Mam died. Those memories are like snapshots in time and hold precious reminders of happy and carefree days. I sometimes look at my own children when they're doing something and wonder will they be looking back on these times as adults and what experiences will be theirs in the intervening years. For the moment though, I just want them to be happy and healthy and to enjoy life as we did when we were youngsters.

When I look back on my childhood years I feel that my life was perfect and running on an even keel. I was living in a very secure environment in Clondalkin, which was then a small but growing village on the outskirts of Dublin, with my parents, brothers John and Tony and my sister Deirdre. There wasn't any money to spare but we all lived very happy lives and laughed and played a lot. Having your cousins living next door seemed like the most natural thing in the world, hardly worthy of comment because there were so many children on the road anyway and we all played together. The summer nights were the best. We'd play chasing games like King, which involved somebody being 'on' and chasing the others (which could number up to 20), along the road, over the walls, through the garages and into the back gardens. Once you were caught, i.e. hit with the tennis ball, it was your turn to be on. It was great fun, the running and jumping and hiding and avoiding being hit. There were however, one or two houses on the road occupied by older couples who didn't have children and who didn't appreciate balls going into their gardens. Sometimes they rang the guards and sometimes the guards came up to give out to us. This only added to the excitement of the game. I remember one night, we saw the guard arrive on his motorbike and we scarpered into the nearest house, which happened to be ours, in the front garden, through the garage, into the back garden and over the stile into the cousins and then over a couple of more back walls to complete our escape. What we didn't realise was that the guard had got off his bike and was coming after us just as my mother was coming out the kitchen door with a basin of washing to hang on the line. They came face to face in the garage and my mother nearly died of fright to see this tall figure in black with a helmet on standing in front of her. She dropped the washing and had to listen to his complaint which in fairness to him he had to make. We were in trouble when we finally came back and I think we were all grounded for a few nights after that. That was okay for us because there were two families of us and we could be kept in one house and play Monopoly or something.

They were certainly fun times and innocent times for us, but as an adult when I think back I realise that while we were all getting on with life and going to school other children, our age, were living in fear and brutality. All of us (boys and girls) went to the Presentation Convent. The boys left after their First Communion and went to the Marist Brothers in Moyle Park. Those were the days of corporal punishment and we all got a few slaps from time to time which we were cute enough not to tell our parents about because they'd always take the side of the teacher and want to know the precise details of the misdemeanour. You could then end up with a double whammy, getting punished by the folks as well.

None of this had any ill effects on us whatsoever. We were getting a good education and learning respect for others and the difference between right and wrong. A few short miles up the road though, other children our age were being brutalised and living in fear and trepidation. We had no idea at the time that the children in Goldenbridge orphanage run by the Sisters of Mercy were being badly treated, as we now know from the exposure in Christine Buckley's documentary *Dear Daughter*. I passed Goldenbridge on the bus on Fridays and Saturdays when I was being brought into town to Irish dancing and elocution lessons. None of us had any idea that it was a place where children were being beaten and abused by the people who were entrusted with their care. When I think about it now I feel almost shell shocked to realise that as we were passing by on the bus, some child the same age as me, was perhaps down on their hands and knees scrubbing floors, or being beaten for not scrubbing them correctly; all the time living in fear. And all that was worrying us was whether we'd get a tongue lashing for not knowing our dance or our poem and whether we'd be allowed buy sweets on the way home. We were very privileged but we didn't realise it at the time.

Both of my brothers and my three cousins next door were altar boys. It was the done thing in the '60s and '70s. As we know now, terrible things happened in those days. Members of the clergy abused many young boys. Thank God, my brothers and cousins escaped. We've spoken about this as adults and wonder why they were so lucky. The obvious reason is because the priests they were working with were honest and upright men.

My brothers and cousins were as bold as brass. They never learnt their Latin Mass and would mutter any old thing as quietly as possible and then proclaim a loud and confident 'Amen' thinking they were fooling the priest. My brother John got his comeuppance one day when he was serving on his own with the Monsignor and as they arrived back into the sacristy the Monsignor swept by, pointing his finger at John and saying to Sr Bernard, who was in charge of the altar boys, 'This boy doesn't know his Latin!' He did by the next week though because she gave him a couple of lines a night to learn and she tested him on them too.

The only hassle from those times was inflicted on my mother because she was the one who had to dig John, and in later years, Tony, out of the bed when they were serving the 7.30 a.m. Mass. She didn't want them to be late of course and if she didn't badger them, they would have been. She and Uncle Tom went to that Mass together every weekday morning of their lives. He had a few hassles with his altar boy sons as well. One morning, when the two brothers, William and Brian were serving the 7.30 Mass and he and my mother were waiting in the church for the start of Mass, Uncle Tom had to leave the pew and go around to the sacristy to break up a fight. The two boys were engaged in fisticuffs over who would do what during the Mass and the noise was travelling from the sacristy into the church. The most lethal combination on the steps of the altar was my brother John and his cousin Brian. If you were at Mass and Benediction when they were serving you'd nearly want to bring a gas mask because they seemed to be intent on completely filling the church with incense. The place would be full of it and the priest would be coughing and have to signal to them to desist. They fought over who would ring the bells and would hold down the other's hand to make the bell ringing impossible. Often as not, when it was time to move the Sacramentary from the lectern on one side of the altar to the other, the one who was getting up from kneeling at the foot of the altar would stumble because the other one was kneeling on his soutane. They blew out each other's candles and argued about who would serve at Communion and any member of the family (parents excluded) who received from them would get a sharp dig of the paten under the chin. I threatened John that I would tell on him if he did it again because I arrived home from Mass one Sunday, looked in the mirror and realised I had a red mark under my chin from where he had assaulted me with the paten.

They were bold certainly and yet they wondered why they never got to serve weddings where they would be guaranteed a few bob. Sr Bernard had their measure and kept those perks for the better-behaved lads. Again, when I think of the five of them and how happy and carefree they were and the mischief they got up to as altar boys I realise how lucky and privileged they were to come through childhood unscathed. I've met men who suffered abuse at the hands of the clergy and even though these priests have been brought to justice and the men have had counselling and compensation, the hurt, the fear and the pain will never fully go away. I can see it in their eyes and hear it in their words. Their childhood was shattered and they show enormous courage in dealing with that awful injustice and rebuilding their lives in a way that they shouldn't have had to ever think about. The same is true of anyone who has been abused as a child, whether the abuser is a person in a position of authority or a member of the family and let's face it, that's where most abuse happens. In fact, although there's a feeding frenzy in the media when the church and abuse are mentioned, according to figures realeased by the catholic press information office, only 3% of sexual abuse of children can be attributed to members of the clergy and other religious. That's 3% too much of course, but we have to realise that children are being brutalised and abused in their own homes and there's still a terrible veil of silence around that scenario.

It's impossible for us to comprehend how those horrific experiences can have terrorised those children who, like the rest of us, looked to adults with respect and for protection.

I remember two incidents from my childhood that seem completely trivial by comparison with the stories of abuse we've heard about in the media but which scared the living daylights out of me at the time and make me wonder what it can have been like to experience the fear that those children suffered. The first involves a priest and the second a male stranger.

The Saturday after I made my First Communion, I went along to confession. We went every week in those days. I went into the confession box, feeling a bit nervous. This was my first time on my own, after all, without the whole class lining up and the teacher telling us which box to go to. We had been so well drilled for our Holy Communion that instead of saying 'Bless me Father, for I have sinned. It is a week since my last Confession', I, in my nervous state and because I had practised it so often, said instead, 'Bless me Father, for I have sinned. This is my first Confession'. I didn't even realise my mistake and was very taken aback when the priest replied immediately, 'That's a lie. Start again'. I hadn't a clue what he was referring to and had to ask him to explain, which he did in a gruff, curt way, pointing out to me that I obviously wasn't thinking about what I was saying. I was so scared and intimidated by the experience that if I were there yet I would still be saying, 'This is my first confession'. Every time I began again I said the same thing. Eventually after about six attempts, he told me to just get on with my sins and not to forget to include that lie. I did confess that lie to him and I was shaking when I eventually left the box. I never went back to him for confession again and if he was the only priest hearing confessions I left the church and told my mother I'd been. Another lie; caused by him. I was seven years of age at the time and I remember that day as if it were yesterday. I was frightened and intimidated. I didn't tell my parents because I was convinced I had done wrong. That trivial little incident which scared me hugely makes me realise that we cannot begin to imagine the fear, intimidation and guilt, the whole nightmare that victims of abuse are subjected to.

The other experience was equally trivial but it also affected me greatly and once again I remember it in detail as if it had just happened. I was about ten and my mother sent me up to the shops at the top of the road. It was a summer's day and as I was walking up the road, a car on the opposite side crossed over and drew up alongside me. It was a light blue Austin A40 with the driver's window rolled fully down. I continued to walk but the driver, who was alone in the car, called me and asked me for directions to another part of the village. I gave them but he seemed not to understand fully and pointed through the windscreen down the road. I moved closer to the car to repeat the directions and realised that I was vulnerable and that this was a potentially dangerous situation. It was obvious at that point that this man was a pervert because he had exposed himself. I felt sick. I actually thought I would throw up. I said nothing, turned away and continued the last few yards to the shops, shaking and in a daze, wondering why this had happened to me. Like I said, I was ten at the time but I can remember every detail about that incident: the dress I was wearing, the house I was standing outside, what he looked like, the colour of his shirt, the car. I know I was shocked and disgusted. I wanted to cry but I couldn't and I know I said nothing to my mother or to anybody at all because I felt dirty and that somehow I'd be in trouble. I know now that I should have gone home immediately and told my mother who could have reported him to the police. Who's to say that he didn't try the same thing somewhere else and the girl he approached might not have known to walk away? I also know that my mother would have wanted to know. I would certainly hate something like that to happen to a child of mine and for them to bottle it up but I couldn't bring myself to speak about it. Once again it was a trivial incident by comparison with the stories of sexual abuse we read about but my reaction of shock, disgust and an element of guilt makes me realise that we can't even begin to imagine the turmoil and horror suffered by victims of sexual abuse.

Those two incidents stand out in my memory because they were in such stark contrast to the rest of my childhood, which was a time of joy and innocence with a wealth of stories that weren't buried under the weight of life's complexities. We were happy and carefree and loved and well looked after and we assumed every other child was too. I now know that while I was enjoying those early years, children of my own age were being abused and terrorised. Joy and innocence weren't an option for these youngsters and it was a shameful time in our land. I know how I would feel if it happened to one of my children and my heart breaks at the thought of childhood innocence being destroyed. I'm sad too that the legacy of that brutality has tainted the work of so many good priests and nuns whose only intention is to work for and on behalf of the people who seek their care. I have some good friends, men and women, in religious life who are sickened by these revelations and disappointed by the way the church has handled them. They are people of commitment and dedication though and they continue to do great work out of love for the people and for God. And as I sit here, writing this I can see my children chatting and laughing in the back garden. The sun is shining. They're enjoying the lack of routine during the school holidays. The only concern they have at the moment is who's going to feed the rabbits. They'll argue as to whose turn it is, there'll be bribes offered to do the job if someone has a few spare euro, there'll be bargains struck about doing it twice next time if there's a reprieve now and do you know what will happen in the end . . . I'll do it! I don't mind though. They're young, they're healthy and happy and that's good enough for me.

Geesala Summer

As you approach the village, you can see for miles to the right and the left because the land is so flat and expansive. The bog cotton and the grasses sway in keeping with the force and the direction of the wind. The force is considerable and the direction is from the sea. This is the village of Geesala, Gaoth Sáile in Irish, on the western seaboard of county Mayo. There's an air of tranquillity about the place and comely maidens could quite safely dance at the crossroads because they are wide and fairly free of traffic. There's a mare with her foal in a field to the right, you can see the church steeple up one road, the sea over the hill in another direction, and the pub is still called The High Chaparral. My first impressions tell me that very little has changed in Geesala since I spent a holiday here with my family more than 30 years ago. Very little except for the major changes that is. Teach Iorrais, the hotel, is built on the site of the house we stayed in and the primary school which was located beside that is now moved up the road beside the church and the handball alley is gone. I mention those landmarks because they are central to the story of that holiday. When someone listens to that story and says, 'Maeve Binchy would get a novel out of this', you'd be forgiven for thinking romance. Not so in this case, but rather one of those chance encounters that make up this rich tapestry of life and which remind us that we connect with people in different ways and at different times along the path of life. During the summer this year, I met somebody I hadn't seen or heard of in more than 30

years and even then, back in 1969, our paths crossed very
fleetingly and casually. It's a nice story though.

Our two families, the Kennedys and the Whites, always
went on holidays together. I was saying in the previous
chapter that all that really matters is that my children are
healthy and happy. That's my priority as a parent and it
clearly echoes the concerns of my parents and my aunt
and uncle when I was growing up. They gave us such good
times and one of the highlights of our year always was the
joint summer holiday. The trip to Geesala was one of
many great adventures that the two families shared. Early
in '69, my mother and my aunt were scouring the newspapers for houses to rent that would accommodate the 11
of us, plus my grandmother and maybe another aunt. The
research was successful and they booked Gunnings house
in Geesala. The price was right; the house was spacious
but where exactly was Geesala? We hadn't a clue and it
took careful perusal of a pretty detailed map to find it.
Geesala is north of Mulrany and Achill, about eight miles
west of Bangor Erris and about 11 miles south east of
Belmullet. At the time it was a tiny little village on the
western seaboard with a pub, a couple of shops, a church
and a school. My Dad's reaction when we arrived there
was 'Next stop America'. It hasn't changed much in the
intervening years. The pub, The High Chaparral, named
after the TV western that was popular at the time is still
there, as are the shops and the church. The school has
only 30 pupils now and they were very sad to lose a
teacher last year. All in all though, Geesala is still remote,
still charming and is aptly named Gaoth Sáile, because the
wind from the sea would cut you in two at times.

I have very vivid and fond memories of that holiday,
over and above others the two families spent together and

when I try to figure out why I think part of the reason must be because as a thirteen-year-old, my heart was set a flutter there for the very first time. We arrived in Geesala after a two-day journey from Dublin – neither the roads nor the cars were conducive to making good time so we stayed overnight in Elphin in county Roscommon on the Saturday night. The key to Gunnings house had to be collected from a neighbour across the road from the church. Julia Barrett was her name and I remember her as a warm friendly woman who got on extremely well with my mother and my aunt and who baked the most delicious brown bread for us during our stay in Geesala. Julia had a large family: three girls and eight boys. Now, with that many boys in the one family, there was bound to be one of an age that a thirteen-year-old girl might set her cap at. And there was.

He was about fifteen or sixteen, a boarder at St Jarlath's in Tuam and in the evenings he would go into the ball alley which was behind the school, right next door to the house we were renting and sit on the wall. Meanwhile, I would go upstairs to the boys' bedroom, stand on the windowsill, open the top part of the sash window, lean out and we'd chat. I know, I know; visions of the balcony scene in Romeo and Juliet spring to mind. I tell you I looked forward to those evenings. My parents couldn't get over how agreeable I was when I was told it was bedtime. Little did they realise what delights awaited me upstairs. I don't remember having any contact with this young lad during the day. I suppose I wouldn't have been allowed, given my age and considering the fact that even to talk to him from the bedroom window I had to bribe my brothers and cousins every night so that they wouldn't blow my cover to the parents who were playing cards downstairs, happy in the knowledge that all seven children were tucked up in their beds. The boys had a great laugh at my expense every evening and they got rich too. They didn't usually have so much spending money on holidays.

As is the case in all such holiday romances, it fizzled out. At the end of the two weeks, I went back to Dublin and he went back to school in Tuam. We exchanged addresses I know because he sent me a letter from Jarlath's and I replied. I can't remember if there was a second letter but that would have been the height of it anyway. It's a nice sweet story, but that's not the end of it. Fast forward to summer 2003, and I am back in Geesala making a programme for TG4 called *Mo Laethanta Saoire*. I'd spent a weekend there last year with my children and showed them the area. That was my first time back since 1969 but this year was a different experience altogether. Christine Reddin phoned me and asked if I would be interested in taking part in a series of programmes that Adare Productions had been commissioned to make where people revisit a place where they spent a lot of holidays as a child. 'Certainly Christine, Barbados was where we used to hang out as youngsters!' Well it was worth a try.

Actually, Skerries in north county Dublin was where we spent many holidays as small children. Like a lot of Dubliners, we were restricted by funds and transport and had many happy holidays in our own county. The two families would decamp to Skerries for a month in those days and my Dad and Uncle Tom would take the bus or the train into work in the city every day and Mam and Auntie Eilish would take us to the beach with our buckets and spades and we'd happily play away while the two women supervised us from the rocks, sometimes wrapped up in fur coats. I know it's often said that we remember

our childhood summers as having been drenched in sunshine, well that was definitely not the case for us in those
early years because the camera does not lie. And we have
some really cute black and white photos of those fur coats
wrapped warmly around legs to keep out the biting cold.
We were oblivious to the chill it seems because we played
away in togs and t-shirts in the sometimes damp sand
without a care in the world. There must be an element of
truth in the saying that 'a cardigan is something a child
wears when an adult feels cold!' They were happy holidays
and we reminisce about them a fair bit these days because
my younger brother Tony and his wife and family now live
in Skerries. It takes us about an hour to drive to their
house along the M50 and we're fascinated by the fact that
for us to go there on holidays was a day-long expedition,
planned way in advance, with almost military precision
because it would involve borrowed transport and food
shopping.

Anyway, during the course of the conversation about
Mo Laethanta Saoire with Christine, we discussed those
holidays in Skerries when we were very young and then we
got talking about our one holiday in Mayo which all of my
family seem to remember very clearly, probably because
we were that bit older then, so we agreed that Geesala
would be my destination for that trip down memory lane.
I filled her in on all the relevant details, including the chats
between the bedroom window and the ball alley and off
she went to set up the filming schedule. When she came
back to me and said that she had contacted the guy and
that he was willing to be interviewed for the programme
I nearly collapsed. He has a good sense of fun and was 'up
for it' as they say. The fact that he is now the headmaster
of the local primary school, a pillar of the community and

very highly regarded by one and all didn't dissuade him from taking part and that impressed me.

There are a lot of people who would decline the invitation for fear of what 'people might say' and I believe that's a terrible affliction, an affliction I suffered from myself formerly. The way I view things now is that the people I care about know me and understand me. What others choose to think of me is up to them. I cannot let what other people may or may not think appropriate influence the way I live my life. It's a sad fact though that many people are restricted in this way and allow other people's opinions of them to influence their actions. How can you allow that to happen and still live a fulfilling and satisfying life? How can there be things that you want to do and you quite simply don't, even though you're happy in your own heart and soul that they are worth doing? If I'm ever in danger of falling into that old trap of being held back by what people might think or say, I remind myself of Polonius' advice to his son Laertes in *Hamlet*:

> This, above all, to thine own self be true,
> And it must follow, as the night the day,
> Thou canst not then be false to any man.

The recording dates were organised and at the beginning of June, the crew and I hit Geesala and stayed in Teach Iorrais. I was taken back in time quite dramatically when we were sitting in the dining room and I realised I was looking out the window at exactly the same vista as I had from that spot more than 30 years ago. The memories came flooding back of our sense of awe at the coastal landscape, so different from what we were used to in the city, the freedom we had to run in the fields and on the beach, and of course the heart fluttering experience of the ball alley.

Séamus Barrett wasn't so much interviewed for the programme as door stepped in his classroom – after the children had gone home from school for the day of course. We'd already set up the story 'pictorially', if you like. In 1969, the ball alley was behind the national school, right next door to Gunning's house. The school is now the community centre, the house is now the hotel and all that remains of the ball alley is a bit of a concrete wall. We filmed that bit of concrete wall though and I was filmed leaning out of the hotel window which looked onto that spot. The cameraman said he couldn't decide whether I reminded him more of Juliet or Rapunzel. I think we were getting a bit carried away with ourselves. At about 3.45 p.m. we went around to the school and I recorded a piece at the entrance to Scoil Náisiúnta, Gaoth Sáile. Then the camera followed me as I made my way into the building and found the classroom with Mr Barrett on it and a sign underneath saying 'Fáilte Isteach'. Promising. He was in the classroom, he knew we were coming but we hadn't met before starting to film the piece. I felt a bit shy but I walked in and introduced myself to this man that I hadn't seen or heard of in over 30 years and who had no idea until this programme was being made that he was the very first person to set my heart a flutter so many years ago.

It was lovely to meet him again. I reminded him of the ball alley evenings. We talked about teaching and family. He has a huge interest in the GAA. I remembered him having a hurley with him on a couple of occasions. But really it wasn't about the ball alley anymore. It was just nice to meet somebody that I'd known before and find out a little bit about how that person's life had evolved since. I honestly believe that connecting with people is one of life's great pleasures and that sharing stories is a dynamic and versatile tool available to us humans for the exploration of meaning in life. He was friendly, warm and welcoming to me and the camera crew who landed in Geesala that day; and fair play to him for his willingness to be a part of it.

It was Seamus who told us that the school had lost a teacher last year because of falling numbers. This saddened him greatly. His dedication to the school is obvious. The place is coming down with trophies and photographs and examples of the children's work. Everybody in Geesala speaks of him with the utmost respect and warmth. He gives his all for the children. I was thinking as we were leaving the school that it's a great privilege for those children to have him as their master, somebody who is so in tune with the area. He grew up across the road from that school. He went away to become a teacher and has returned to the home place as máistir. What better person to understand the qualities, the nuances and the needs of a place than somebody whose roots are there.

Another highlight of that trip down memory lane 'ar mo laethanta saoire' was the opportunity to meet Julia Barrett, Séamus's mother, again the woman from whom we picked up the key to the house in 1969. She's moved from that house and lives now with one of her sons and his family next door to the school. After saying goodbye to Séamus, we went in next door and the welcome there was just as warm. Julia is eighty-seven years old now, but she oozes love and warmth and that is exactly how I remember her all those years ago. She remembered my mother and aunt well and me as one of the gang of seven that didn't seem capable of walking anywhere. We ran and jumped along the street in Geesala. It must have been the sense of freedom and space we had there. Whenever Mam or Auntie Eilish wanted information about something in the area, they'd ask Julia. We'd stop by her house to pick up brown bread that she'd have hot out of the oven. She always stood in the porch and waved us off, full of life and energy. Rearing 11 children didn't seem to drain her. She was the first person I'd ever met called Julia and I thought it was a most beautiful and romantic name. Her son's attentions had me in a romantic frame of mind perhaps.

Julia and I chatted in the living room. I told her that neither of my parents was still alive and that Uncle Tom had died too. But that Auntie Eilish had been thrilled to hear I was going back to Geesala and that she'd be delighted to know I'd met Julia again and that she was well. She told me about her family, and we reminisced about that summer of '69 and discussed the little things that went to make up a holiday that was a great adventure for all of us and a very relaxing and pleasurable time for my parents and my uncle and aunt. Things like the sherbet flyers that Mam and Auntie Eilish found in the sweet shop while they were out walking and hadn't had for years previously. They bought the whole box and brought them back to the house. I needn't tell you they didn't last long. Things like the fishing expeditions that the men and boys went on and which yielded no catch . . . ever. The boys and the Dads would set off with all the gear and tackle, well wrapped up against the rain, and the womenfolk, who had more sense than to sit in the rain and have the fish thumb their nose at them, would wave them off with good wishes and mock relief that it would be great not to have to go shopping for the dinner. We'd have the pan out ready to fry the fish.

We laughed a lot on that holiday. As I think back to that summer, I'm amazed at how easily entertained and pleased we were as children. Soon after we arrived, Julia told us about a man in Doohoma who had a horse that we could ride. So every other morning, we'd travel the couple of miles from Geesala and hire out Bob. We rode him bareback, not because we were accomplished horse riders but because he didn't have a saddle. Up and down the football pitch he'd slowly trot with one of us on his back. Remember there were seven of us, all wanting our turn and some of us, me especially, less than comfortable at the prospect of climbing on his back. Uncle Tom took cine film of those holidays and the footage of me being helped onto the horse by my Dad and then escorted down the pitch as I held on for dear life is very unglamorous. Through all of this, Bob maintained his composure, which is more than can be said for us. He was the quietest, most patient animal you could meet. I'm sure he's long gone to his eternal reward and if there's a heaven for horses, he deserves to be there.

As well as horse riding, fishing and walking, we swam every day. It must have been cold but our blood was young and we loved every minute of it. Apart from that we played around the house. It had a huge garden. There was a kind of annexe to the side of the house that was locked when we arrived and we thought nothing of it. Until the following Tuesday that is, when I went into the sitting room, opened the curtains and fell backwards with fright because I wasn't expecting to be looking at the backs of three local men sitting outside on the windowsill. I ran into the kitchen to tell the folks and it transpired that they were queuing to see the doctor. The annexe was in fact the local dispensary and the doctor and nurse came on a Tuesday. Once that mystery was solved, we went out into the garden and the local people made a great fuss of us. We looked forward to the following Tuesday and had fun with more of the locals.

Another endearing feature of that house was the fact that at high tide, there was a stream that flowed across the kitchen floor. This caused us no inconvenience whatsoever because the floor was flagged and the water came in at one side of the kitchen and went down underground again at the other side. In fact, it was one of the things that went to make that holiday such a memorable one for all of us. I can still see my cousin Brian jumping high over the stream on his way from the sink to the kitchen table. He was always jumping as we grew up; over walls, over railings, over anything he could. Mind you, one of my abiding memories of our childhood years is of Brian with his arm in a sling. He broke his arm on more than one occasion . . . jumping.

I'm so glad we had that holiday in Geesala. I've spoken to the others about it and they have great memories of that time too. It was a special time shared by two branches of the one family and now that some of them are no longer with us, the memories are all the more precious. It was lovely to relive that time last June in Geesala while making that programme for TG4; to stand at the crossroads again, to see the football pitch where we went horse riding, to walk the beach, to stay in the hotel and remember the house, to meet Séamus and Julia and roll back the years to such happy simple times; to have a laugh with them and to feel their friendship, even after more than 30 years. It makes me think of that excerpt from Kahlil Gibran where The Prophet speaks of friendship:

And in the sweetness of friendship, let there be laughter and sharing of pleasures

For in the dew of little things,

The heart finds its morning and is refreshed.

My heart was certainly refreshed by that trip last June. And I'm so glad that my parents went to the trouble of taking us on those family holidays because they make up part of our knowledge bank, our store of experiences that influence the way we view the world. We were city children and that holiday in Geesala gave us an insight into a life and a place that we had never experienced before. John Millington Synge wrote *The Playboy of the Western World* while he was staying in the area and if you're familiar with the play you'll have some appreciation of the place; the wind from the sea, the isolation, the rugged coastline, the wild and free spirit of the area. My children were mesmerised and amused by the stories I told them about our holiday there. They found it hard to believe we had such fun in such a quiet and peaceful location. In fact I took them to Achill during our weekend there last year and insisted that we climb up a hill to see a dolmen. They protested as we climbed the hill and I pointed out to them that this dolmen was part of our heritage and we were lucky to have the opportunity to see it at close range. Eoin who was twelve at the time piped up from behind me; 'Mum, we're the MTV generation. To us, The Beatles are history.' That may be true but I have no doubt that in the fullness of time that trip up the hill in Achill will come into its own, maybe even in a school essay and give him a sense of our history, of what went before. It's gone into his memory bank and will shape his outlook on life in the same way as that holiday in Geesala shaped mine. Those experiences make us what we are. The places I bring my children and the way we spend our time are all being digested by them now and I hope that in the future, they will remember holidays and gatherings that I organise for them with the same affection and fondness as I do my childhood excursions and holidays.

It's funny too the way history has a way of repeating itself. My children spend two weeks every summer on holidays with their cousins. I'm glad to say, that in spite of the fact that the children think we were out of the ark, they are amazingly content with a relatively simple and unsophisticated way of spending the holidays. Long may it continue. Their memory bank is being filled with the good things in life. They're connecting with their cousins and uncles and aunts in a relaxed and laughter-filled environment and I reckon that connecting with other people is the ultimate reason for being and for doing.

Chalk and Cheese

L ife may well be all about connecting with people and certainly for me that's what makes life wonderful. It's not all about summer holidays though, much as we might like that to be the way of things. We spend a huge proportion of our lives working let's face it. I am constantly amazed at the arbitrary way in which we choose our careers and I think it's a really tough choice to have to make at such a young age. I look at my children and I wonder what careers they'll have and what detours they'll take along the way. I've been working in television for a long time now but I started off as a school teacher. In fact, there are times when we're all in the *Open House* office, working away, exchanging ideas and out of the blue, I'll say something to which there'll come the reply 'Jayney, ye'd know you were a teacher.' What is it about me? Is it a turn of phrase, a raised eyebrow or a look of incredulity? Is it a certain mindset? I don't know. I suppose the fact that I always have a pen (sometimes a red pen), stuck behind my right ear doesn't help. That's a legacy of my teaching days. There were no pockets in those long black gowns and it was my solution to the problem of juggling books and copies and chalk and a pen. My mother used to joke that I must have been a carpenter in a former life. Nowadays though it's a way of always knowing I have a pen to hand. I don't think about it at all. Others do that. Every day before we go on air with *Open House*, the floor manager will do a last minute check and invariably say; 'Mary, have you got a pen behind your ear'? It does

happen on occasion that it's still there when the programme starts, but it's hardly noticeable tucked under my
hair and it's only when I go looking for a pen that I realise
where it is and 'slip it' as they say. Nobody's any the wiser.

Just thinking about that reminds me of other things that
people don't see on television but which can keep a
presenter on his or her toes. I have a comb and a mirror
that I bring on the set with me and carry from one area of
the studio to the other as the show progresses. I remember
one day, I'd moved on to the couches and Marty was in the
armchair that I had just vacated and where I had left my
comb and mirror. I didn't have to wait too long to discover
my mistake because while I was interviewing a guest I
realised that there was a very strong light shining straight
into my eye. I couldn't make out what was going on for a
while and then I looked over and saw my esteemed co-
presenter with my mirror positioned at an angle so that it
caught the studio light and shone straight into my eye. He
must have been great at signalling in the boy scouts because
he had the mirror at just the right angle to catch the light
and my eye. The challenge then was to keep going without
laughing. I explained to the guest afterwards why I was
moving around so much during the interview. I was trying
to avoid the glare.

We drink a fair amount of tea and coffee during the
morning rehearsals and just before the programme starts.
We use those very fetching white polystyrene cups and
there can be quite a collection of them on the set's coffee
table before we go on air. Naturally, they're removed but
the odd time, one can slip through the net. They don't
enhance the look of the programme so it's a question of
removing the offending cup as surreptitiously as possible. I
remember one afternoon, being in the middle of an item

with one of our regular contributors when the director came through on my earpiece to tell me there was a coffee cup on the table. I knew what I had to do; wait until the camera was off me and on our contributor and then get rid of the cup. I kept an eye on the monitor and when he was onscreen I bent over, picked up the cup and flung it over my left shoulder and behind the couch. As far as I was concerned the problem was solved. However, I hadn't taken the reaction of the poor contributor into account. To say he was surprised to see me launch this missile behind me while he was talking away is to put it mildly. He thought I'd taken leave of my senses and found it very hard to keep a straight face for the remainder of the item.

Such are the joys of live television. This chapter began though with the red pen syndrome and the throw back to the days I was a teacher. I spent 11 years as a full-time secondary school teacher in Coláiste Bríde in Clondalkin and I have fond memories of that time. It was a lot more enjoyable than the years I spent there as a pupil. I was a bit of a messer and a bit lax about the whole study thing in first year but after that I knuckled down and didn't put my head above the parapet from September to June. I'm aghast at students nowadays preparing for State exams who just hedge their bets. They look through the previous few years of exam papers and decide to leave out certain aspects of courses that are unlikely to come up. I never took that risk. For me it was a case of belt and braces when it came to preparing for exams. I went into them, having studied every iota of the courses. 'Nerd' is the word my children use to describe what I was like then. It was bad enough to be like that in secondary school but sadly the nerd bit continued in to university and I do feel I could have enjoyed my college days more. Apart from being a

member of the Athletics club, which I thoroughly enjoyed
I spent my time either at lectures, tutorials or studying in
the library. How sad is that?

When I think back to those days at UCD and I ask
myself why I was so studious and nervous about exams,
the memory of feeling totally out of my depth springs to
mind. I studied Irish, English and French at honours level
in first year, even though it was only necessary to take two
at honours and one at pass level. Why? Because I was
afraid of failing one of them. I gave myself an awful lot of
extra work especially as I got honours in all three and
ended up dropping English. I needn't have spent all that
time doing Old and Middle English in first year but I
suppose it gave me a chance to study the *Canterbury Tales*
and the like. Unfortunately, because I was so nervous and
insecure I didn't actually enjoy studying. In Irish I was in
class with native speakers and people who'd gone to
gaelscoileanna and I felt like I didn't belong. I admit the
problem was all mine. I lacked confidence in my ability. I
know that if I went back to college now I'd enjoy the
learning, the people, and the atmosphere and live it in a
way that I just didn't then. For me it was a period of
concentration and intense work. In the heel of the hunt I
did well in college but I was never relaxed about it. My
daughter Eva is studying in Belfield now and I went on a
tour of the campus with her one day. It's changed a lot but
it wasn't the changes that registered with me as we walked
around. It was the return of those old feelings, the burden
of endless reading lists and assignments to be submitted by
a certain date, the tiredness from having to leave Clondalkin
so early in the morning to get the 51 bus in to town and
then the number 10 out to Belfield. As we walked along
the corridors of the Arts block I remembered feeling too

warm indoors and yet it was easier to wear the coat than carry it along with all the books. For me it was a time of struggle and push and very little enjoyment apart from the time I spent running on the track. It's so different now. Eva and her friends are enjoying the college experience. We had tea in the Arts café, which didn't exist in my day. Its exterior window was where the exam results used to be posted and I remember the heart-stopping experience of scanning the lists to see if my name was there. It always was and why wouldn't it be? I never stopped studying. If I had the time over again I would be much more philosophical about the whole thing and try to strike a better balance between work and play.

We underestimate our own abilities hugely. I meet people all the time who are surprised by how well they've succeeded in some course of study. I present certificates and diplomas every September to adults who left school early and who've gone back to second chance learning. We celebrate the achievement and the success and there is no doubt that we all thrive on both. There's a saying that:

> Life's battles don't always go to the stronger or faster man. But sooner or later the man who wins, is the man who thinks he can.

It's just a pity that so many people, myself included, have to wait a long time for that feeling of confidence.

Maybe it's because of that whole experience that I tried always to instil a sense of confidence in the girls I was teaching. I wanted them to feel they could achieve if they put their minds to it. I don't know how often I quoted Thomas Edison's line to them about genius being 'one per cent inspiration, ninety-nine per cent perspiration'.

I wasn't an easy teacher. I know I was demanding. I know I'd be on their case if their homework wasn't done. I know I wasn't a barrel of laughs with a new class until we had an understanding of each other, until they knew what I expected. Then I felt I could safely let my guard down. I had a face that could resemble a bag of hammers at times. My children sometimes tell me I have my 'teacher face' on. I never asked too much of them though. I didn't want them to be nerds like me. And I know I got greatest satisfaction from the pupils who started off in secondary school by informing me that 'I hate Irish, Miss' or alternatively 'I'm no good at Irish, Miss' and who ended up passing the exam. That's achievement and that's a confidence builder.

People sometimes ask me was it strange going back to teach with some of the teachers who had taught me. It wasn't. It's funny actually. We always imagine our teachers are years older than us. It wasn't till I began teaching alongside them that I realised they were only a couple of years older than me in some cases. I enjoyed the years I spent in Coláiste Bríde. We worked hard. But we had fun too. I always looked forward to our end of year staff dinners. The principal of the school at the time, Sr Paul, was a great character who loved a party and was always game for a laugh. We used to dress up in the costumes that were used for the school plays and perform parodies and skits, composed by the music teacher and highlighting, in a tongue-in-cheek sort of way, the events of the previous academic year. All behind closed doors of course. No partners allowed at those shindigs. It was funny really. We'd all arrive, dressed in our finery to celebrate the beginning of the summer holidays and the end of another academic year and no sooner was the dinner over than

Paper Tigers

we'd be off to the classrooms to change into the rags and old clothes for the 'show', Sr Paul leading the way.

I remember on one occasion as the school year was drawing to a close, Sr Paul was in her office with a few of us who had a free class. We were rummaging through the box of costumes trying to decide what weird and wonderful things we'd don at the staff dinner. There was a knock at the office door and Sr Paul went to answer it, wearing a grass skirt over her habit and a long brown wig. She reckoned it was one of the other teachers and that she'd give her a laugh. Only it wasn't one of the other teachers. It was a young graduate who was there for a job interview! Sr Paul had lost track of time and forgotten she'd made this appointment. I can't remember whether that young teacher joined the staff the following September. She certainly got the shock of her life when she came for her interview.

Sr Paul was principal of the school when I was a student there as well and could be very cross at times. Some of that I think now was due to the fact that she had terrible arthritis which could be very debilitating. When I joined the staff though and got to know her better, I was amazed by her big heart in spite of her awful suffering and her mischievous sense of fun. Sometimes you couldn't keep up with her. I remember being called out of class one day. I was teaching away when Sr Paul's voice came over the intercom. 'Would Miss Kennedy come to the office now please'. No matter how mature and sensible you are, an announcement like that can make you wonder what you've done wrong. I got a bit of a start all right, I left the girls with something to do and somebody 'in charge' of the class and made my way towards the holy of holies. Sr Paul met me half way and walked towards the office with me saying that there was a parent there who was spitting fire about her daughter being given detention for something or other and she was baying for my blood because I was the year head. She said she just wanted me to know that, before going into the office because forewarned is forearmed and all that. I felt I was being fed to the lions as I went into the principal's office. This woman stood up and proceeded to rant on about her daughter being a good girl and there was no way she was staying back after school because she had a music lesson in town. I hadn't a clue what she was on about but tried to get a word in about the rules being useless if they're not observed, about not making exceptions for one particular girl, about the need to follow through on decisions. To be honest, however, every time I opened my mouth she was off on another rant. Meanwhile Sr Paul was behind the desk, nodding at me and making soothing noises to the woman. Then all of a sudden, this irate mother bent her head and started to sob uncontrollably. Or so I thought. She wasn't sobbing, she was breaking her heart laughing. This irate mother was none other than a fellow teacher, another nun, dressed up in coat, wig and glasses. Sr Paul had put her up to it. I was had totally and it wasn't even April Fool's Day.

That was the sort of thing Sr Paul would get up to and I'm fully convinced that it made the school a happy place. The standards were high, the discipline was strict, the results were good but there was still room for flexibility and fun. I have very happy memories of my time teaching in Coláiste Bríde and of the people I met there. Sr Paul died about four years ago although she had retired as school principal sometime before that. I remember being at her funeral with the other teachers and reminiscing about those days, her spirit and her sense of fun. There's a way in which we renew our sense of spontaneity by being with people like her. She had that gift of making others realise that life and work can be very serious but there is also a place for laughter and fun.

There's one person who stands out from the others from those days in Coláiste Bríde. She started off as my teacher and we ended up as teaching colleagues. She was also the Vice Principal. Most importantly, she is somebody who influenced me in a number of ways; the subjects I chose at college, the way I taught my classes and the way I viewed the pastoral aspects of the job as well. Her name is Mrs Redmond and she's retired a number of years now. She does have a first name, but even when we were working alongside each other she was always Mrs Redmond. Not because she's the kind of person to stand on ceremony, but because that's who she is to me, quite simply. She's a diminutive, dignified, soft-spoken woman who oozed authority always. She also had a great sense of fun, although that didn't become apparent to any of her pupils until the boundaries were well established and we knew the score. The score was hard work, precision and attention to detail. Mrs Redmond was my Irish and French teacher all through secondary school and I ended up loving languages, their literature and their culture. She's from Kerry and gave us every encouragement. She organised for a group of us to go and stay in houses in Corcha Dhuibhne in the summer after 5th year. There were no classes, we just lived with a family and soaked up the language and went for walks. She knew what she was doing. We all came back in love with the place, the people, the language and the culture.

For most of us it was our first taste of the gaeltacht. A few of us had been to an Irish college, just outside Gorey, at the end of 6th class. Personally speaking, I might just as well have spent three weeks on Mars for all the good it did me. I had no sense of where I was or what was expected of me. My one memory of the sojourn is of being caught having a midnight feast. There was a group of us from Clondalkin in a dormitory and there had been a visit from the parents on this particular Sunday afternoon. They brought the customary tins of shortbread and buns for us in case we got peckish. Anyway, that night, after lights out, we decided to investigate the contents of the tins. They were all placed on one bed and we were just about to dive in to them when we heard footsteps on the stairs. Everyone scarpered back to her own bed and Joan, whose bed had been used as the picnic table, raced around putting the tins under her bed. The teacher came in and turned on the lights. There was nothing untoward. She was suspicious but all she could see was a room full of sleeping twelve-year-olds. Then, just as she was leaving, Joan, in a valiant effort to make us look all the more authentic and innocent, turned and pulled the covers up over her. Unfortunately, there were a couple of biscuit tin lids caught in her covers and they clattered spectacularly as they hit the ground. That noise was followed by a succession of muffled sniggers. Eyes remained tightly shut in the hope that 'it' might go away. No chance. 'It' came storming back into the room in the shape of a furious teacher who was seriously not amused. I can't remember what punishment ensued but I do know that I learnt no Irish that year, in marked contrast to the time I spent in Corcha Dhuibhne where not only did I learn the language but I fell in love with everything it stood for.

I know that when I began teaching I used Mrs Redmond as my role model. She was thorough and demanding and I knew that if I did the work she set I would get the desired results. I wanted my pupils to feel that way too. She was very strict when we started off as 1st years but as the years progressed and we were in a rhythm of work, she relaxed hugely and we had lots of laughs in class. She had that healthy balance of work and fun that we sometimes lose sight of in these pressured times. I'm lucky to have been taught by Mrs Redmond and I'm glad her influence put me on the path to studying Irish and French at college because even though I no longer teach the subjects I get great pleasure from both languages, particularly Irish which for me is an integral part of our make up as Irish people and which we speak even when we're using the English language, with our colourful turns of phrase and idiom.

My female friends are very important to me and there's a group of them that I met through teaching that are good friends still. We taught together and made a point of getting together socially every so often, as well. When our children were small, we'd organise a meal in someone's house. Everyone would make something and bring it along. We had some great lunches and dinners and looking at the photos of those gatherings now brings back happy memories of those times. We still keep in touch. One of our group, Barbara Ann, or Babs as I call her, has been a friend of mine since we grew up together on Brigid's Road and she's a wonderful person for keeping us all in touch. She and I were in class together from Junior Infants right through to Leaving Cert, we were in college together and ended up teaching together in Coláiste Bríde. Our mothers were friends too and although we don't work together any more and there can be times when we don't see a lot of each other, there's a strong bond there that goes back to our childhood days. Babs is a brilliant organiser and is great for making that call and getting everyone together. The more I live the more I realise how important those friendships are. Connecting with people is definitely one of the riches of this life.

That's also why I love to hear from former pupils and find out how they're getting on. It's when I hear that they're married with children that I realise how quickly time flies. A reminder that we get one swing on this merry-go-round called life and it's up to us to make the most of every opportunity and to have dreams and goals but to make a conscious effort to pursue them with energy. Wasn't it Eleanor Roosevelt who said 'it takes as much energy to wish as it does to plan'?

La Belle Vie!

How would you feel about spending the summer looking after a two-year-old girl in Paris whose parents were extremely wealthy and whose grandparents had a shipping business and lived on the Avenue Foch, the most expensive and the grandest of the avenues that spread out in a star shape from the Arc de Triomphe? You'd be living with the little girl and her parents on another of those avenues, the Avenue Klèber, in a luxurious apartment about twice the size of a normal semi d in Ireland. You'd travel with the family to the Pays Basque, near the border with Spain, and stay with friends of theirs in a spacious villa with a pool and sunloungers and be able to visit San Sebastian on your free days. You'd also spend some time with their relatives who lived in an old French Chateau in the heart of the country; a building full of character and history. You'd sleep in a circular bedroom in one of the turrets and get to meet lots of other French country folk because the chateau had a sizeable domestic staff. You'd then return to Paris where you'd spend most of July and then fly down to Nice to spend the month of August on the family estate, complete with vineyards on the Côte d'Azur, a few miles inland from St Tropez. It sounds idyllic, doesn't it? Well it wasn't. I know because it happened to me.

I was nineteen years of age, ready and willing to practise what I preach about making the most of every opportunity, having dreams and goals and pursuing them according to the advice of Eleanor Roosevelt. It was a big step for me to leave home and spend a summer in France; neither of my parents had any experience of this and I was the eldest so nobody had gone before me and blazed a trail. I'd just finished second year Irish and French in UCD, and when I landed in Paris I might just as well have been landing on the moon. I hadn't a clue where I was in relation to where I was going and there was nobody there to meet me. I should have smelt a rat straight away. I took a taxi, which I could ill afford and showed him the address on a piece of paper. I was going to spend the summer as an au pair looking after one delightful two-year-old girl so that I could improve my oral French. And she was delightful. Sadly the same cannot be said for some adult members of her family. I think it was during that summer that I developed an abhorrence of meanness and a realisation that generosity is a gift which bears no correlation to the amount of money a person has at their disposal. It's a state of mind that can manifest itself materially but if a person lacks generosity of spirit it permeates all aspects of their lives. It's telling also that the people I met during that summer whose faces I remember and can still visualise in my mind's eye are the ones who were kind and generous and warm. They shone out like a beacon of light and compensated for the lack of warmth in others.

It was my first time in France and when we arrived at the incredibly grand apartment on the Avenue Klèber, my eyes were out on stalks. The entrance hall to this apartment was more spacious than the whole of the downstairs at home. The reception rooms were beautifully furnished in a classic French style. The bathroom was fully tiled with tiny blue mosaic tiles. The taps were brass, and a devil to polish every day. Sophie's (not her real name) bedroom was a little girl's dream, the like of which I had only ever seen in the movies. You'd sink into the thick, shaggy cream carpet. There were shelves and shelves of fabulous teddies and dolls and Sophie's wardrobe was filled with designer clothes. The name Christian Dior comes to mind for a start. It was not surprising that she would be wearing miniature versions of his creations because her mother, my boss, was a valued client. I remember answering a knock at the apartment door one lunchtime and a courier handed in an invitation for Madame, beautifully wrapped with an orchid attached, to a private Christian Dior showing.

Madame was very watchful of what I would pick out for Sophie to wear each day. There was no way you'd put a top from one outfit with the bottom of another for this little toddler. She was also very particular about her own clothes and was always beautifully dressed. But as my grandmother used to say if anyone admired someone's appearance or clothes: 'handsome is as handsome does' and in this case the doings were not handsome. She seemed to have no understanding of the philosophy of 'au pair' whereby you take somebody into your home and treat them as one of the family in exchange for a set number of hours of childminding each week for which you pay them pocket money. I replaced a Mauritian girl who had worked as a domestique (maid), for about three times the amount of money I was paid. I was expected however to do all the housework that she had done, which posed problems on two fronts. First of all, I lived at home in Ireland and because I was studying, my mother didn't ask too much of me on the domestic front so I wasn't exactly efficient in that regard in the beginning. I tell you I got good at housework though. I had plenty of practice that summer. I spring-cleaned that apartment from top to bottom. I washed, ironed, shopped and cooked. It was great training, especially the shopping because I got to talk to the shopkeepers and practise my French. The only other outlet for speaking French in Paris was by babbling away to Sophie who at two was only learning to talk herself and wasn't at all critical of my hesitant and mistake-ridden French.

The other problem about replacing the domestique rather than being an au pair was that there were times when I had very little contact with Sophie during the day and I regretted that because we grew very fond of each other and I missed her terribly for a long time after I came home to Ireland. I think she took to me because I actually played with her. I remember coming back to the apartment after a day off; I'd bought her a cheap plastic doll in a bath so that we could play at bathtime. I know her room was coming down with the most beautiful teddies and dolls but they were not for messing about. Sophie and I had great fun bathing this really cheap baby doll and washing her hair and the following day she was going to visit friends with her mother for lunch and wanted to bring this doll but mother was having none of it. I reckon the thought of her daughter arriving at some swanky place with this cheap naked plastic doll in tow was more than she could stomach.

Appearances were very important for Madame. The one and only time I showed a bit of spunk was one evening shortly after I arrived when she was having a dinner party. She and I prepared and cooked the meal and then before she went off to get ready, she gave me my instructions about how to serve at table. I wasn't surprised by that really because I never ate with her even though her husband was an engineer who was working on a project in Africa from Monday to Friday and only spent weekends in

France. If she was staying in for the evening, she preferred to eat alone, which suited me fine at the time because I wasn't really at ease with her and preferred to eat with Sophie but when I look back now I think it was a pity when you consider that there wasn't a huge age gap between us: I was nineteen and she was about thirty. We could have had good conversations about our different lives and boy were they different. The cultural exchange didn't seem to interest her. I find that difficult to understand because when I went on to have au pairs when my children were small there was a lovely feeling of learning about another culture, another way of life, other ways of doing things that I know my children enjoyed. In fact in one case, we had two sisters from the same German family as au pairs within a couple of years of each other and they have remained good friends ever since and we visit backwards and forwards from time to time.

Back to the dinner party. I listened dutifully as Madame showed me how to serve at table, even though I had that skill. I worked through the winter in the Little Chef restaurant (now Joel's) at Newland's Cross, for goodness sake. I didn't share that with her though. I don't think it would have rated in Paris 16ième terms. What happened next floored me. I thought first of all she was joking, but she was deadly serious. Madame produced a little bell and said that she would ring it once when I should clear away and twice when it was time to serve the next course. And that's not all. She also produced a black dress with a white lace apron and cap and assured me it would fit me nicely. Can you imagine? I almost laughed until I realised this wasn't a joke and I had two choices: wear the uniform and answer to the bell or not. I don't know where I got the courage because I was quite intimidated by Madame in those first weeks. Maybe it was the memory of the 800 years of oppression and subservience that rushed through my consciousness at that moment. Whatever the source I stood up for myself then in a way that I hadn't before and didn't afterwards. I told her I would wear my own clothes and I didn't mind if they got splashed. (It's not as if I was decked out in Christian Dior or his ilk.) I also told her that she could 'give me a shout' when she needed me in the dining room but that I would not under any circumstances budge if I heard that bell tinkle. And that's how the dinner party proceeded. And the walls didn't come crashing in. And everybody got fed. She didn't like it though and she got her own back on me quite soon afterwards.

It was a Sunday evening. Madame was at the cinema with friends. Her husband was at home, having dinner with his younger brother, who was in his early twenties and a student, like me. I was on duty that evening, so after I put Sophie to bed, I cooked for the two men, served them and cleaned up afterwards. It was now about 9.30 and Monsieur went off to bed because he had to catch his early flight back to Africa the next morning. His younger brother asked me if I would like to go for a coffee on the Champs Elysées and because I had done all my jobs and would normally have gone to my room at that stage, I said yes. It would be nice to see Paris by night. We walked down the Avenue Klèber and turned on to the Avenue des Champs Elysées; had a coffee and chatted and then he walked me back to the door of the apartment. It was now about 11.30 p.m. It was a nice evening, but it had been noted.

Friday was my day off and I had arranged to meet a friend from Clondalkin who was also au pairing in Paris in much less affluent but much more convivial circumstances. She wasn't free on Fridays but her family welcomed me to spend the day with Susan and their small son and I used to stay and have dinner with them when they'd return from work. This wouldn't have happened in my gaff on the Avenue Klèber. Anyway, on this Friday I went into the living room to say goodbye to Madame and Sophie before I left for the day and I was surprised when Madame told me to be back by 6.00 because she and her husband were going out for the evening. I explained to her that I had arrangements made because I was normally free for the whole day. Not this Friday, she said. Didn't you have time off on Sunday evening? I pointed out to her that I had all my jobs done and that if I hadn't gone out I would have been in my room but the lady was not for turning. It was a mean thing for her to do but it was teaching me a life lesson that I got more and more insight into as that summer progressed.

For a start, it made me appreciate my home and the easy-going lifestyle that I had taken totally for granted until then. And I was aware of Madame's lack of generosity in spite of all the comforts and luxuries she enjoyed in life. I should point out that we never had rows and there were never raised voices between us. She might throw her arms in the air from time to time in exasperation at something I'd done wrong but we got on fine on a superficial level. I didn't rise her I suppose. It's always been a trait of mine, and not one I'm proud of, that I avoid confrontation. I just put up with it and thanked my lucky stars that I lived with a mother and father who had very little materially but who showered all of us with love unconditionally and for whom appearances mattered not a bit. There were, of course, times during those first weeks in Paris when I wanted to go home and I must have said as much in a letter because although it was usually my mother who wrote to me I got a letter from my Dad one day saying that if I really wanted to leave I could but this was a wonderful opportunity to see another country and to learn the language. He talked about times when he was away from home as a young lad and the feelings of homesickness that I recognised. He assured me those feelings would subside, that three months was a very short time in the overall scale of things and that in years to come I would be glad I stuck it out because I would learn something new about myself and about other people with every passing day. He also made some suggestions as to what I should say and do to Madame, but they remained our secret. I took his advice to heart and weathered the heavy feelings of loneliness in the pit of my stomach and he was right. They did subside and boy did I learn that 'there's nought as quare as folk'.

The first glimmer of light entered my life when Madame, Sophie and I drove from Paris to stay with her friend in her villa in the Pays Basque. We drove all day through the French countryside which was a whole new experience for me. I loved the towns and villages that we passed through. We stopped at a roadside restaurant and my French was still pretty rudimentary so when I saw the word for egg on one of the dishes I went for it. I ordered a plate of spinach with a fried egg on top. I love that combination now but that first time, I nearly threw up at the sight of it, not to mention my reaction to the taste.

When we arrived at our destination at the foot of the Pyrénées, not far from Biarritz I was enthralled. The villa was white-washed with a hacienda style: big, open plan, and sprawling. The garden was a sea of colour and scent with flowers everywhere and to the side a great big swimming pool. But my favourite memory of that time is

Madame's friend who was there with her two small boys
and her French au pair. She was kindness itself. The contrast
between her and Madame was huge. While Madame was
a very beautiful and expensively dressed woman, she
looked nothing beside this friend of hers who always had
a smile and a kind word and who in my mind's eye seemed
to glide rather than walk around the place. The evening
we arrived, she was so welcoming and warm. She asked
me questions about Ireland and my family and gently
corrected my French. She insisted that I eat with her and
Madame and her French au pair. I must have been
desperate for a bit of kindness and affection because when
I went to bed that night I cried myself to sleep. I didn't
understand what was happening then but now, many years
and many experiences later, I realise that it must have been
a release after all the tension of being around Madame
and enduring her coldness. It also strikes me that Madame
was the unfortunate person in this scenario because
although she was beautiful and wealthy and had a very
comfortable and luxurious lifestyle, she was closed to the
value of widening her circle and truly welcoming another
person into her life. It was such a shame. Her friend was
also beautiful and wealthy and lived a life of luxury but her
heart was open to embrace others. She had the confidence
to reach out. She didn't feel threatened. She was always
showering gifts on me; like a lovely sweater that she said
didn't fit her anymore. Or books that she'd read and she felt
I'd enjoy and learn a bit of French from. Part of me thought
even then that she was saddened by Madame's coldness and
tried to make up for it. She was certainly capable of feeling
for other people and her spontaneous acts of kindness
towards me are a good illustration of what John O'Donohue
wrote in *Anam Cara*:

Spontaneity is one of the greatest spiritual gifts. To be spontaneous is to escape the cage of the ego by trusting that which is beyond self. One of the greatest enemies of spiritual belonging is the ego . . . The ego is threatened, competitive, and stressed, whereas the soul is drawn towards surprise, spontaneity, the new and the fresh.

When I remember how differently I felt around those two women, how one of them made me feel good about myself and the other intimidated me, I realise the power we have to influence the happiness of other people. I can see that we can be a positive and a loving presence in others' lives, because our confidence grows and flourishes when we are praised and loved.

The warmth of that interlude in the Basque country had to sustain me for quite a while because we went from there to Madame's aunt's Chateau, in the Loire, and the old regime returned. The demarcation zone between the family and the hired help was re-established but having had the positive experience, I didn't care. In fact, instead of feeling hard done by and improperly treated I was strengthened in my view that these people were restricted and disadvantaged by their inability to look outside themselves and outside their own circle for social interaction.

There was another example of meanness that I encountered during that summer which taught me another life lesson; that our children learn their value systems from many different sources, but principally from their parents. What a huge responsibility that is. And what a wonderful opportunity to open their minds to the ways of dealing with people and events. If Madame was mean-spirited, her mother was even worse. To a comical degree, actually.

Here's what happened on her estate, where we spent the month of August. It was a beautiful spot, high up in the hills with acres of vines ripening under the intense heat of the sun. The house was enormous and built in the Provençal style. There was a winter house and a summer house. The dining section for summer had no walls, just a Provençal roof with bougainvillea growing up through the uprights, and a tiled floor. There was an enormous wooden table in the middle around which sat the many guests that stayed for a couple of days at a time. There were film directors, politicians, actors; all very pleasant and chatty. Madame's mother also had an Irish au pair, Deirdre, who was a year behind me in college and who ended up as a work colleague in RTÉ in later years. We'd never met before but we hit it off straight away and we had a lot of laughs together. It was nice too to have company on our days off, on the odd occasion that they dovetailed. Our two bosses weren't all that concerned about facilitating us and letting us have time off together, because that would leave them without that extra pair of hands.

One night, all the adults went off to dinner in Saint Tropez and Deirdre and I were left with Sophie. Before she left, Madame senior told us that there were tomatoes in the fridge and that we could make 'tomates provençales' for our dinner. That was fine. I put Sophie to bed and Deirdre set about preparing our dinner. She washed the lettuce, cut the bread, set the table. We then decided that we would luxuriate in the absence of our host family and we went for a swim in the pool. We then sat by the barside pool and had an apéritif. Then we came back and Deirdre stuffed the tomatoes and put them in the oven. We noticed that there were a few sausages in the fridge so we cooked them too. Now it wasn't an extravagant meal by any stretch of the imagination: sausages, tomatoes, salad and bread. But we enjoyed it and didn't envy them their posh restaurant in Saint Tropez one little bit.

Fast forward to lunchtime the following day. I was upstairs with Sophie and I heard Madame senior bellow from the garden below. She was calling Deirdre and when Deirdre meekly replied 'Oui Madame', the bellowing continued. She was a big woman with an equally big set of lungs. She wanted to know where the sausages were. I kept a very low profile as Deirdre explained that we had eaten them for dinner. Madame told her that the tomatoes were for our dinner and the sausages were for our lunch today and that seeing as we had eaten both we would have nothing but bread and salad. And we were starving. It felt like a scene from *Oliver Twist*. Except that this woman was married to a shipping magnate and lived on the Avenue Foch in Paris in the 16th arrondissement. That's what I call mean and that's also what I call comical. But wouldn't you much rather be on the receiving end than be the person capable of that kind of meanness?

One of the reasons I love travelling to other countries is to view a different culture and to appreciate the different ways people live their lives. By looking outside of ourselves, travel broadens the mind. And by looking inside of ourselves, travel makes us appreciate life and relationships at home. This was my first time to be with people who really had no interest in finding out anything about me or my life. They just weren't interested in having a conversation or finding out about life in Ireland. Deirdre and I were the help and that was that. There was a guest there at one stage who was friendly and his overtures were discouraged. He was a nephew of François Mitterrand and perhaps because of his Socialist background, he always wanted to help us. When Deirdre and I would go into the summer dining room after they'd all had lunch or dinner, he'd stand up and start to gather up plates. And no sooner had he done that than Madame senior would more or less tell him not to be stupid; wasn't that what we were there for. Every day he was there, he'd make the gesture and every day he'd be slapped down. It was comical and Deirdre and I enjoyed the farce immensely.

Another comical interlude that had Deirdre in the wings in stitches and me centre stage just brought home to me the lack of regard these people had for our customs. From the time I was a child, I watched my mother empty basins of soapy water over the rose bushes in the back garden. It was part of the summer routine of washing the dishes. When the job was done, she'd go out through the back door, with basin in hand and douse the roses in the suds. I also knew from a very early age that the reason she did that was to keep greenfly at bay. So there I was in the garden in the south of France one day and I noticed that some insects had visited a lovely rose. Later, as I was washing Sophie's cup and plate in the sink, I thought of the roses again and decided that if soapy water was good enough for greenfly, sure it would probably do the job for other infestations as well. So I went out to the garden with the basin and tossed its contents over the rose bush just as Madame senior was passing by. I can only assume from the level of her roars that she thought this was an act of deliberate sabotage on my part and that I'd be setting my sights on the vineyards next and that by the time I left I'd have devastated every living creature in her garden and ruined her summer retreat. When I recovered from the fright of her reaction, I tried to explain to her what I was doing but I could see by the way she was looking at me that she thought I was stone mad. My efforts to convince her of the validity of what I'd done weren't helped by the fact that I found it hard to keep a straight face because over her shoulder I could see Deirdre, a safe distance away, in fits of laughter at my dilemma.

After that episode I think Madame was convinced that we lived in mud huts in Ireland. And that she was introducing us to levels of sophistication beyond our wildest dreams. This was not true; certainly their lifestyle was way beyond anything I had encountered previously but even then, as a nineteen-year-old student I could see that their sophistication was very superficial; appearances were everything. It was all about expensive clothes, jewellery and cars and influential guests. I remember one day Madame senior came into my room and saw that I was reading *Du Cote de Chez Swann, A la Recherche Du Temps Perdu*, a weighty tome by Marcel Proust. It was part of my third year reading list. She was impressed. I suppose it would be the equivalent of a young French student with very little English wading through *Ulysses*. I was just trying to make life easier for myself in my final year by having one or two of the books read during the summer. She viewed me differently after that. Yet I hadn't changed one bit. She was less disparaging and dropped her joke that I heard about a hundred times, about Irish people throwing their dirty water on the flowers instead of down the sink. However, her tolerance of me did nothing to change my opinion of her or her daughter. They were shallow, unfriendly and mean people and I got one further example of that meanness when we returned to Paris at the end of August.

With about a month left of my stint as an au pair and just as I was settling back in to the Paris routine of cleaning the apartment and looking after Sophie, who I really adored at this stage, I developed awful pains in my stomach. I said nothing about them initially, convinced they'd just go away, but one day Madame came into the kitchen and found me doubled over and holding onto the sink for support. She must have got a bit of a fright because she was on the phone to her doctor straight away and made an appointment for me to see him that afternoon. She drove me over to his surgery . . . and left me there! I'm sorry but I do not know anybody in this country who would do that. He diagnosed appendicitis and asked me whether I'd like to be operated on in Paris or at home in Dublin. It would be done free in Dublin because of my student medical card. He gave me his bill that I couldn't pay obviously. This was the very posh part of town but he said not to worry. He'd post it to Madame. I think I took a taxi back to the apartment. I couldn't have managed the metro with the pain that was coming and going.

The rest of the day was spent on the phone to change my flight arrangements and I was amazed at how helpful Madame was through all of this. She made all the arrangements and I was on a plane home the following day, which was awful because I was pretty weak from the pain and I was heartbroken to be leaving little Sophie. I had no time to prepare for this sudden departure and it was very hard. I held her and she cried and didn't want me to go and I cried too because I knew I wouldn't see her again. I was amazed at how attached I'd become to this little one. But then we were together all the time and she really was my French teacher that summer. I'd chat and chat to her and if I made a grammar mistake I'd correct it and say the sentence again. She didn't mind. At two years of age, children love repetition. I learned that from my own children, many years later when they'd want to hear the same bedtime story over and over. I missed Sophie for a long time after I came home. I sent her cards at Christmas and for her birthday for a while. I loved her.

When I got home everything happened quite quickly. I went to my GP, then the Mater Hospital and before too long I was minus my appendix. It was only afterwards that I fully understood Madame's helpfulness in getting me back to Dublin. She didn't have insurance for me. She didn't need it for somebody staying in the country for three months. After that length of time, it's a requirement. I had been there three months and one week at that time and if I had stayed the full time I would have spent four months with her family. So she should have had insurance but she probably thought for the sake of one month it was worth the risk and she'd save a few bob. I also now understood why her doctor tried so hard to persuade me to have the job done in Paris. He was quite concerned about me travelling back to Ireland in case the appendix might burst whereas I was thinking my whole family would be bankrupt if I stayed. The doctor assumed Madame had me insured and that my hospital costs would be covered. Silly man.

What topped the whole episode for me was the arrival through the post of his bill, which he had duly sent to Madame and which she had redirected to me. She was this super rich woman in Paris and I was a penniless student in Dublin. I couldn't believe she could be that mean. Doctors in the 16th arrondissement do not come cheap and this bill was for more French francs than I earned in a week while I was an au pair there. I couldn't pay it and when I found out about the insurance scam I decided not to pay it. I ignored it and continued to write to Sophie and she continued to send me little drawings she did for me that Madame obviously went to the trouble of putting in envelopes and posting. It was a bit bizarre in a way to continue the communication on one level as if the bills didn't exist. Every time the doctor sent her reminders she sent them on to me. And every time, I ignored them. This continued for a number of months. And then eventually, she gave up. I was glad I made that little stand. It wasn't even about the money at that point. I could have borrowed it from my parents. It was a matter of principle. I didn't want to give in to what was a form of exploitation in my mind.

It was an amazing summer for many reasons. 'Far from it ye were reared', as my Dad said often after I'd come home and was regaling the family with stories of the Chateaux and swimming pools and vineyards and summer and winter dining rooms. There are life lessons contained within the events that happen to us on a daily basis and certainly I learnt a lot about life during that stint. Handsome certainly is as handsome does. In spite of the meanness and lack of warmth I encountered in the family, my time with them gave me a feel for France. I love the country and am very at ease with the people.

Another life lesson picked up very clearly involved how to treat an au pair. Or more precisely how not to treat them. When Lucy was born, 18 months after Eoin and with Tom and Eva quite young as well, we decided to try having an au pair to live with us. Over the years we had six altogether, four German and two Spanish, and except for two that didn't work out they were great successes. I have no doubt that because of what I went through I was aware of how to make it a good experience for all concerned. In one case, we had a German girl who'd just left school and a couple of years later, we had her younger sister. Their mother came over to visit while they were with us and the two families have become friends. In fact that's where the children and I stayed when we went to Germany for a long weekend last June and Eva and Tom spent several Easter holidays with them over the years. All of the children enjoyed the au pairs being in the house. They learnt some nice German customs for Christmas and Easter from Karin and the two sisters Ari and Isi. Esther made super Spanish omelettes and told us great stories of her family and their set up in Barcelona. In fact, Esther enjoyed Ireland so much that she came back to Dublin some time later and worked in a restaurant. Ari came back years later after she'd finished her degree in Germany and worked as a German translator in Dublin.

I'm glad all of those girls were part of our family life for a while. They were a great help with the children once they settled in. Settling in takes a while. That was something else I appreciated from my own experience. I could sense their homesickness in the beginning and helped them through it with phone calls home and reassurances that it would pass. They ate with us. They watched TV with us. When they arrived first we showed them around a little. They always knew they were welcome and viewed as part of the family. And as they settled in they made friends and would be up and out on their days off which meant that we all had our own space and lots to talk about at the end of the day. When I compare what I'm just writing to what I experienced as an au pair, I feel as if I could have been working and living with people from another planet, not another country. I don't regret it though. Life is about embracing different experiences, extracting the good and discarding the bad. And in this case, saying with a sigh of relief and a bit of a smile, ' There but for the grace of God, goes any of us'.

On Your Marks . . .

There are times when I wonder if I've taken the notion of embracing different experiences a bit too far. I know my mother thought so whenever there was talk of my need for exercise and running in particular. She couldn't see the sense of it, felt I was overstretching myself and that was without her having even a vague notion that I was training for the Dublin City Marathon . . . all 26 plus miles of it. That was a different experience and I'm really glad I persevered because when people ask me what I'd most hate to give up, the answer has to be running. It's not that I actually enjoy running when I go out, but I am in no doubt as to the benefits it brings, not just physically, but psychologically as well. I get out for a six-mile run four times a week during the summer and as often as work commitments allow during the *Open House* season. I never really look forward to a run. Sometimes I'm tired and sluggish and I'd rather do something completely different . . . like washing the floor or ironing. There are times when I'd do anything rather than put on that gear and take to the outdoors. I know it's going to be hard work. What I also know though is that when I finish the run and arrive back at the house, sweaty, exhausted and very thirsty, I will feel great. So, if you're of the mindset that wakes up every Monday morning determined to start an exercise regime but by breakfast time that resolve is weakening and you can't bear the thought of going out in the cold or the rain and by midmorning you've decided you'll leave it till tomorrow to start walking or swimming or jogging or cycling or going to the gym or whatever, remember that simple fact. Exercise does work. It makes you fit, it tones your body and you'll return in a much more positive frame of mind.

I have never been sorry I went for a run. I have often been sorry I didn't. The late Noel Carroll had this bit of advice for reluctant runners like me. Put on the gear, go out and give yourself six minutes. If after that time you still don't feel like running, go home. The fact is that after the six minutes you won't want to throw in the towel. You'll continue, do your stint and feel the better for it afterwards. I think it's great that something as simple as a bit of exercise can have such a positive effect on our psyche. The sense of physical and mental well-being that comes my way from a bit of physical activity is worth its weight in gold.

Sometimes I go out running in the early morning and there's an added bonus because in this country, even if it's going to be a grey and miserable day, chances are the early morning will be pleasant. There's a stillness then too that allows you to really embrace the moment. You can hear the birdsong, the rustle of the leaves; you can feel the wind on your face, or the sun on your back, or the rain falling on you and actually enjoy it.

During the early summer, I came across a few bunches of cowslips growing on a green while I was out running. I hadn't seen any in years and they were all over the place when I was a child. That was a real treat for me and an opportunity to let my mind wander back to those times when we used to pick cowslips and bring them in for the May altar in school. Even now the scent of cowslips, lilac and sweet Williams bring me right back to my school days. We'd have glass vases arranged around the statue of Our Lady which was standing on a starched and embroidered

white cloth on a table under the window. In my mind's eye
I could see the array of flowers. I could smell them. I
could remember us singing the Bells of the Angelus at the
end of the morning prayers. Before I knew it I had another
mile or two under my belt and the happy hormones were
doing their stuff.

That's one of the great things about running. It provides
a wonderful opportunity for thought. If there's something
on my mind, I often consider the options while I'm running
and I'm much more likely to come up with positive solutions
to a problem under those circumstances. The glass is half
full when I'm running. Other times I daydream. Sometimes
I reminisce like the day of the cowslips. After my mother
died I had a real sense of her presence around me when
I went out running in the early morning. Maybe it was the
stillness that allowed me to concentrate on her voice, her
smell, and her words. Mind you, her words would not have
been supportive. She always hated me running, she felt I
was doing too much and pushing myself too hard. Maybe
now she can appreciate just how important and therapeutic
running is in my life.

I remember when I was training for the Dublin City
Marathon for the first time in 1981, I was still single and
living at home and I knew that it would be more than my
life would be worth to let my mother know what I was
working towards. As I said, she didn't like me running and
could barely tolerate my doing a 30-minute run so I
devised a very strategic approach to my training that
meant that she never actually realised I was running long
distances. For instance, Mam was a member of the church
choir and always sang at the 10.30 Mass on Sundays,
which meant she'd leave the house at 10.15 and she would
return around 11.45. I would be togged out and ready to

go as soon as her car left the driveway and when I got back to the house at 12.15, she assumed I'd left for my run just before she returned home from the church. It wasn't always easy though to be bright and chirpy and pretend I'd been out for a short hop when I was ready to collapse in a heap after running for up to two hours.

One Sunday in September, about a month before the marathon, I was looking after a friend's dog for the weekend and I needed to go for an 18-mile run as part of my training schedule so I suggested to my mother that I take Tiger for a long walk in Belfield after lunch. A long walk is right. The dog was in a state of near collapse when we returned home because, while I was running 18 miles and no more, Tiger was running ahead at times and then back to me and then maybe ahead again. I reckon he must have clocked up about 22 miles on that afternoon. No wonder he couldn't wag when I got him home. He took up a position on the rug in front of the fire and didn't budge until the next day. Mam thought he was dying and worried about how we'd console Dick and Brid, Tiger's owners, when they'd come to pick him up on Monday evening. What could I say? I played it down and said I was sure he'd be fine and that dogs sleep things off. He was fine and probably the fittest dog in Dublin to boot.

And so, by stealth and skulduggery, I managed to train for and run the Dublin City Marathon without my mother finding out; until the day of the race that is. That morning Mam left the house very early to go to take care of her mother who was in her 90s at the time. She left me and my brothers and sister in bed on that October Bank Holiday Monday. As soon as she was gone, I set off for the city centre and the starting point, well prepared and ready for this project. It went well until about the 22-mile point anyway. I paced myself and thought positive thoughts all along the way and got great encouragement from the numbers of people who turned out to line and route and cheer everybody on. This was only the third ever Dublin City Marathon and the novelty hadn't worn off so the streets were packed with well-wishers. My steady pace continued until I turned onto the seafront in Clontarf and I noticed two things. The wind from the sea was cold and cutting. And there were a lot more St John's ambulances than before! This was where the 'wall' kicked in. Every step from there to the finish on St Stephen's Green was torture. I was one of the lucky ones though. There were runners keeling over, throwing in the towel. I repeated five words to myself over and over 'Pain is only physical force' and I kept reminding myself that every step was taking me closer to the finish. I struggled on and made it to the end and when I stopped there my legs quite simply turned to jelly. I was so glad I hadn't allowed myself to take a rest at any stage along the route, because I know now that if I had stopped, I could not have started again. I reckon that's why so many people gave up at that 22-mile stage. The wind was desperate and they took a breather and the legs either seized up or turned to jelly and the engine just wouldn't restart. I was the twelfth woman home in a time of 3 hours 40 minutes which was quite respectable. Emily Dowling won the women's race that year and when I came through the finishing line I was met by the late Brendan O'Reilly who said he was off to present the racing from Leopardstown that afternoon and would Emily and I come down and be interviewed between the races. No problem there I thought. The only difficulty was actually getting out of the car at Leopardstown because after 26 miles of running around the streets of Dublin my legs had locked into the sitting position!

Meanwhile, over in Ellesmere Avenue, off the North Circular Road, my mother and my grandmother were having lunch and decided to turn on the horse racing because Granny was always an avid fan. I can only imagine my mother's reaction when up I popped up on screen telling Brendan O'Reilly how the going was tough around the 22-mile mark and that yes the wall does exist and that my legs felt as if they didn't belong to me as soon as I crossed the finish line and so on and so on. My grandmother told me afterwards that Mam was speechless and the only consolation for her was that it was all over and I had survived.

Not only had I survived, but the feeling of achievement and well-being was enormous. It's a great confidence enhancer to set yourself a target and stick with it to the very end and then enjoy the results. And the harder the struggle, the sweeter the success. It was a huge undertaking and it acted as a template for other struggles over the years. I've often used it as an encouragement to myself. 'If I can run 26 plus miles without stopping, surely I can . . .' I ran the Dublin City Marathon again in 2000. It was my New Year resolution on the eve of the millennium. And I survived it again. The training went well throughout the summer. I enjoyed the runs and the feeling of being really fit again. I didn't enjoy the actual marathon though on the October Bank Holiday. It was bitterly cold and wet. I always carry a face cloth to wipe the perspiration during a long run. I ended up wrapping it around first one hand, then the other to try to get some feeling back into them. The numbers were down on 1981 but up on recent years because I wasn't the only one who decided to mark the millennium this way. There were about nine thousand runners taking part, about a third of them from the States. And they brought a lot of supporters with them, who lined the routes and cheered everybody on.

The American accent was the predominant one on the Marathon route that day. Everybody was in good form and they were handing out high-energy sweets to all comers as we passed by. There was a carnival atmosphere that went some way to relieve the agony of the run itself. The cold wind was biting and the going was tough. This was understandable, given the 19-year gap between the two outings. The body was older, the time was slower but the sense of achievement and well-being was just as great.

I suppose it helps that I never smoked. I was involved in sport from the time I started secondary school so it just wasn't an option. I did feel the peer pressure though and had the odd puff just to look cool; although in those days cool was a word that was used solely to describe temperature. I remember one Saturday afternoon on the way in to our elocution lessons. Yes they were called that in those days. Speech and drama were elements of elocution for us. Anyway, we three pals decided to throw caution to the wind and risk the wrath of parents by buying a cigarette each. How daring was that. It seemed very adventurous at the time. I can remember distinctly the feeling of foreboding once we had purchased the deadly weed. I couldn't have felt guiltier if I had emerged from robbing a bank instead of from buying three woodbines and a match in a corner shop. We stood at the bus stop at Islandbridge waiting for the bus home full of dread and fear that somebody might pass by in a car and see us smoking so we decided to defer the experiment. I never actually got to sample that fag because I hid mine up my sleeve and it broke in two. I remember a small feeling of relief that I now couldn't actually take the final step and commit the sin. And a sin it seemed in our eyes.

Now I view smoking as a great shame. I look at young people who start, quite simply to look cool in front of their pals and I know in my heart and soul that they will spend a small fortune on cigarettes over the years and another fortune on various devices to help them kick the habit. As a parent, I'm under no illusions about the pressures my children will face to take that first drag. We do our best for them. We point out the stupidity of the whole thing. We encourage them to be involved in lots of sport because 'ye need all your puff when you're out on that pitch'. We tell them of the cars and holidays they can kiss goodbye to if they start smoking. We assure them that they will in the fullness of time, regret the fact that they ever started and go through the wringer in efforts to give them up. And then we wait and we hope for the best. It's a lottery. It's about peer pressure and where they see themselves in their social circle. Some will smoke and some won't. As I said, we do our best and we hope for the best.

When I'm asked if I ever smoked I say I'm glad I never started because I have the willpower of a gnat. And then I'm reminded that it takes willpower to go running when you don't want to. Therefore I do have willpower and so do many people who underestimate their own resolve and ability to achieve. It's a great shame that we don't revel in our own powers to get things done. We take ourselves for granted so often. We sell ourselves short. I know there are days when I feel positive about myself and my worth and there are days when I don't. And I believe there are many people who can relate to that sentiment. I admire women who have a positive attitude to life and a high regard for themselves and their contribution to their home, their workplace, and their community. It's called self-confidence and it's something so many of us have to work at all the time. Mind you, exercise helps. My outlook is much more positive and my self-confidence much higher when I'm running regularly and taking in all that oxygen and working that body. And if the annual phenomenon that is the Women's Mini Marathon is anything to go by, there are an awful lot of people out there who would agree with me. This year's event, on the June Bank Holiday was a spectacular occasion. The sun shone for one thing; strange but true. Everybody was in high spirits and it was a huge success. This was the twenty-first Women's Mini Marathon and in that time the numbers of women who take part and raise valuable money for charity has grown from 8,000 in 1983 to 37,473 this year. This year seven million euro was raised, bringing the total for the 21 years to 70 million. That's an awful lot of money, raised by the women of Ireland for charitable organisations at home and abroad through this one sporting occasion.

The women come from all over the country. They've trained in their own communities and groups and have raised sponsorship for their chosen charities and then on the day, arrive in the city ready to run or walk and to party. There's no doubting the qualities of these women: their determination, their generosity of spirit and their sense of fun. The atmosphere, from beginning to end is fantastic. You begin to feel the sense of occasion walking to the start and passing the buses from all around the country. Waiting at the start is fun too. There's chat, laughs and upbeat music from the gig rig.

The music has a way of keeping you going along the route. The bands are strategically placed at spots where you might be faltering a bit, like at the bottom of an incline. I can tell you that when you hear these musicians belting out numbers like *Uptown Girl*, *Simply the Best*, or Joe Dolan's *Good Lookin' Woman*, it puts the spring back into your step.

Sonia O'Sullivan was first home this year in a time of 33 minutes and 12 seconds. It was undoubtedly a wonderful performance, and for all of the other 37 thousand plus women, it was also a wonderful performance. There's the accomplishment of training for and walking or jogging or running ten kilometres. There's the camaraderie of the rest of the group you've trained and travelled with and there's the knowledge that your efforts have raised valuable funds to benefit others. What a way to boost your self-confidence, not to mention your fitness levels and health. If you've never done the Mini Marathon, think about it for next year. I can't recommend it highly enough.

There's no doubt that for me physical strength brings with it inner strength – the strength to deal with problems, to realise goals, to lift the phone and call a friend, to feel good about myself. And that's as it should be.

The greatest living person, for me, is Nelson Mandela and this is what he has to say on this subject. These words have been attributed to him at the time of his inauguration in 1994, as South Africa's first black president.

> We ask ourselves, who am I to be brilliant, gorgeous, talented and fabulous? Actually, who are you not to be? Your playing small doesn't serve the world. There's nothing enlightened about shrinking so that other people won't feel insecure around you. We were born to make manifest the glory that is within us. It's not just in some of us: it's in everyone. And as we let our own light shine, we unconsciously give other people permission to do the same.

Now that's a nice thought. By feeling good about ourselves, we make others feel good too.

Giving Something Back

There are of course, many practical ways in which we can make people feel better about themselves. We're all members of a community and in every community there are charitable organisations that work to improve the lot of people less well off in some way. One thing these charitable organisations have in common is their need for more workers and more resources. Sometimes people say I do a lot of work for charity. The fact is I don't do as much as an awful lot of people. I have huge admiration for people who sit on committees and work tirelessly for the benefit of others. My work and domestic commitments mean that I can't do that kind of continuous voluntary work and no organisation worth its salt would want me as a fundraiser because I am useless at it. I just can't bring myself to ask people for money. I think it goes back to when I was at school and we would be given books of raffle tickets to bring home and sell. My mother would never let me go around the neighbour's houses to sell them. She felt they had enough expense without having to shell out to me. So she would always just buy the whole book of tickets herself, which meant of course that I never got used to knocking on doors and asking people for money – a skill that is much easier to acquire when you're young. I just can't bring myself to do it now as an adult, which is strange because I'm happy to contribute if somebody asks me to. I can help out on the night though and I will gladly contribute that way when I can.

But, as I said earlier I have huge admiration for the many many people in this country who give so freely of their time and energies to enhance the lives of others. When I travel around the country to host an event, I'm always struck by the warmth of the people who've organised it, their awareness of others, their boundless energy, their commitment and most of all their good humour. It's hard work organising a charity fashion show or concert or gala ball, but they have great craic and it's infectious. For all of these reasons, I'd recommend voluntary work to anyone who has time on their hands, or who's feeling lonely and isolated. There's great fun to be had out there and great satisfaction in knowing that you're doing something for somebody else who's been dealt a difficult hand of cards in life. We gain so much personally when we open our minds and our hearts to the plight of other people. We come out of our little self-sufficient cosy cocoon and get a real sense of belonging to a community, to a group of people who are living life the best way they can and helping others so that we can all aspire, at least, to be healthy, happy and fulfilled during our time on this earth. And we all have different skills that can benefit others: some people are great organisers; others are good time givers or great fundraisers and some of us, because of the job that we do, can quite simply raise awareness of whatever charities we're involved with.

One charity with which I have a particular affiliation is The Carers' Association, the organisation that works to raise awareness and support for the people who care for loved ones in their own homes. They asked me to be the patron of the association and I was happy to agree because I've met a number of carers over the years on *Open House* and I've been deeply moved and in awe of their devotion to the person they're caring for in the home, be it an elderly parent, a partner or spouse or maybe a child with special needs. Their dedication to the role of carer, their energy and stamina and their selfless love are worthy of recognition and reward. Sadly though, recognition and reward are in short supply.

There are in this country, 120,000 full-time carers in the home. A mere fraction of them receive any financial support from the state, one sixth to be precise. Only 20,000 carers receive any kind of carers' allowance and by the way, the maximum amount payable is the princely sum of €129.60 a week. Not a lot when you consider that by caring for their family member in the home these people are saving the state an estimated two billion euro a year, because if it weren't for their commitment, the person being cared for would have to reside in a state nursing home or some other institution.

We have a long tradition of caring for others in an un-selfish way in this country. Maybe it goes back to missionary times when Irish priests and nuns travelled to other continents to spread the Christian message. These days, Irish aid agencies work tirelessly to improve the lot of those less fortunate than ourselves in the third world. Look at the work of Goal, Trócaire, Concern and Self Help to mention but a few. Look at the work done at home on behalf of others by organisations like the St Vincent de Paul Society, Alone, the Simon Community and others. That outward looking mentality, that concern for the plight of others less well off than ourselves is one of those wholesome Irish qualities that in a way we take for granted. It's that same mentality that prompts people to care for a loved one in the home. It shouldn't be taken for granted though or exploited and that's one of the aims of the Carers' Association; to work on behalf of the carers, to lobby for funding, to provide support and respite care where the carer can get a break.

One of the questions often asked is 'Who's caring for the carers?' It can be a lonely life for them. Often they're quite simply unable to leave the person being cared for alone. They lose contact with friends. They get tired, depressed even. They need to know there are people who are looking out for their interests. And to know that they are not alone. Any time we have a carer on *Open House*, we receive letters and phone calls from people saying it's nice to know other people are living the same kind of lives. They get consolation from the knowledge that they are not alone and I must say that's one of the satisfying aspects of working on the programme for me – knowing that people can tap into a real life story and find a connection with their own situation.

Another charity that I'm associated with is Aoibhneas, (which is the Irish word for delight) a branch of Women's Aid, the organisation that provides a refuge from domestic violence for women and children. Here again, the workers are tireless, unselfish and provide a sanctuary for very vulnerable people at a very fragile stage of their lives. Such is the success of the service provided that a number of the women who sought refuge in Aoibhneas are now working there for the benefit of others. My involvement began when I was asked to lead their team of runners one year in the Women's Mini Marathon. This was no problem to me, because I was going to run it anyway and if they felt I could help out in that way, I was happy to oblige. I really feel that someone like me, because of the job that I do, gets off very lightly and while it might seem like a lot of charity work it's not labour intensive and I genuinely believe that we all have a moral responsibility to help out where we can and where our involvement can help to improve the lot of other people.

The reason that Terry Morrissey from Aoibhneas approached me in 1998 to run the Mini Marathon was because she had seen a TV programme I presented on Good Friday that spring about women who endure very difficult situations in life. It came from the Cathedral of the Assumption in Carlow, as part of the Easter ceremonies. Fr Dermod McCarthy, Head of Religious Programmes, asked me to interview five women in a programme, the idea for which had grown out of Roddy Doyle's book, *The Woman Who Walked into Doors*, the story of Paula Spencer, married to Charlo who physically abuses her. She endures great hardship, fear and misery before finally opening the bedroom window and throwing a suitcase stuffed with his clothes at Charlo in the front garden as he pleads yet again for forgiveness for his brutality. But in vain this time.

The programme was called *The Women Who Stayed* (as Mary stayed at the foot of the cross of Calvary after Jesus was crucified, along with her sister and Mary, the wife of Clopas and Mary Magdalene). It was a humbling experience for me to hear the heartbreaking stories of these women. One woman's son had committed suicide; another's son was a heroin addict. One woman was the mother of a daughter with special needs, and another woman had buried her son, just three months previously. He had been a cross community worker in Belfast, married with a five-year-old and a two-year-old daughter. He was shot dead by loyalist gunmen. This programme happened on Good Friday 1998, the day of the announcement of the Northern Ireland Agreement, but the announcement came too late for this mother who was heartbroken understandably and by her own admission was 'living a nightmare'. She said there were days when she wondered if she would ever smile again. She realised

I really like this photo
of my parents. It was
taken before they
were married.

My grandmother
married Chris
Dowdall from
her aunt's house
on St Stephen's
Green in 1911.
He worked in
Guinness's
Brewery until he
died in 1948.

This is the photo with my Granny that got me thinking of times past. Those curls didn't come easy. I had to sleep with pins sticking into my head the night before.

First Communion before the pony bolted!

The Family: Mam, Dad, Deirdre, Tony, John and Mary. This photo always sat on the piano at home.

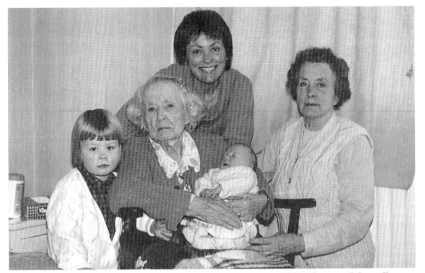

Tom as a baby with four generations of Kennedy women, 1986: Granny, Mam, Eva and I. I'm glad to have it because my Granny died the following year.

UCD Graduation – Granny, Mam and Dad were as proud as punch that day. I'm glad you can't see the platform boots. Mam was right, talk about dating the photo!

My first Saint Patrick's Day as a continuity announcer.

Marty, Maureen Potter and myself on *Open House*. I remember listening to
Maureen and Dinjo on the radio as a child while we were having Sunday lunch.

Taken at the *Open House Special* for Jimmy
Magee: his knowledge of sport is amazing.
He really is the Memory Man!

Bob Geldof's contribution to the
people of Africa has been enormous
and he richly deserves all the
accolades he's got.

Self-help trek, October 2002, Eritrea: this photo kept my spirits up during the long hours I spent at my desk over the summer.

Eva and I on a rusted tank in Asmara: a reminder of the Eritreans' 30-year struggle for independence from Ethiopia.

People had to walk miles to fill water drums. Now this Self Help water pump services three villages.

I was thrilled when Mary Robinson became our first woman president and it was great to meet her during Eurovision week in '95.

If I had one Euro for every time somebody has asked me 'What's Gay like?' I'd never see a poor day again. He's warm, calm, softly spoken, good company and great fun!

September 1997, Mother Teresa's Funeral, Calcutta. I can still remember the scent of the lotus blossom wreaths.

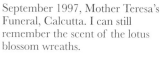

Back in Plan de la Tour, France, where I au paired for a month. It was great to be there with my children and 'beholden to no one!'

Interviewing Daniel O'Donnell in Kincasslagh, 1996. Daniel was very welcoming and friendly to us and to the endless streams of fans who besieged the place.

Rolf Harris is a dynamo. You'd be breathless trying to keep up with him.

John Hume has given huge amounts of energy to the pursuit of peace in our land. A great singer and raconteur too!

I wonder how many people who meet Gabriel Byrne end up extolling the virtues of Peig Sayers? He was an Irish teacher too and he's one of the few, who, like me, actually enjoyed Peig's autobiography!

The post-premiere dinner for *Dancing at Lughnasa*: Meryl Streep was, of course, the guest of honour.

that she had to keep going for her son's young wife and his two young daughters. What all of these women had in common was an amazing strength of character, an acceptance of their situation and a determination to come to terms with tragedy and life. The programme paid tribute to the women through their stories and through music. Kieran Goss sang *Somebody's Love*, a song about a man warning his friend that he should treat his wife properly. Otherwise he would take care of her because he loved her too but she had married the other. 'If I had your luck this time, You'd be gone, she'd be mine'.

Nóirín Ní Riain sang *Stabat Mater*, and Liam Lawton composed a piece specially for the programme called *The Silence and the Sorrow*, which echoed the heartbreak of Mary holding the crucified body of her only son when it was taken down from the cross.

The love of those mothers, those women who stayed, for their children, no matter what the circumstances was total and unconditional, their perseverance in spite of their sadness was obvious and the support they got in their tragedy from family and from the community in which they lived helped them to cope and get on with their lives. The same could be said of the women who seek refuge from abusive domestic situations in the women's aid refuge in Coolock in Dublin. They rebuild their lives with the support of the people around them. It's an organisation that works very hard and which is grossly under funded, like so many others in this country, so once again I'm happy to help in ways that I can.

I'd feel as if something was missing from my life if I wasn't doing some sort of charitable work from time to time. I grew up in a house where one or other of my parents was always doing something for the community. When they moved to Clondalkin after their marriage, it was a small country village where new houses were being built and bought by young couples starting families. The onus was on them to develop an infrastructure and there was always a wonderful sense of teamwork in the village as we were growing up. My father was a member of the St Vincent de Paul society. Their work involved visiting the long-term patients in Peamount Hospital and I know Dad got very fond of some of the men there who had few visitors because they were from the country and their families didn't have transport. He and Uncle Tom went out to Peamount every Sunday morning without fail and on Christmas morning as well. They were both involved in Muintir na Tíre and organised talent contests and debating and public speaking competitions for the young people in the parish. They set up, with others, the Clondalkin Amateur Dramatic Society and enjoyed that so much. I have memories of them rehearsing their productions in our front room. I'd be listening to the voices from upstairs in bed and they seemed to spend more time roaring laughing than actually rehearsing lines. They had fun onstage too and used to do some awful things to each other, like throw in an ad lib at some point that would have nothing whatsoever to do with the script and you'd have to follow on and hope that you weren't being led up a blind alley until the practical joker decided to revert to the right track. My Dad really enjoyed those improvisation sessions onstage and he'd regale us with accounts of them the next morning at breakfast. He was also a founder member of the Credit Union in Clondalkin. He helped run the draw in the village to raise money to build a swimming pool. It took a long time but they got there in the end. He was also a member of the Parents' Association of the girl's secondary school where Deirdre and I went and where I taught. And he was on the Tidy Town's committee as well. Uncle Tom set up the Church collection and they both went to count the money in the envelopes every Tuesday night. My mother was a member of Glór na nGael and the church choir and she and Auntie Eilish were active in the ICA. They all had a strong sense of community and felt an obligation to help develop Clondalkin for the benefit of their children. The words of Saint Francis come to mind, because in giving of their time and energy, they received great satisfaction and enjoyment in return.

Now I'm not suggesting for a minute that I do anything like that amount of community or charity work. As I said before my work circumstances don't allow me to commit to committee work on a regular basis but they do allow me to help organisations in other ways and that's why, when I can, I do. I know people who give a huge amount of their spare time to charity and I admire them greatly. We're very lucky to have such selfless people who ensure that things get done and lives are improved. There are also of course, people who dedicate their lives entirely to others and I often ask myself at what point they realise this is the life path they want to follow. A woman who acknowledged her calling to look to the needs of others at an early age was Mother Teresa of Calcutta who actually trained to be a nun here in Ireland. I was asked to travel to India to provide the television commentary at her funeral in 1997.

Over the years, I've worked on a number of occasions with the Religious Programmes department in RTÉ. I've already mentioned that incredibly moving programme from Carlow Cathedral on Good Friday, 1998. I enjoyed presenting the station's programmes of Christmas Carols from different parts of the country. John Bowman and I provided the commentary for the ceremony from the Pro-Cathedral to mark the National Day of Mourning in the wake of September 11th. The saddest part of that was looking at the faces of the congregation as they appeared on the monitor. The place was packed and everybody was reeling from the shock of what had happened in the States three days beforehand. I was back in the Pro-Cathedral a month later to commentate on the reinterment of Kevin Barry and his comrades. It was nice to see the relatives of these men present in the Pro-Cathedral as the ten coffins, draped in the tri colour were placed in front of the altar and given full military honours 80 years after their executions. In November of that year, 2001, I did the commentary for the Unifil Stand Down Parade, in the Garden of Remembrance in Dublin, which marked the end of the Irish Defence Forces peace-keeping mission in Lebanon. The ceremony paid tribute to the soldiers who had lost their lives in Lebanon and a family member pinned a white rose to a frame in the shape of a dove, the symbol of peace. Last year, I commentated on the Mass in the RDS that celebrated the bicentenary of Blessed Edmund Rice, the founder of the Christian Brothers. It was a privilege for me to be a part of all of those special occasions, especially the funeral Mass for Mother Teresa, a woman who epitomises the whole notion of charitable work and dedication to others.

Poorest of the Poor

It's Saturday, 13 September 1997. It's 5.00 a.m., a lovely time in Calcutta. The day has begun but the noise hasn't. The city is waking slowly and savouring the moments of quiet and calm which won't last too long in this city teeming with up to 15 million people. When the alarm clock goes off it takes me a minute or two to orient myself. I've slept well in spite of the hard horsehair mattress on the iron frame in this Spartan and drably decorated room. The previous day's flights, from Dublin to London and then on to Bangladesh and from there to Calcutta, followed by the race around the city's streets to get photos taken and accreditation organised, coupled with the intense heat and humidity obviously worked magic because I'm normally not a good sleeper but I never stirred all night. I look forward to a shower because even at 5.00 a.m. the heat is building. The shower is just a metal rose protruding from the wall of the bathroom and only gives a trickle of water. I remember to use bottled water to brush my teeth and to spray my clothes with Mosi Guard before I venture downstairs. The smell of that stuff is disgusting and returns to my consciousness every time I remember my time in Calcutta.

Yesterday, Fr Dermod McCarthy, head of Religious Programmes in RTÉ, met me at the airport and we drove at what seemed like break-neck speed in a taxi to get to a passport photo shop on the other side of the city before it closed. I needed two photos before they'd consider me for accreditation. The reason it seemed we were travelling so fast was because we were weaving in and out of traffic of all sorts, other dilapidated cars, buses with people hanging out the windows and sitting on top of the roof, bicycles, rickshaws, donkeys carrying heavy loads. All this on dirt track backstreets and accompanied by a constant blowing of horns and screeching of brakes. It was a huge culture shock for me. As was an incident when we stopped at the first set of traffic lights. I had opened my window; more to let the awful petrol fumes out of the car than in any deluded notion of letting fresh air in because there is no fresh air in Calcutta. No sooner had the driver stopped than the car was besieged by a crowd of women with sleeping babies wrapped up in their saris. They'd noticed the open window, which I didn't realise was a big no-no and they came looking for money. Their upturned hands were in through my window like a shot. I put a dollar in the hand nearest to me, which, let's face it, is not a huge amount of money but in Calcutta in 1997, it was more than a lot of those people would see in a month. The taxi driver nearly had apoplexy and shooed the women away. I think he actually threw caution to the wind and took off before the lights were green to get away from the situation. The effect the incident had on me was a realisation that the women's urgency was an indication of their desperation. The babies and small children they had on their shoulders seemed to be dozing and sleeping for want of something stimulating to do. I was also struck by the incredible beauty of the women despite their malnourished condition. Is it any wonder that Mother Teresa took them to her heart and that they returned her love and respect.

The passport photo shop was actually at the back of a house which had a long corridor partitioned off, behind which there were a couple of people sewing in a dim, dingy alcove and a dim dingy light. They were bent over their whirring machines and they didn't even look up as we passed by and made our way into this room where the photos were taken and developed on the spot. Then it was off to the municipal buildings to stand in queues and fill out forms and answer questions before standing in more queues and repeating the process over and over. Finally, after a number of hours the mission was accomplished and we made our way to our hotel, clutching those valuable documents that would allow us access to Netaji Stadium for Mother Teresa's funeral the following morning.

Our hotel was like something out of a Graham Greene novel, a little bit of old colonial England, shabby but cosy and run by an English woman who'd been living there for years. The street outside the hotel was teeming with people as we arrived there at about nine o'clock at night. It was as busy as Dublin's Henry Street on a Saturday afternoon, except the people here were there for the night. To walk on that street, you had to step over men, women and children who had bedded down for the night. The area was in stark contrast to the hotel around the corner, the Oberoi Grand Hotel, which we walked through just to see what it was like. It was like stepping into another world; Rolls Royces parked outside the colonnaded entrance, a tiled and mirrored hallway, and marble staircase. It was the last word in opulence and a million miles away from the reality of what was happening a few hundred yards up the street.

When I think back to all of the things that happened in those first few hours in Calcutta, is it any wonder I slept well that night, in spite of the strange room, the hard mattress, the humming of a generator and the heat, because the shutters were closed as a mosquito preventative. I was in sensory overload. Little did I realise what experiences were in store when I woke up to the quiet of the new day at 5.00 a.m. the following morning.

After breakfast – more bottled water and a banana because you can peel it (I lusted after a hard boiled egg but I was afraid to chance it even though it had its shell); it's out onto the streets that are now beginning to fill up with people. It's a strange sight to be walking in the centre of the city and see men shaving and washing their teeth on the streets, using water from the gutters. Like me, they've just woken after a night's rest but theirs has been spent outdoors, some under canvas, some lying on cardboard, others just lying on the concrete. I'm aware that there are a lot more men than women. These men have left their families in the countryside and come into the city in the hope of finding work and sending money back home. That rings a bell for Irish people of course. As we pass by and see them performing their ablutions on the city streets, I feel sorry that they're away from their families, but then a little further on I see groups of families and I realise the loneliness of the men is the better option. I see small babies and children being bathed in tin basins that have been filled from the waters sent into the gutters early in the morning to clean away the dirt and dust of the previous day. I see women filling billycans from those same gutters to make tea over gas stoves before the daily task of eking out a living, probably by begging, begins. The traffic is building up now. The wooden buses have slats inside of windows, which let the air flow through but which also allow people to stick their heads and sometimes upper bodies out of the crush of the packed buses. Every bus that passes is packed to overflowing and is heading in the same direction as we are – the Netaji Indoor Stadium where the funeral of Mother Teresa will take place.

We're making our way through the now thronged streets to the stadium to do the commentary on the funeral which will be transmitted live on television back home in Ireland. We're dragging two oversized shopping trolley type cases on wheels with microphones and a tiny monitor and books and notes while trying to find out which gate we should enter. We're turned away from the first one and so we proceed around the perimeter of this pretty expansive building until we finally get to an entrance that allows access to our particular type of accreditation. Security is understandably tight with heads of state coming from all over the world to pay their last respects to this amazingly charismatic woman: kings, queens, duchesses, presidents and first ladies, prime ministers, shahs, generals. An operation of this magnitude is a huge challenge to these people who are relying on pretty primitive infrastructure and facilities but the one thing everybody has in common is a determination that this should be a fitting tribute to this tiny founder of the Missionaries of Charity who dedicated every ounce of her being to the outcasts of society. As she said herself:

> I realised that I had the call to take care of the sick and the dying, the hungry, the naked, the homeless – to be God's Love in action to the poorest of the poor.

Once inside the building, Dermod and I walk across the main hall where last minute preparations are being made. Most of the seating is already in place and big velour couches are being hauled into position in the front rows for the visiting heads of state. Across the floor from them is the altar, set on a rostrum covered in the blue and white colours of Mother Teresa's Missionaries of Charity. All

around the edges of the rostrum are pinned lotus blossoms.
The scent of those flowers as we enter and right through the
morning is uplifting and fragile; in keeping with the woman
they are there to honour. We climb the back stairs to the
commentary boxes and set out our bits and pieces. The
facilities are pretty rudimentary but that's okay because the
technicians are so obliging and willing to do whatever we
need done in so far as they can. We begin to get ourselves
ready. We pin lists of the dignitaries and where they're
sitting up on the wall. The order of the ceremony is up
there too, the route of the cortege and the different
elements of the funeral Mass. The microphones are plugged
in, the lines to Dublin are checked, the notes are in order
and we can sit down for the first time in hours and draw
breath. We're pretty exhausted by the effort of actually
getting there and the ceremony hasn't even begun yet.

Eventually, the stadium is full, everything is in place and
the funeral of Mother Teresa begins with the cortege
leaving Saint Thomas's church in the compound of the
Provincial House of the Loreto order in Middleton Row.
It passes through the streets of Calcutta which she walked
for so many years taking in the sick and dying. Dermod
and I point out the famous landmarks like the Howrah
Bridge, the Victoria Memorial, a huge white-marble
structure, a reminder of the days of the British Raj; Fort
William, built in 1781 after a number of British soldiers
were killed in the city and around it the large patch of
green, the Maidan which is known as the lung of Calcutta.
Everywhere the cortege passes is thronged with the people
of Calcutta who are there to pay their final respects to this
woman who made her home in their city and who they
knew simply as Mother.

Mother Teresa first came to Calcutta in January 1929, as a Loreto nun to teach at a girls' school. She'd joined the Loreto order in Rathfarnham at the age of eighteen, having travelled to Ireland from her home in Skopje, in Macedonia where she was born Agnes Gonxha Bojaxhiu in August 1910, the youngest of three children.

All the time she was teaching in Calcutta, Mother Teresa was deeply moved by the presence of the sick and dying on the city's streets and eventually she got permission from Pope Pius XII to leave the Loreto congregation and set up a new order which she named the Missionaries of Charity and for whom she chose a simple white sari with sapphire-blue bands. She received permission from Calcutta officials to use a portion of the abandoned temple to Kali, the Hindu goddess of transition and destroyer of demons. Mother Teresa was pleased to be offered these premises because they had been a centre of prayer for Hindus and it was here that she founded the Kalighat Home for the Dying that she named Nirmal Hriday, which means Pure Heart. Mother Teresa and her sisters spent their days taking the poor, the destitute and the dying off the streets of Calcutta and restoring dignity to their lives. She opened her first orphanage in 1953 and in 1957 began working with lepers, outcasts to everybody but Mother Teresa, 'I see God in every human being. When I wash the leper's wounds, I feel I am nursing the Lord himself. Is that not a beautiful experience?' For her, 'the dying, the cripple, the mental, the unwanted, the unloved – they are Jesus in disguise.'

Mother Teresa was eighty-seven when she died and in spite of her tiny frame she was a tower of strength to the poorest of the poor. As well as ministering to the physical needs of the people she cared for, she was aware that there were other problems besetting humankind.

'We think sometimes that poverty is only being hungry, naked, homeless. The poverty of being unwanted, unloved and uncared for is the greatest poverty.' The people cared for in Nirmal Hriday were enveloped in an atmosphere of kindness, love and dignity, something that had been taken from them as a result of their circumstances. Mother Teresa was a world figure who spoke out on numerous occasions not only on behalf of the destitute and the dying but also to warn people in the more affluent parts of the world of the dangers of putting too much store by material wealth. For her, loneliness was the 'leprosy of the West'. She was greatly admired the world over and the list of heads of state and other dignitaries who travelled to Calcutta for her funeral bears testimony to that. It was sad that one of her great admirers and champions, Princess Diana died so tragically a week before her. They had become friends and Mother Teresa paid tribute to Diana for being devoted to the poor. She said at the time of her death, 'All the sisters and I are praying for her and all the members of her family to know God's speed and peace and comfort in this moment.' So many people around the world were plunged into grief by the untimely and tragic death of Diana and were grieving for a second time at the passing of Mother Teresa. Those heads of state who travelled to London for Diana's funeral found themselves together again a week later at the funeral Mass for Mother Teresa.

As Dermod and I looked down over the stadium from our commentary position above the altar we could see the dignitaries sitting in the comfortable velour couches in the front rows. I was fascinated to see so many women of note from around the world. Hilary Clinton was there, so was the Duchess of Kent, Queen Sofia of Spain, Sonia

Ghandi from India, Queen Fabiola of Belgium, Madame Chirac, wife of the French president, Queen Noor of Jordan, President Aquino of the Philippines. All of these influential women were gathered to pay their last respects to another powerful woman who devoted all her energies to the poorest of the world's poor.

It was a privilege for me to be given the opportunity to be present at that funeral and to savour the atmosphere in the city and in the stadium during the Mass. There was a quiet in the hall, a calm, a peace and sadness at the passing of this great woman. Mother Teresa lay in repose in front of the altar; her mortal remains covered in one of her saris. You would be in no doubt as to the slightness of frame of this otherwise powerful woman because her feet were uncovered and they were tiny. Enormous wreaths of those highly scented lotus blossoms surrounded her. Archbishop Henry D'Sousa the archbishop of Calcutta celebrated the Mass and her fellow missionaries of charity sang. It was a very moving and gentle occasion, dignified and unhurried. There were funny moments too during the funeral Mass. Our commentary position had a makeshift chipboard tabletop with a tiny black and white monitor which only sometimes had a picture on it. When the signal became snowy, Dermod and I looked down to the German commentary position about three booths away where there was a big colour monitor. These were times when it literally was a question of long distance commentary. We were more fortunate than the BBC commentator who was in the booth next to ours because at one point during the transmission, his tabletop collapsed and all of his notes were scattered over the floor. Dermod and I looked at each other and there was a real feeling of 'there but for the grace of God go we'.

That and a resolution not to put anything weighty on the tabletop.

The broadcast lasted five and three quarter hours. That's a lot of commentary, even when two people are sharing it. It was nice though to have the opportunity during that time to tell the story of Mother Teresa and to share some of her thoughts and her beliefs with the Irish viewers. She taught a lesson of love always and felt that if you judge people, you have no time to love them. Although she realised the need for aid for the poor, her belief was that mere aid is not enough.

'Let us not be satisfied with just giving money. Money is not enough, money can be got, but they need your hearts to love them. So, spread your love everywhere you go.' Mother Teresa spread love and acceptance everywhere she went and the people of Calcutta returned that love to her during her life and at this moment of her passing. I knew before going there the high regard in which she was held. I'd seen the pictures, I'd read the articles and the interviews, but it wasn't until I was in Calcutta and witnessed that outpouring of love and grief first hand that I fully appreciated the effect this diminutive figure had on the lives of the poorest of the poor. When we emerged from Netaji Stadium after the funeral, I was amazed to see old and frail Hindu women kneeling on the streets, praying in front of cardboard boxes that they had covered with satin and bedecked with incense sticks and little nightlights shining in front of pictures of Mother Teresa. This was their way of marking her passing and honouring the contribution she had made to the lives of all the people of Calcutta, regardless of their creed. This was the culmination of a week of grieving among the Christian and the non-Christian communities. From the moment of her death a week previously the people had come from all sides of the city to pay their respects to Mother. There were mile-long queues, day and night, outside Saint Thomas's church while she lay in state. And as the people of Calcutta filed past her remains, they cried, prayed, kissed her feet, lifted small children to touch her robes and left flowers by her side. There were banners, posters and billboards with messages of love for Mother Teresa all over the city. I remember one written in English in big bold black letters, 'We mourn for the loss of our Mother'. There was a huge sense of loss among the people but also a huge sense of gratitude and a dignity which these beautiful people seemed to exude effortlessly, in spite of their poverty and their hunger.

This was my first visit to this part of the world and the level of poverty and destitution in the city shocked me. The first thing that struck me when I landed on Indian soil was how dark it seemed even though it was the middle of the afternoon. The pollution in Calcutta is so bad that the sky is like a dense grey ceiling, which sits just above your head. Although there's great heat during the day, the sun never actually shines. It can't penetrate the layer of pollution. The smell of petrol fumes was constantly in my nostrils and on my clothes. The noise of clapped out, spluttering engines was relentless as the cars and buses packed the streets and there wasn't an inch of pavement on view because of the absolute sea of people, some walking, some begging, some just lying down on the path asleep. As I said earlier, I found myself literally stepping over sleeping men and women as I walked along, all of them emaciated, all of them poor and hungry. The whole experience was an assault on the senses and you'd have to be made of stone not to be moved by the plight of those gentle and beautiful people. Within an hour of my arrival in Calcutta, I was in no doubt as to how very very lucky we are to live in a land that is green and fertile and where we can have food and shelter in abundance. And that's before we even begin to consider the levels of luxuries and the amount of waste that we encounter in Ireland every day.

Now, as I recall that day of Mother Teresa's funeral, I appreciate how special the whole experience was. In spite of the fact that Calcutta is polluted, overcrowded, extremely poor and very noisy, what I remember is the peace and calm and beauty of the people, and the love associated with Mother Teresa. It's nice to have the opportunity to recall that visit to Calcutta now that Mother Teresa has been beatified and to celebrate the message of love that she spread by the way she lived her life. That message of reaching out to others and remembering that every living soul on this earth is worthy of respect and care. I've said it before and I don't mind repeating my belief that the circumstances into which we are born are fortuitous and we in the more affluent parts of the world have a moral responsibility to look to the needs of those who by an accident of birth are less well off than ourselves, and to be caring in our dealings with those around us. To finish with some more words of Mother Teresa: 'Kind words can be short and easy to speak, but their echoes are truly endless'.

Memory of Mam

I have often been reminded of the truth of those simple words of Mother Teresa about kind words having endless echoes, but never more profoundly and with such comforting effect than in the days, weeks and months after my mother died. It gave me great consolation that people sought me out and shared their memories of my mother with me, and invariably those memories seemed to revolve around some kindness she had shown them. Her kind words were echoing even though she had passed on from this life. She died on the 23rd December 2001, so she'll be dead two years this Christmas and I can honestly say I missed her more this summer than ever before. There were days when I longed to be able to lift the phone and share a problem with her, to ask her advice. That longing was deep and awful and I hope that stage of the grieving process will end soon. It seems to come in six-month stages and I've written about them at various intervals. In this chapter are the thoughts and feelings that I had in the first stages of grieving my darling mother.

When the phone call came at 11.45 p.m. on 23rd December, 15 minutes to the start of Christmas Eve, to say that my mother had died, a chill ran down my spine. I felt something drain from me, right down to my toes. I wanted to reach out my hand and physically pull her back from wherever she had gone. But her time had finally come. It's not that her death was unexpected. For seven weeks, since she had a stroke while in Tallaght Hospital for tests and treatment for cancer, we had been waiting for that phone call. I had rehearsed how I would feel so many times in those seven weeks. I wondered every time I went into the hospital, just how she would be that day. It became automatic, on exiting the lift on the third floor, to brace myself, both physically and mentally for a possible dramatic deterioration in her demeanour. I had gotten well used to her frailty on the one hand and her incredible fighting spirit on the other. The stroke had left her totally paralysed except for the movement of her right arm, and she exercised that right arm until the last few days. At regular intervals, she would raise and lower her arm time after time, just as an athlete might do press-ups. We'd all praise her and encourage her to continue. We knew this was one of her ways of holding on and staying alert.

It's not that she was afraid to die. She had a deep, deep faith and believed always that when she died, she would be re-united in heaven, with her husband, my father, Tom, who had died of a heart attack while on a golf outing 26 years ago, at the age of 59. But she loved life and people and she was very concerned for the well-being of her four children: John, Deirdre, Tony and me, and our families. The fact that we are all adults didn't matter one bit. She worried about us and I'd say these concerns occupied her thoughts a lot in those seven weeks. Would we be okay when she was no longer there? Would I be able to find somebody to be there when the children would come home from school? (Something she had done for me from the time Eva was born almost eighteen years previously.) All my friends used to remind me how lucky I was to have my mother to look after my children, but I didn't need reminding. It was a great privilege for me in life and also a privilege for my four children and the outpouring of sadness and loss and pure love that they displayed when their precious Nana died bore witness to the bond that existed between them.

One of the nice things about having those weeks with her was the opportunity it afforded me to reassure her that we would be fine; that she had done a wonderful job of rearing us and that the values she had instilled in us as we were growing up would stand us in good stead now. I remember the stillness of her hospital room while she'd be sleeping and I'd look at her tiny, emaciated frame. My tears would flow with heartache and sadness at what had happened to her and what would be the inevitable outcome of this period in hospital and then the absolute quiet would be broken by her stirring in the bed and I'd say: 'Are you awake, Ma?' She'd struggle out a 'Yes' and I'd compose myself and just talk to her. I told her so often then how much I loved her, how grateful I was for all she had done for me and for my children and that she was not to worry about any of us. I promised her that, being the eldest, I would keep an eye out for John, Deirdre and Tony, I'd visit Nell in the hospice on her behalf and that she was a beautiful person who touched the lives of so many people with a positive, friendly and loving force. I lay beside her in her hospital bed sometimes and let her hair touch my face. I wanted to be physically close to her and for her to feel the love that was in my heart and in my words for her. It was a great privilege to be able to do that.

On the day before she died, while I was talking to her, I suddenly remembered that every year since Daddy died she had made a Christmas wreath and put it on his grave on Christmas Eve, so I told her that she shouldn't worry. Daddy would have his wreath. It wouldn't be a homemade one – my mother knows my limitations. When I told her I'd be bringing a Christmas arrangement to Esker cemetery for Dad, she gave my hand a squeeze and I thought my heart would break. I was so grateful that something made me think of saying it to her. It was obviously on her mind. That same afternoon, I put a basket of holly and Christmas flowers on my Dad's grave. Days later they were placed to one side as the grave was reopened to take his wife's coffin. One journey had ended. A new one was just about to begin.

When Mam had the stroke initially, the four of us, her children, decided to divide the 24 hours of the day between us so that she would never be alone. We had been told that the first 48 hours would be crucial and that if she survived those hours she could survive indefinitely. We knew she was not going to 'get better'. She was unable to take any food whatsoever and the only attachment was a drip to prevent dehydration. But she rallied to some extent and it was pointed out to us that we would be exhausted very quickly if we persisted with this regime because there was no way of telling how long this situation might continue. So, we worked out a roster, week by week, of two six hour shifts a day so that in her waking hours, Mam always had one of us at her bedside. And I know that I speak for the others when I say that it was a great privilege to be able to do that. Although life was ebbing away, there was an intense feeling of life and living in the moment once we went through that hospital bedroom door.

The nursing staff were kind and gentle and always dignified and respectful in their dealings with Mam. Her make-up was applied every day. Her nails were painted, her hair was combed. In fact, at one stage, Sr Taylor asked us to bring in her hair colour so that they could put it in for her. It took four nurses to do the job – two to hold Mam over the side of the bed, one to hold the basin of water under her head and the other to wash the hair and apply the colour and then dry and set the hair. It took hours, it was exhausting, but they were delighted to do it and thrilled with the results. Those women who cared for my mother were angels.

We all had our different routines when we were with Mam and we'd compare notes as to how she had been. At weekends, John used to watch the horse racing on television while he was with her. He'd call out the runners' names and their prices (Mam's eyes were closed from the time she had the stroke) and they'd both have an imaginary flutter. During the week, if he was there in the afternoon, he'd put on *Open House* and talk her through it, not without the odd added joke at my expense. Tony would do the crossword with her, call out the clues and wait for her answer which would take time but which she would force out of her mouth. (I said already she was a determined fighter.) Her answers were always correct. She was a great crossword person. I would read to her while I was sitting with her. A couple of days after her stroke, I was in the library with Lucy and my eye fell on *Little Women*, which she always loved and which was one of the bedtime stories she used to tell me when I was very young. Seeing the book on the shelf in front of me reminded me of those bedtime story sessions. I felt this was meant to be and so I borrowed the book and began reading it to her – a couple of chapters each evening. Not a lot happens for a long time in *Little Women* and one evening I said to her, 'Ma, I'm getting bored with this. If something doesn't happen soon, I'll go mad'. She summoned her energies and said slowly and with great effort 'Read on!' And so I did. I was under orders.

Probably the most beautiful and uplifting aspects of Mam's stay in Tallaght were the music sessions that happened in her room. Deirdre and her friend and singing

partner Fionnuala Gill, would set up with the harp and
perform lots of very beautiful songs that my mother loved,
always ending with her favourite – *The Castle of Dromore*,
which they also sang at her funeral Mass. The word went
round the hospital that there was lovely music in room
nine in the Gogarty ward and Deirdre and Fionnuala were
asked to perform at the lunchtime Mass in the hospital
chapel anytime they were there in the middle of the day.
They were happy to oblige and my mother was thrilled
that they were asked and had agreed.

Tom is learning to play the guitar and one day he came
to me and asked if he could play for Nana in the hospital.
I told him she'd love that and he brought the guitar up to
her room and played all his pieces. When he was finished,
Mam clapped that strong right arm on her right knee. You
could sense her delight. Not surprising really, when I
remember the very special relationship she and Tom
shared. Because of his half day on Wednesdays, she'd pick
him up in a taxi and they'd either go for lunch to a little
café locally or come home to Coolamber. Either way, they
enjoyed endless cups of tea together and lots of chat. They
were like two old pals who'd known each other all their
lives. But then they had.

Another special musical memory of Mam's time in
Tallaght was the day Uncle Tom sang his party piece for
her. It's *Scarlet Ribbons*, the song about the man who heard
his little daughter praying for some scarlet ribbons to be
left on her bed at night. The father walked the town
looking for them but all the shops 'were shut and shut-
tered'. In the morning, when he peeped into his little girl's
room, what did he see 'in gay profusion lying there – some
scarlet ribbons, lovely ribbons, scarlet ribbons for her hair.'
My mother loved that song and she loved Uncle Tom

singing it. He wasn't all that well at the time – he was on
dialysis twice a week but he made the effort and it was a very
loving and moving moment in room nine, which was recalled
five short months after Mam's death when we were back in
Clondalkin church for Uncle Tom's funeral Mass and
Deirdre and Fionnuala sang *Scarlet Ribbons* in his memory.

The nurses responded brilliantly to Mam's love of
music too and every morning when they'd wake her they'd
turn on the tape recorder that Deirdre had brought in and
play one of her tapes for her till whichever one of us
arrived. They also installed an aromatherapy steamer,
which gave off a lovely scent of lavender in the room. And
we were privileged in another way too, because in spite of
the fact that Mam was dying and having no nourishment
whatsoever, she had no pain and no discomfort and was
never agitated. She was at peace and whenever I asked her
was she comfortable, she'd always answer 'very'. She took
sips of water from those sponge lollipop things that the
nurses showed me how to dip in water and let her suck on
and Fionnuala had made up a lavender based lotion which
Deirdre and I would rub on her arm to keep her skin
smooth and also to give her the soothing lavender aroma.

There was a beautiful, gentle, and loving aura in that
room for the whole seven weeks. One of the hospital
chaplains, who had a great affection for Mam and prayed
with her every night, told us after she died that he felt the
room was a sacred place. She would have been pleased
that he thought that. She was a very spiritual woman who
had unconditional love for her church. She had great
devotion to Padre Pio and there was a picture of him
above her hospital bed. Whenever the nurses turned her,
they always remembered to replace her rosary beads and
her crucifix in her hand. One of my memories of that

time is praying with her before leaving for the night. She would raise that good right arm to try to make the sign of the cross and for the first few weeks she'd mouth the prayers as I said them. Later, when she didn't have the strength to do that, she'd squeeze my hand at the beginning and at the end of praying.

John Kelly was the chaplain who was with Mam when she died. He had just left her room, having prayed with her as usual, he chatted with the nurses at the nurses' station and then he went back in to say goodnight and realised this was the end of Mam's life. The nurses called us immediately and I was there within minutes living closest to the hospital. Mam was still warm when I kissed her. In spite of the fact that we knew this was going to happen and had been waiting for that call every day, the reality was horrible. The stillness, the quiet, the finality, the fact that Mam was now getting cold to the touch; all these things were making inroads on our consciousness and the thoughts of her going to a place of eternal rest and peace and tranquillity did nothing to assuage the awful gut-wrenching feeling of loss and helplessness. The four of us were children again, sobbing for the loss of our mother. The years had been rolled back and all I wanted was for my mother not to be gone from this life. There was no point in anyone telling me that she was in a better place, that we had all cared for her so well, that we couldn't have lasted much longer ourselves without dropping from exhaustion. I would have continued to sit by her bedside forever if she could only be breathing and alive. I would have done anything to have her back. I was overcome with grief and the dawning realisation that the bond between a mother and her child is so strong that it's as if the umbilical cord was never fully cut.

Father John prayed with us around Mam's bed. We had tea. The nurses sought us out and sympathised. We each went back into Mam's room and had time on our own with her. Then we left the Gogarty ward for the last time. It felt eerie and strange and very, very lonely. Mam would be taken to the chapel of rest in the hospital. We had planned to wake her at home in Brigid's Road, where she had lived since the day she got married but it was now Christmas Eve and we realised it would be totally impractical and unfair to her nine grandchildren, most of whom would be awaiting a visit from Santa Claus that night. The four of us hugged each other in front of the hospital and went to our cars and home to a totally new and strange reality. When Dad died, we still had our mother. Now, we were without either parent. It seemed as if we were being projected into the front line. Being an adult meant something different altogether now that there was no adult above us, as it were. Tony, I think it was, joked that we'd have to grow up and be responsible people now.

Christmas Eve was an emotional and physical roller coaster. Deirdre had come back from the hospital to stay with me. We'd lit a fire, sat up till 5.00 a.m., had two stiff gin and tonics each and talked and planned and finally decided we were going around in circles of exhaustion so we went to bed for a couple of hours. By 9.00 a.m. we were having breakfast and then it was a case of getting a funeral organised by close of business, which on Christmas Eve was about 3.00 p.m. We managed somehow. John and Tony went to the undertakers, Deirdre organised the readings and the music and I organised the flowers and the food because we had decided that given our disappointment at being unable to bring Mam home to her own house, we were determined that people should go back to her house after the burial. She would have wanted that. As John said at the Mass: 'Our mother kept an open house long, long before it was a television programme.'

I don't remember much of the rest of Christmas Eve or Christmas Day. Santa came. We went through the motions of Christmas Day. John, Deirdre, Tony and I met at the chapel of rest during the day and had a little prayer and hymn service there. Mam was wearing her Child of Mary medal and was dressed in her pink knitted suit and her Child of Mary cloak for which we had to search high and low the day before. She had always said she wanted to be laid out in that cloak and John, being 'helpful' during the search, said that he had put it back in the third drawer of her chest of drawers the last time he had used it – as a Batman cloak, 30 plus years ago!

A number of people have said it was so unfortunate that Mam had to die right at Christmas time but I don't view it like that. There was great comfort and consolation in seeing the crib and the Christmas tree on the altar when we walked into the church in Clondalkin at six o'clock on Saint Stephen's Day. This church, where we had all been baptised, received Holy Communion and Confirmation and where three of us were married, is an integral part of our family background and that sense of family and community was emphasised for me by the family in the crib.

Mam's final journey was actually very beautiful and very moving. It began in the chapel of rest in Tallaght Hospital where Fr John said prayers, Deirdre and Clare (John's fifteen-year-old daughter) sang *Oíche Chiúin* and *A Mhuire Mháthair*. and the grandchildren had an opportunity to kiss their granny goodbye. It was then that I realised fully the incredible bond between my children and my mother. They were genuinely grief-stricken. With an eleven-year-old's logic, Eoin offered, through his tears, 'if she only didn't get sick that one time, she wouldn't be dead now'. I don't remember feeling like that when my grandmother died, but then I didn't have such regular contact with her. Mam was great for helping my children with their homework and she was great at the Irish although it annoyed them always when she insisted on referring to 'h' in the aimsir caite as 'séimhiú'. She sewed their teddies when they were a bit the worse for wear. And when it came to school concerts, they always knew she'd come up with the costume they needed from the endless boxes of old dresses and materials in her attic that she would cut up and sew into fabulous new creations. And she'd be there in the audience to watch them. In fact, when Eva was in *Oklahoma* during transition year and Mam was in hospital for the first time, not knowing what was wrong with her but losing weight and feeling very ill, she insisted on leaving the hospital to be in the audience to see Eva. She encouraged them always, she chastised them when she deemed it necessary and most of all she loved them to bits and they knew it. Their heartrending grief in the chapel of rest bore testimony to that shared love which will always be part of their lives.

My brothers, two of my cousins from next door and two neighbours, friends of John and Tony, shouldered Mam's coffin up the centre aisle and placed her in front of the altar where she had worshipped faithfully for so many years. The choir, of which she had been a member for about 20 years, sang to welcome her into the church. There were three priests to receive her: Father Wall, the parish priest; Dermod McCarthy, my colleague from RTÉ, and Gearóid Conroy, a friend of Deirdre's, who works in Rome but was home for Christmas.

Deirdre sang and Fionnuala played the harp. They performed a song that Deirdre wrote when Mam was dying and we included a piece from it on her memory card:

> Walk me to the water, hold me at the edge,
> Gently release me to the breathless sky
> Opening to take me as I soar.
> Light me on my journey, echo words of love,
> Light me on my journey to the other side.

The support of the people was phenomenal. There is nothing to compare with the feeling of comfort you get when people queue up at the end of the removal service and take the trouble to sympathise with you. Before my father died, I always felt awkward joining that queue and sympathising with the bereaved but when Dad died and I was in that front row, I realised, even though I was only twenty-one, that this meant an awful lot to Mam, to my brothers and sister and to me and from that day on I have never had any difficulty joining the queue. This time round, there was just the four of us in the front row and we were comforted in our loss and our grief by the good wishes of friends, neighbours, work colleagues and class-mates who wanted us to know that they were thinking of us with warm thoughts. I hope that custom always endures. It's not till you've been on the receiving end of it that you can possibly understand how comforting it is.

After the removal service, we all came back to Coolamber. I had bought a turkey and ham and two of my wonderful friends had been beavering away in the kitchen since early morning. There were about 24 plus people to be fed. It seems like a lot but we were always used to crowds at Christmas. The two families, living side by side, always spent Christmas Day together. That's why I refer to my three cousins from next door as brothers. We grew up together.

I have good memories of being brought up in that extended family situation. I remember we used to play cowboys by putting a rug over the back wall with a stone for the horse's head and a hurley for the rifle. I remember the boys playing 'hangings' one day and my father coming out into the back garden to see Brian standing on a wooden box, with a noose around his neck which was slung over the washing line. William was just about to issue the order to John to kick the box! Because the three of them were so close in age they got up to all sorts of mischief.

I remember the saga of the Rosary, which we said every evening in our house after tea – even in the summer – even when the sun was splitting the stones and the pals were calling. Sometimes we'd think Mam might have forgotten and we'd be clearing away the tea things and just as we'd finish, you'd hear 'hand me down the beads'. There was no point in suggesting that we might say the Rosary later. We'd go down on our knees at the kitchen chairs. John used to get great satisfaction if he heard the back door open because that meant Brian or William was calling for him and when they unwittingly opened the kitchen door, John would bellow out their name so they couldn't creep back out and they would then be invited by my mother to join in – which they did or their mother would hear about it.

I remember too the time Auntie Eilish was in town and Mam was minding the boys in our house. William had gone into the sitting room to do his piano practice and was messing with a souvenir box of matches from Spain. He set the net curtains and then the whole sitting room on fire. The firemen hosed from the hall door and the place was destroyed but Mam was just relieved that nobody was hurt and I distinctly remember when my Dad came home from work she sent him in next door to make sure Uncle Tom or Auntie Eilish didn't give out to William, because she felt the shock of what had happened was enough for him.

I remember my mother taking Irish conversation classes in the boys' school so that she could help John and Brian with their Irish as they were coming up to Inter Cert and didn't seem to be making much progress. The two cousins viewed the 'grinds' as great entertainment. She might ask Brian a verb and he often replied: 'I think you should ask my learned friend beside me'. John's favourite answer was 'Stop the lights'. And the problem was that my mother, after a while, would start to laugh at the two of them and the lesson would disintegrate into a fit of the giggles which let the two boys off the hook.

Anyway, we survived and grew up and have remained very close as a family to the extent that, as well as sharing each other's celebrations, we also feel each other's losses very deeply. And I know that William, Brian and Barry felt the loss of Mam as that of a second mother. They carried her coffin, they did some of the readings, and their children played a part in the funeral proceedings. Mam's funeral Mass was truly a celebration of her life. Her choir was there, Deirdre and Fionnuala, the three priests, and all of her friends and neighbours and relatives. People who didn't know Mam, said afterwards, that they got a great sense of the person she was from the Mass. There was a bit meascán of Gaeilge and English in the readings and the prayers, which were recited by the people who wrote them. The smaller grandchildren brought up the offertory gifts including things that were significant in Mam's life, like that rosary beads which she held in her hands all the time she was in the hospital and the crucifix which Nancy

Breslin, her friend and neighbour had left her when she died in 1984, her sheet music for the choir, a montage of photographs of her grandchildren and the little Christmas presents that the grandchildren had bought and wrapped for her about a week earlier. And once again, the support of the many, many people who attended the Mass was a great comfort to us at that sad time.

People said there was an atmosphere of love and belonging in the church. In fact, I had a phone call from a woman who'd been in school in Clondalkin around the same time as me to say that she had just come back from a trip abroad with her mother, who had been asking her to accompany her for years. She wanted me to know that after Mam's funeral Mass she made up her mind to bring her own mother on that trip and it had been a wonderful success. I was delighted to get the phone call and to hear that my mother had that effect on another person.

There have been other instances of people giving me an insight into aspects of Mam's personality of which I was unaware. About six months after the funeral, I was at a concert in the Bank of Ireland Arts Centre, organised by another of my mother's sisters, Auntie Phyllis, and I was sitting beside a woman, a childhood friend of Phyllis's, who explained to me that as a youngster she was very shy and she was always very relieved when she'd go to play with Phyllis and find my mother at home, because Mam always went out of her way to put her at her ease. I shouldn't be surprised by that really because as we were growing up and forming opinions and making to take sides in arguments she would always, always, tell us to think of ourselves in the other person's shoes and see if we'd like to be talked about in such a way. If we wouldn't be happy in that position, we shouldn't dream of inflicting it on anyone else.

I had a letter of sympathy from my French and Irish teacher in school who was subsequently a teaching colleague when I went back to Colaiste Bride. That's Mrs Redmond and I've spoken about her earlier as someone who influenced me as I was growing up. She would have known my mother as a parent at parent-teacher meetings for myself and later on for Deirdre. She described her as 'an exceptionally nice lady, an unsung heroine, comme ceux qui, dans l'ombre, accomplissent leur tache', 'like those who accomplish their task in the shadow, away from the limelight'.

Mam was a totally devoted wife and mother. Her day began with 7.30 a.m. Mass to which she would drive with Uncle Tom and they'd sit in the same seats day in, day out, year in, year out. She was a gifted seamstress, knitter and embroiderer. She was a great cook, loved woodwork, did all her own painting and decorating, and threw nothing out, believing that it might come in useful some day. One of the hardest things for me was having to go through her things after she died. It was here that I, too, got an insight into aspects of her personality of which I wasn't aware. I didn't realise that as a young woman she kept scrapbooks of important news events that make very interesting historical reading now. She also used to cut out prayers and motivational thoughts from magazines and stick them into scrapbooks and copybooks. I was shocked to find that she had kept everything that was ever written about any of us, including newspaper photographs of my brothers' football teams and the programmes from every event I was ever involved in. I used to love bringing her to events and she enjoyed being there and meeting the people I'd be working with. Since she died, there have been lots of events I've presented that I know she would have loved to attend and that makes me very sad.

Going through my mother's papers was hard enough but a breeze compared to having to dispose of her clothes. I hated having to put her outfits into black sacks and take them to the clothes-recycling bank. The fact that some person in a cold country would benefit from the warmth of her woollens was small comfort as I was emptying her things into the big yellow bin in the Rathfarnham Shopping Centre car park. Memories of times she had worn certain things came flooding back and I was over-come by a feeling of regret that she didn't have any really good or fancy clothes. She spent very, very little on herself ever. I would have just loved to have had an opportunity now to quite simply spoil her. I cried my eyes out as I was emptying those sacks of clothes and I have no doubt some passers by thought I had flipped, especially as there were one or two things I just couldn't part with, like an Aran cardigan that she had knit for herself and a woollen scarf that I realised still had her smell. I put them back in the car and left quickly.

Mam was a strong and healthy woman who never smoked or drank and yet at the age of eighty-one, she developed an obstruction, which turned out to be a malig-nant growth in her small intestine. That they operated on her was an act of faith in her strong constitution, that she came directly from the recovery room back to her hospital bed after the operation was further testimony to her strong disposition and that she got two more years of good health after that is something for which we must be grateful. But you see, her own mother lived to be a hundred and two and I had no notion of anything happening to my mother for a very long time yet. I wanted her to be there for Eva's eighteenth birthday party in January, just as she had been at the surprise 'pink-themed' party I had for Eva for her seventeenth. She enjoyed herself so much that night, dressed in a grey suit with a pink blouse, looking at her sons, daughters, nephews and nieces and their offspring dressed in all kinds of pink everything including John's pink thong, worn over his trousers, thankfully. His mother was not impressed and referred to him as a 'disgrace' all night. Even the dog wore a pink bow. She told us we should have more sense.

I wanted her to be there for Eoin's Confirmation in March. She would have been a great support to Tom and Eva as they prepared to take their Junior and Leaving Cert exams. She was so much a part of my life and I miss her terribly.

Mind you, there are also times when I feel her presence and those times are a great consolation. About a month after she died, I was driving home from somewhere and feeling very low and lonely and all of a sudden, I felt this energy surge in my stomach, which took me totally by surprise. I didn't know what it was but I thought of her at that moment and then I felt it again. An almost breath-taking experience which I haven't had since but which I did associate with her presence at that time.

The following Easter, I was trying to get my head around masses of information for work – a commentary that I'd been asked to do with about three days notice. I spent one day gathering the information, a day editing out the superfluous material and then very little time to put an order of priority and probability on what was left. Added to that was a late night on Saturday night, so there I was at 7.00 a.m. on the Sunday morning, transmission day, pouring over the sheets of paper at the kitchen table and beginning to panic. I remember saying: 'Ma, I'm not on top of this. I need a dig out.' And within a couple of seconds, a shaft of sunlight came in through the kitchen door and spread at an angle right across the pages on the table. It was incredibly beautiful and then it was gone. Coincidence perhaps, but a very happy and pleasant coincidence, during which I felt my mother's presence. I got stuck into the work with renewed vigour and had it all categorised in my head and was ready for action by noon.

At times, when I'm out running, particularly if I go very early in the morning, at around 6.00 a.m. I am over-whelmed by a feeling of well-being looking up into the trees and hearing the birdsong. It's at times like these that I feel my mother's presence around me.

Mam would have celebrated her eighty-fourth birthday on the 22nd of June 2002. Instead she was six months dead on the 23rd of June. On that day, Tony and Sharon's fourth child, Ailbhe, who was born in March, was baptised. She wore the christening robe that Mam made when their first child, Niamh was born and which Niamh, who's now eight, insisted on bringing along and offering as a gift during Mam's month's mind.

That was a very emotional and in a way uplifting Mass too. Fr John, the chaplain from the hospital, celebrated the Mass in the dining room in Brigid's Road. The two families were there, also some neighbours from the road and Deirdre and Fionnuala sang again. So did Clare, and Tom performed a song that he had written on New Year's Eve in memory of his granny. He played it on the guitar and Deirdre and Fionnuala sang it in two parts. It's called *The Other Side*. It tells of his reaction when he heard that Mam had died; disbelief, wonderings. The chorus goes:

> I know you're in a place where the sun shines, rivers flow,

Someday, I'll be there too but for now, I have to
Wait a little longer, be a little stronger,
See you in the place where the rivers flow.

Another aspect of the month's mind of which I have fond
memories is the blessing of little shiny coloured stones –
one for everybody who was there to take away with them
as a memento of that woman whose quiet life seemed to
have a ripple effect way beyond anything I had anticipated.

November is the month of the Holy Souls and during
that month, there's a special Mass every year in Clondalkin
church to celebrate the lives of people from the parish who
have died over the previous 12 months. November 2002
saw Kennedys and Whites there along with the families of
the other 88 parishioners who'd died. It was a lovely occasion in the general sense . . . a gathering of the community
to celebrate the lives of those 90 people from the parish
and there was a candle lit to represent each of them. They
were positioned at the foot of the altar in the shape of a
cross. The candles were very beautiful and touching and it
was nice to have John, Deirdre, Tony and my children
altogether in the same pew with Auntie Eilish, and their
family just a few rows ahead. But when the bell rang and
the priest came out from the sacristy and the choir began
to sing I quite simply lost it. A multitude of thoughts and
impressions and memories and visualisations bombarded
me at that moment. And all to do with Mam and the
choir. She was so loyal to that group of people and never
ever missed an occasion when the choir was asked to sing.
She would have been up there if she were still alive.
I listened intently to those voices and there's not much I
wouldn't give to have heard my mother's voice among
them. I looked at the altar as they sang but my mind's eye

was actually panning the organ gallery and thinking of Mam's friends who were up there paying their tribute to her and to the other parishioners who had passed on in the previous 12 months. I thought of my mother getting ready to go to her choir practice on a Tuesday evening at seven o'clock with her friend Kitty. She took that choir practice very seriously and wanted never to miss a practice or a recital. There were times when I had tickets for concerts or 'do's' that I know she would have enjoyed but she wouldn't let her fellow choir members down. Her philosophy always was one of commitment. She'd joined the choir and therefore on a Tuesday, that was her commitment. But she loved it and she loved the people that she met there every Tuesday evening and every Sunday morning when they'd sing the 10.30 Mass.

I'm only now beginning to appreciate how much that church meant to my mother. It's hugely important in my life and I love having occasion to bring my children there, it's just a pity that all of the occasions on which they go to the church seem to be sad ones these days. Although I do remember and I hope they do too, when Eva and Tom were small and I was down at Mam's house with them I'd always make a point of taking them to the church and telling them, that was where we all had our class Masses and confessions and communions and confirmations and weddings. I particularly enjoyed bringing them to see 'Nana's other crib' in that church over Christmas. There was always a huge Christmas tree with hundreds of white lights on the altar beside the crib, which had the same figures that were in it when I was at school and visiting it with my parents every time we went out for a walk over the Christmas period. Sitting in the church on that November night, my mind wandered back to those

Christmases that the two families always celebrated together,
the fun we had, the ease with which we moved from one
house to the other. We took it all in our stride. We didn't
realise it at the time but we were very lucky and led a
charmed life. I felt very sad, sitting there with my children
and my brothers and sister and looking at Auntie Eilish,
because I realised that those charmed days were well and
truly over. The figures in the crib may be the same as
when I was brought there as a child, those same figures
that were there when I brought my children to visit
'Nana's other crib', those same figures that were in the crib
when my mother was brought to this church from Tallaght
Hospital after she died. So many other things had changed
though and were lost to us forever.

Back to Ailbhe's Christening. I think it was a nice way
to mark the half year. We were celebrating new life. We
were all together again – the four of us and our families
and the cousins next door and their families, and Auntie
Eilish was there too. Sadly, Uncle Tom died, following a
week's illness in May. He was cremated and his ashes were
buried on what would have been his seventy-eighth
birthday, 15 May 2002. And just as I said the cousins felt
the loss of my mother very deeply, I felt that I had lost my
second father when Uncle Tom died. He had taken us all
totally under his wing when our Dad died 26 years ago.
We were all back in the same church for the same reason
far too soon.

Those two houses were bursting with a minimum of 11
people at any given time for so many years. They were full
of laughter and love; they were a sanctuary for us when we
were in difficulties of any sort and now one of them is sold
and the other has two people living in it – Auntie Eilish

and Barry. I count myself extremely lucky to have had the childhood I lived and I hope Eva, Tom, Eoin and Lucy will use this memoir to remind them of their beloved Nana. I hope they'll tell the story to their children in times to come; times that will be very different in lots of ways, but hopefully similar in the ways of love and belonging and strong family ties.

Unforeseen Circumstances

A sense of love, a sense of belonging and a sense of strong family ties are some of the qualities of life that I dearly want for my children so that they will always feel the support and security of being around people who want the very best for them. I think I'm probably over sensitive with regard to their emotional well-being because of their circumstances. They are the most important part of their parents' lives but their parents are separated. Sometimes that reality weighs very heavily on my mind, like right now for instance.

I'm sitting in idyllic surroundings on the patio of a spacious ground floor apartment in a tiny little village on the Côte d'Azur. The sea is across the road and to the right is the little marina where yachts are moored. They're impressive to my eyes but seem like dinghies compared to the sea going hotels you can see if you walk along the prom in Saint Tropez. St Trop, as they call it, is 20 kilometres away. It's buzzing, it's full of Ferraris and designer people as well as designer clothes and it's well worth a visit in the cool of the evening. You can sit and people watch to your heart's content, which is perfectly acceptable over there because the people very definitely want to be looked at. They haven't spent a small mortgage on lifts and tucks and clothes and bags, and sometimes designer dogs, so that they can strut their stuff unnoticed. The other evening I was sitting on the port in Saint Tropez and who sat down at the next table but Ivana Trump and her escort. I heard he's her personal trainer. It's a strange feeling to be sitting beside somebody that is so so well-known and so so wealthy and that everybody feels they know well. I sat and watched and wondered what must it be like for her because there was no doubt about a couple of things that evening. She has had her lips done. They were massive. She's got an expensive look about her. I'd seen her yacht in the port on previous occasions. Well not in the port exactly because it's so big that it won't fit in the port. She has another one that she uses to come ashore and I'd read in a magazine a few weeks ago that she bases herself in the south of France from May until September. Her trousers were snow white and her silk shirt was pretty special too. Nothing could prepare you for the almost black heart-shaped sapphire ring she was wearing. The man with her was about a third of her age. It'd remind you of the story Paul Daniels tells about his wife Debbie being interviewed. She's a lot younger than him and apparently the interviewer's first question was 'So what was it first attracted you to the millionaire Paul Daniels?' Similar situation I'd imagine with Ivana and her man. He was extremely handsome. Good for Ivana, you'd think. I don't know though. There was only cursory conversation and no laughter between the two of them. It made me wonder what must be going through her head as she realises everyone is watching her and thinking of her extreme wealth.

Mind you, she's not the only extremely wealthy person in Saint Tropez. She'd be up there with the best of them though. It's an amazing place but I couldn't stay there. It's far too busy and noisy. This little village, between Saint Raphael and Sainte Maxime is ideal. It's no more than one street with the sea on one side of the road. The little supermarket is so narrow that if you're at the end of an aisle and you realise you've forgotten something, it's easier to go out and come back in again than to retrace your steps against the flow.

This is my favourite part of the world outside of Ireland. I love the Provençal way of life. I read Carol Drinkwater's book about renovating an old olive farm in the area full of envy. I thoroughly enjoyed her account and I'm looking forward to reading the sequel, *The Olive Season*. I love everything about this part of France: the sunshine, the language, the straw baskets, the olives; the smell of the lavender on the air, the sound of the crickets in the undergrowth, the brightly coloured tablecloths and aprons, the juicy ripe peaches, nectarines and apricots, the 'tomates provençales', stuffed with breadcrumbs, garlic and herbes de Provence. Those same tasty tomatoes that got Deirdre and myself into trouble when we were au pairs down here many years ago. I fell in love with the area back then and I suppose you could say that it's a mark of what I've achieved in life that I'm back here now and 'beholdin' to no one'.

I'm writing at the patio table, looking out at a clear blue sky. It's about 28 degrees but there's a light breeze. I'm wearing a swimsuit and sarong. Anything else would be just too heavy. There's a small lawn in front of the patio, an olive tree with tiny olives maturing at the end of it, a cordyline beside that and a huge palm tree. The hedging on either side of the apartment is made up of bougainvillea; pink to my right and white to my left. If I want a break from the writing, I'll throw on a pair of flip-flops and walk the 100 yards to the pool. Or I can cross the road and swim in the clear warm water of the Med. What more could I ask for? Good question. I'm lucky to be here and to savour this very beautiful and relaxing part of this earth. But I'm sad and I know why.

I'm looking at families passing by on the footpath at the end of the lawn, on their way to the pool or the beach:

mother, father, sometimes grandparents (the French are great for going on holidays with grandparents) and children with their towels and their inflatable mattresses and all the other bits and bobs that you think you'll need but just end up carrying to the beach and back. Watching those processions gives me a heavy feeling in my heart because my children aren't here. They're on a two-week holiday with their Dad in Rosslare. I know I had a two-week holiday with them also and we had great fun in spite of the fact that the weather wasn't wonderful.

My children have a special place in their hearts for Rosslare in the same way I suppose that I love the south of France. They've been spending the month of July there since they were very small and that has continued since their Dad and I separated. They spend the first fortnight with me and the second with him. They love that month and I should be content about that. Most of the time I am but just at the moment, I'm missing them and wishing that life had dealt me a different hand of cards and that separation wasn't one of them.

I grew up in a very ordinary, decent, happy home. I've already spoken about my parents. They also grew up in similar setups. They lived in the same area. Mam was one of seven and they lived first on Murtagh Road and then moved to Ellesmere Avenue, off the North Circular Road in Dublin 7 to a nice three-bedroom house, my aunt Kathleen still lives there. The five girls slept in one room, the two boys in the box room and the parents in the third room. Downstairs, there was a sitting room, dining room, a small kitchen with a fireplace and off that, a scullery where the cooking and washing was done. Outside the back door there was a meat safe. I remember the eggs and milk and meat being stored in that wooden raised box with a mesh front on it. My grandfather worked in Guinness and was, by all accounts, a gentle, mild-mannered man. He died in 1948. My grandmother had her fair share of heartbreak during her life, having already lost her brother Peter when he was shot during the Troubles and her twenty-six-year-old son Billy to TB in 1939 but she was a woman of great character and great faith, and she passed those qualities onto her children. She also loved company and enjoyed a good laugh and a game of cards and I know that my mother, her daughter was the same: great company, great faith and a strong character.

My father grew up on St Joseph's Road, which joined Prussia Street and Aughrim Street, a stone's throw from Ellesmere Avenue and they got married in the local church in Aughrim Street, a double wedding, remember, with Eilish, Mam's sister and her husband Tom. Dad was the eldest of four, two boys and two girls. His father was in the RIC, a tall handsome man who lived to ninety-three. He was a gentle, kind grandfather and I have an abiding memory of him at my father's funeral. My heart went out to him even though I was consumed with gut wrenching grief and a feeling of injustice that my Dad should die at the age of fifty-nine, while playing golf and that I hadn't seen him in the previous three months because I was teaching English in Brittany at the time. The funeral Mass was over and Mam and I were sitting in the black funeral car while people commiserated. It was a grey, wet day, 26 March 1977. Granddad walked slowly over with the aid of a walking stick, his tall frame stooped over with age and grief. There were tears in his eyes and as he embraced my mother I heard him say that he wished it was him in the coffin. He'd lived his life and he felt it was wrong for him to be alive and his son to be taken while he was still rearing his family. I could understand that generosity of spirit and as I say my heart went out to him at that moment. It was only years later, when I had children of my own that the full magnitude of that moment struck home. The worst nightmare for any parent is to bury their child. I know my father was a grown man with four children but your child is always your child. My grandfather was trying to make sense of the death of his son and yet his thoughts were not for his own heartbreak but for his daughter-in-law and her loss. I don't know if I would be so magnanimous in a similar situation. But like I said he was a very kind hearted, easy-going man with a big heart and those qualities he most certainly passed on to his son, my father.

This was my first experience of death and I remember finding it impossible to reconcile myself to the thought of my Dad lying in a coffin in the ground in Esker cemetery on a dark wet March night. That vision entered my head as I was sitting beside my mother in the funeral car. The vision stayed with me through the burial and was almost unbearable that night when I was lying in bed in Brigid's Road. I wanted to go to Esker and sit by the grave and keep my Dad company. I can understand how people feel the urge to throw themselves on top of a coffin. I felt differently when my mother was being buried even though it too, was a bitterly cold and wet day, the 27 December 2001. This time around, there was no stomach churning grief at her being put in the ground because that wasn't how I viewed it. I was more aware of her spiritual life continuing in a different place and in a different way and of her being reunited with my Dad. A friend sent me a poem by Joyce Fossen after she died and it gave me a great reassurance as to what had happened to her. Here is an extract from it:

Do not stand at my grave and weep
I am not there. I do not sleep.
I am a thousand winds that blow.
I am the diamond glint on snow.
I am the sunlight on ripened grain.
I am the gentle autumn rain.

My acceptance of her death in a way that I couldn't accept my father's is due to the way my own life evolved in the intervening years. The good things and the bad things; the people whose paths crossed mine: love, marriage, children and separation as well. Everything we experience colours our perception of life and the world and for that reason we have to take that deck of cards that destiny has for us all and make the most of the hand we're dealt. There's no point in falling into the quagmire of regret over things that have happened or things that haven't. There are times when we have to trust our instinct and do what we believe is the right thing. Otherwise, there's a danger that life will pass us by. Think of the words of Mark Twain:

> Twenty years from now you will be more disappointed by the things that you didn't do than by the ones you did do. So throw off the bowlines, sail away from the safe harbor. Catch the trade wind in your sails. Explore. Dream. Discover.

That's not to say that the fact that my marriage ended in separation doesn't fill me with sadness. Look at me now. Sitting in this little piece of paradise and pining for my children who are having a lovely time with their Dad and who I text every evening to hear how their day has been. And it's been fine. They're enjoying themselves and I have to accept that this is the way my life has evolved but I would rather it were different. I do envy those French families passing by on their way to the beach. I miss my children when they're with their Dad and I'm sure he feels the same way when they're with me. We both love them dearly and they know that. But it didn't work out. I wish it had. I'd like to be sharing the rearing and educating of my children with their father in one family unit. To be encouraging them in their studies and their extra cur-ricular pursuits together. To be sitting at the kitchen table over dinner and hearing their stories of the day, of what happened in school, with pals, at football matches. To be taking one or two of them into town maybe while the others are happy at home. But that was not to be. Nobody goes into marriage wanting anything other than for it to last. Everybody wants to be married till death do us part. But the reality is that for some, that's not to be. The circumstances differ from couple to couple and they are nobody else's business but the reality of separation is a difficult and imperfect one. It is not something I would recommend. However, when it happens, life goes on.

There are times when I lie awake at night and wonder how my children will be. There are also times when I look at them and realise that they're fine. They're bright, sociable, they have a sense of right and wrong and above all they know that both parents cherish them. I also know they'd prefer to be in a family environment with both parents in the one house. And that makes me sad and depending on my frame of mind, makes me feel pretty miserable because they don't have that. What I have to learn and what all of us in difficult circumstances have to learn is to rid ourselves of that misery. It's corrosive and futile. When I'm having a bad day and the negative feelings are to the fore I remind myself of these words, from the Book of Proverbs, 17:22.

> All healing comes from within. All misery comes from within. Our thoughts have tremendous power. We can create our own spiral of despair or we can create a trampoline of happiness and attainment.

The Feel Good Factor

There are people who think I have a positive outlook on life. And for the most part that's true. I enjoy my work, I adore my children, I have great friends and I embrace opportunities as they present themselves. There can be no doubt however in the light of the previous two chapters that I am not immune to the 'slings and arrows of outrageous fortune'. Like everybody else, I have my ups and downs. There are mornings when I wake up full of the joys of spring, ready to take on whatever challenges the day might bring, looking forward to getting up, getting out and getting on with life. There are also mornings when I open the curtains and feel heaviness, sadness, a reluctance to do anything. This can happen for many reasons. I may be in the middle of a heavy and exhausting workload. I may have a problem that is weighing on my mind. I may feel I've handled a situation badly and be wondering how I can resolve it. I may wake up with that empty feeling of loss in the pit of my stomach that reminds me that I'm missing my mother. On these mornings I dread the thought of another day and all that it entails. However, I have not yet won the Lotto and so, I drag myself out of bed and into the shower and downstairs to start the day reluctantly. It's not as if an extra hour in bed would improve the situation either. I am a notoriously bad sleeper and I also know that giving into my lethargy would only make me feel worse.

On these dark days, I know that if I stay in the house and mope around, my mood will not brighten, so even if there's nothing pressing and I don't have anything specific on the agenda, I get out, meet people and I invariably find that the clouds lift. There is nothing like the interaction of conversation to take my mind off a feeling of sadness or greyness and change my focus. I still won't necessarily be a barrel of laughs but I will be able to cope better and will see the light at the end of the tunnel. I'm sure people reading this will relate to what I'm saying because we all have our low days. That's one strategy that I find works for me. There are others and I'll share them because they might just work for someone else as well.

The garden always lifts my spirits. It's my favourite place in my home. I'm lucky too, to have a conservatory that brings the garden into the house on those all too familiar Irish days when the heavens open and we know why this is such a lush green land. I'm not a great gardener nor have I a particularly elaborate or unusual garden. Working in it though, or simply sitting in it gives me a sense of peace and well-being, a feeling that all is right with the world. I enjoy getting my hands dirty. I like digging and planting and the feeling of physical exertion they entail. I am convinced there is a correlation between working the body and feeling good in your head and your spirit. As Margaret Thatcher once said:

> 'Look at a day when you are supremely satisfied at the end. It's not a day when you lounge around doing nothing. It's when you've had everything to do and you've done it'.

If that's the case, it stands to reason that if you wake up in a black mood, an amount of physical exertion will help to lift the clouds.

My interest in gardening goes back to my childhood.

I've already said that my father was a committed committee member. He was involved in all of the organisations
that were working to make the new village of Clondalkin
into a community. One of those was Muintir na Tíre and
one of the activities they organised was a mini Tidy Towns
competition which involved all the different estates in the
village competing for the title of tidiest and prettiest.
There was also a section in the competition for children
and because my Dad was organising the thing, he
persuaded me to enter. A square patch of the flowerbed in
the back garden had to be measured out and boundaries
put in place and then you could literally do what you liked
with the earth. I had never even thought about gardening
and flowers before this, apart from how to avoid having to
cut the grass or weed the beds as a chore during the
summer holidays. I was given a budget of a couple of quid
and off I went to the hardware (there were no garden
centres in those days) in the early spring to buy seeds that
would be in bloom by the end of July, the judging time. I
was nine years of age and I hadn't a clue. So I bought the
most colourful packets, brought them home and without
really expecting anything much to happen I planted them,
following the instructions as to the gap to be left between
the seeds. In fact I was so naïve and so precise that I got
my school ruler out to measure the distance. I had gone
about this task in a scientific manner but I was not hopeful
that those little round pellets would end up looking
anything like the pictures on the front of the packets. But
they did. I watered them and weeded between them. I
checked them everyday; I never went quite so far as talking
to them but by the middle of the summer, my little patch
was a profusion of colour and scent and, if my memory
serves me correctly, the patch stood in sharp contrast to

the rest of the back garden. When I was nine there wasn't a huge amount of time in my parent's lives for gardening and such pursuits. I remember the butterflies in my stomach when the judges arrived to inspect my garden. I didn't know in advance when they might arrive. This was a serious competition after all. The judges wanted to be sure we were tending our gardens lovingly all the time, not just when we were expecting the knock on the door. They came quite late, for a nine-year-old anyway, because I was getting ready for bed when my Dad, who was just as excited as me, called upstairs to me to come down for the inspection. I had to get dressed again quickly and stood quietly as the judges took notes and conferred. I didn't win a prize in the competition but it gave me one of the biggest prizes imaginable, a love of flowers and gardens and other aspects of nature as well. I was bitten by the gardening bug.

For me, the garden is about colour and scents. I have seating in different parts of the garden and it's amazing how the different spots have different charms. There's a little decked area in the bottom right-hand corner and I love to sit there in the morning with the paper and a cup of coffee because the sun shines there then. I look up at the house and the light shines through the cordyline, which also has a magnificent scent when it's in flower and that wafts towards me on the breeze.

There's a garden bench under the conifers and I sit there sometimes and breathe in the pungent smell of those trees. It's beside the clothesline and I sit on the bench and look at the washing on the line. Sounds weird perhaps, but I like the sight of a line of washing blowing in the wind. I could never be happy with a rotary clothesline for that reason. There's freshness, cleaness, a movement about it that appeals to me. I'm not ashamed to say that sitting there quietly with my thoughts watching the clothes on the line can lift my spirit. Simple, everyday things can do that for me. I don't think we should underestimate the power of the ordinary everyday pursuits to give us satisfaction. It's amazing the number of meaningful stories that occur in our lives daily. All too often we miss these life lessons that can remind us that peace and tranquillity don't come from the big occasional events but from the simple and wholesome and people-centred aspects of our lives.

There's a lovely sunny spot just outside the conservatory that looks down the garden at the lawn and the flowerbeds. I've put tubs of brightly coloured bedding plants there. I love to sit there in the late afternoon with a cup of tea. It's a hiatus between the work of the day and the evening. And as I think about how rested I feel when I'm there I'm reminded why so many people refer to their garden as a sanctuary. A feeling of peace and calm envelops me. I generally just sit and chill. And if there are dark clouds in my head, the garden will definitely cheer me up. It's the combination of air, light, trees, plants, smells and colour, birds and animals like our rabbits and dog and cat; all part of the beauty of creation and all there to be enjoyed.

There's one other spot in the garden that's very special to me and that's the patio just outside the kitchen door which gets the sun until it sets and where I love to eat with family and friends. That combination of the good things of nature and the joy of friendship and laughter is a dead cert for lifting my spirits and even if I wake up gloomy and not in a very sociable humour, that interaction with people will, as I said earlier, lift my mood. I hope that description of the pleasure I get from different parts of the garden doesn't give the wrong impression. Mine is not a big garden. Nor is it as I explained earlier, an elaborate garden. It's a suburban space that gives me enormous pleasure and I want to underline that fact because I'm convinced it can be the same for everyone. The garden, if it's tended and enjoyed will repay the gardener ten-fold with a sense of satisfaction at the work accomplished, and a feeling of joy and awe at the beauty and the dignity of the natural world.

Another aspect of gardening that I love is getting slips from friends' gardens. There's continuity in that which appeals to me. The plant gets to share its beauty in another setting and also serves as a reminder of the person who gave it. I get great pleasure from sitting looking at a particular plant and remembering whose garden it came from. It gives me a feeling of warmth, of connection with the friend and that lifts my spirits if I'm feeling a bit low. There's also an undeniable sense of satisfaction that, once lifted from another garden, the plant took root in mine and grew. And the joy of it is that most slips do grow. They wilt and die back and I keep an eye on them and am delighted when I go out one morning and see a little green shoot just above the ground. That can only serve to gladden even the dullest day and the dreariest frame of mind, to open my mind to the wonder of what's around me and what's around me is life.

When I'm feeling low I know the task for me is to bring myself back to a place where I can accept and appreciate that wonder, that energy, that life force that's bubbling and waiting to be tapped again. I have to harness again the optimism that gives that positive outlook on life. I have to tell myself that although things look bleak at the moment, my life is not therefore a mess. All experiences have their worth. There are life lessons all around us. We learn from our failures and we learn from our successes. That's the message in this extract from the Spanish poet Antonio Machado:

Last night as I was sleeping,
I dreamt – marvelous error!
that I had a beehive
here inside my heart.
And the golden bees
were making white combs
and sweet honey
from my old failures.

Isn't that a lovely thought? That failures can be made into sweet honey. I have not blown it just because things aren't working well right now, because everybody else seems to be making a better fist of things than me. When I open up and share these anxieties with others, I realise that none of us is immune to such feelings. They just happen to besiege different people at different times. Talking about our troubles helps. That is easier said than done for a lot of people, myself included up to fairly recently. I used to find it very hard to make the initial move and voice my pain. It felt to me like an admission of failure, of weakness, of helplessness, which of course, is exactly what it was but why hide it? Was it fear that others would think less of me? Or just foolish pride? Maybe both, but totally misplaced. I'm so glad I got over that reluctance to share and open up because I have found since I've begun to share worries that once the first words have been spoken a weight has been lifted from my shoulders. There is absolutely no doubt that a trouble shared is a trouble halved. I'm glad that I can help friends out of those gloomy feelings and they certainly do the same for me. It's when we bottle up our fears and sadness that they can really get us down. On the other hand, when we share our worries and fears with others and are there to listen to their difficulties, we come to realise that no problem is insurmountable and that we can always start again. If we miss the moment, it's all right. There'll be other moments. The important thing is to realise that our spirits will be lifted and the clouds dissipated by that connection with other people. Thomas Moore spells it out very clearly here:

> 'We know we are well on the way toward soul when we feel attachment to the world and the people around us and when we live as much from the heart as from the head . . . and when compassion takes the place of distrust and fear'.

There are other things that lift my spirits if I'm feeling a bit low. I realise it's very much a question of different strokes for different folks and there may be some who don't share this one with me but I love a good bout of house-work. It may sound trivial and flippant but for me it's extremely therapeutic. As with the gardening, I love to get my hands dirty. I like to tackle a job like that and clear off shelves and feel a sense of space by throwing things out and making the place tidy. It's good for the head and being able to see the results of your toil gives that sense of satisfaction with a job well done. I have come to realise that the worst thing to do when I'm feeling low is nothing. Setting myself a task, and doing it may be a diversionary tactic but it works. At least part of my mind has to focus on the task and by the time I'm half way through it, I can feel the clouds beginning to lift. My advice to anyone who's having a bad day, who's feeling low is to force yourself to do something, anything, even though you don't feel like it, even though it's easier to brood and wallow in the sadness. We must use conscious choice to put ourselves in a good and positive place. Action on days when I'm feeling low brings me out of that dark place.

There are two situations when I cannot be sad no matter how difficult life might be at that time. The very fact of being on a mountain or on an island lifts my spirits instantly. There's something about those places that clears away all the accessories to the fact that I am human and that I am part of this natural world, this beauty of creation, that makes troubles seem utterly trivial by comparison. Maybe it's the awesome majesty of a mountain that makes me feel like that, or the self-sufficiency and calm of a small island out at sea. I grew up with that traditional view of heaven being a place above the clouds and while the sophistication of education and maturity might have changed such a notion, there's still a feeling of moving closer to heaven when I climb a mountain. The scenery is invariably breathtaking at a height. I remember climbing Tully Mountain in Connemara on a beautiful summer's day a few years ago and being filled with a feeling of pure delight when I reached the summit. For a start, there's the sense of accomplishment at reaching the top. I know it's not Everest, but any climb requires a bit of effort and Tully is no exception. The exertion is well worth it, not only for the views from the top, but also for the experience of walking through the landscape on the way up, through heather and gorse, over hills, alongside scurrying sheep. There's a pioneering feeling associated with being in deserted places and I relish the vastness of the mountain, especially compared to the often claustro-phobic surroundings of the city. I will always remember being on the top of Tully that day. The sun shone brightly, there was a strong warm breeze and the colours of Connemara were at their most beautiful; on one side the deep blue sea and all around the purple, blue, orange, green, brown and yellow of the land. All the elements were there to make me feel truly close to nature. It's a heavenly feeling. Your spirits couldn't but be lifted in a situation like that. The very nature of the mountain facing upwards towards the skies and the heavens has the effect of giving my thoughts and my feelings an upward, upbeat, positive direction.

The ability of the mountains to keep me positive doesn't depend on good weather though. I climbed Mount Brandon in Kerry on a grey, misty day but it was once again a very gratifying experience, both physically and psychologically. When the weather is bad, there's the extra element of caution required which reminds me of the power of the mountain and the respect that is its due. The rewards are enormous though. I remember at the top of a ridge about half way to the summit, turning a corner and seeing below me a string of lakes, known locally as the Pater Noster. I felt privileged to be standing above looking down on this beautiful sight. At the summit there's a cross and a stone that in former times was used as an altar and on the other side of the mountain, there's an easier climb which is known as the pilgrim's path. Isn't it lovely to be given an insight into the lives of former generations of people and the way they worshipped and it's easy to understand why they would climb to the top of the mountain to pray. My spirits soared on that grey misty day on Brandon.

I've climbed Croagh Patrick on a dull day too; the kind of day that I hate when I'm in the city, but it doesn't matter on the mountain. I just felt glad to be there. What I like about this mountain is the different moods it evokes at the different stages of the climb. A short distance up, when I turned around and looked down at the 365 islands in Clew Bay, I was delighted by their serenity, their stillness, their sense of calm. As I continued the climb and it was getting quite steep, my thoughts turned in admiration to the people who do Reek Sunday every year. Remembering the photos in the newspapers the following day of cut and muddied feet of pilgrims, I felt like a wimp in my walking boots. Then there's an easy bit of a walk across the ridge where I felt comfortable and just plain glad to be there, glad to be alive. In the majesty of these powerful, vast and majestic surroundings all worries and anxieties pale to insignificance. The last bit of the climb is really tough and I ended up on my hands and knees picking my way up the scree to the summit. I felt humbled by this struggle and very close to the physical reality of the earth. Difficult not to be, I suppose, when your nose is only a couple of feet above the ground and you're gasping for breath and praying that you'll make it to the top. And then, on the summit, sitting on the steps of the chapel, all my feelings came together in a positive and uplifting whole: the delight of the islands, the admiration for the pilgrims, the comfort of the walk, the humility of the scree and the satisfaction of the achievement. A moment to be savoured even if it weren't for the breathtaking view from the summit, which I'll have to take on trust because I've not seen it. The summit was shrouded in mist the day I climbed Croagh Patrick but it didn't matter. My memory is of being bathed in a feeling of well-being. I remember sitting there on the chapel steps and just wanting everyone I know to feel the same.

I get that same feeling of contentment on a small island. Again, there's a sense in which you're very close to the physicality of nature, especially when you can almost take in the whole area as you approach in a boat. There's majesty, a calm and a history attached to islands which seems very accessible and in the case of islands that are no longer inhabited, very precious. I remember walking among the ruins of the houses on the Great Blasket and sensing the closeness of the community in a way that is never possible from reading about it in a book. I walked down to the trá bán, sat on the beach and looked back across the sound to the mainland and Dún Chaoin. It was a beautiful day and there were specks of silver light on the sea. A truly beautiful sight that would lift your spirits no matter how low you were feeling. I thought of Peig Sayers and the heartache that same sea brought her when one of her sons drowned while out fishing. On the day of his funeral, she went out and sat looking at the sea and even in the agony of her loss and her anguish at having to bury her child, she took consolation from the sea. I'll never forget this quote from her autobiography; 'Is marbh an croí nach dtógfadh aer bog cúmhra na farraige an smúit agus an brón de'. (Only a heart that is dead would remain unmoved, unconsoled by the soft, sweet air of the sea.) Her heart was broken by this tragedy but it wasn't dead. I think of that day on the Blascaod Mór when I'm feeling sad or lonely. I remember how content and at peace I felt walking on the grass covered pathways, among the ruins of the houses and particularly, sitting on the white sand and remembering how Peig, in her turmoil, took consolation from the beauty of the elements. I'm glad to have had the opportunity to visit the island. It's an experience that, as I say, gives me a sense of well-being, that lifts my spirits and as with the mountains, I can't help feeling that all will be well when I contemplate the tranquillity and beauty that I associate with offshore islands.

The magic begins from the moment I step onboard the ferryboat. A feeling of adventure, of exploration and discovery. I feel as if I'm leaving the world behind and going into nature. The first sight of the island is comforting as well. It's invariably beautiful, lying there in the sea and it's a manageable size; in a way that life sometimes is not. It seems to me to ooze a feeling of serenity and of ease with itself. I can hear its message clearly. 'Here I am. Welcome to my shores. Accept me as I am.' No notions. No pretensions. That lifts my spirits. I brought my children to Clare Island and we were all fascinated by the story of Grace O'Malley, the sixteenth-century sea trader, pirate and clan leader, better known as Granuaile who became a symbol of freedom in an oppressed time, and who is said to be buried in the thirteenth-century abbey on the island. The inscription on the tomb reads Terra Marique Potens O'Máille (O'Malley: Strong on Land and Sea). We saw the lookout tower, explored the ruins on the hill and we hired bikes and rode all over the island. There's no doubt that it's a great way of getting into the soul of the island. It was a glorious sunny day too. The island was particularly beautiful and so too was the sight of the mountains in Mayo sitting in a haze of sunshine on the horizon. I have a friend who, when she wants to underline the fact that something was just great, she says 'Sure I thought I'd died and gone to heaven' I had a similar feeling, sitting on the beach on Clare Island on that Saturday afternoon. Once again my spirits soared.

I've been lucky with the weather when it comes to visiting islands. I accept that it was a safe bet that I'd be seeing the Iles d'Hyères off the Côte d'Azur bathed in sunlight and they were stunning. As were the Greek islands I visited one year as a student. I visited the isles of Skye and Uist in blazing sunshine much to the amazement of Jill, my Scottish friend who spent summer holidays as a child on them and her memories were of Wellingtons and raincoats. Does that sound familiar? Closer to home,

anytime I've been on Inisbofin it's been a scorcher. As for
the Aran Islands, I visited Inis Oirr and Inis Meáin on
beautiful sunny days too but like the mountains, my delight
in islands isn't dependant on the weather. I've spent many
wet and freezing days on Inis Mór as well as sun-soaked
ones and the appeal is certainly different but it's there. The
energy of the sea is uplifting. I'll never forget the force with
which it thundered into Poll na bPéist, the natural pool on
the island, one stormy day. The wind was exhilarating as it
swept over the cliffs at Dún an Dúchathair. The rain has
often come down in sheets as I've walked the quiet lower
road, but I can embrace the elements for what they are on
the island and savour the roar of the sea, the cold of the
wind, the wet of the rain. And the cosiness of returning
indoors to dry off and enjoy the memory of the powerful
elements on this beautiful island where the pace of life
gives me an opportunity to live in the moment and feel my
spirits uplifted.

I think that love of the islands is rubbing off on the next
generation as well because so far two of my children have
attended Irish college on Inis Mór and they both enjoyed
the experience. Eva went to Coláiste Ó Direáin two years
running while she was in secondary school and was
delighted to be able to spend the August Bank Holiday
there this year to see how Tom was getting on on his first
trip there. He was getting on fine as it happens and made
lots of friends. He also learned lots of Irish and got a taste
of island living for three weeks. He was there for the
annual Beannú na mBád ceremony, where all the islands'
boats are decorated with bunting and painted and polished
and then they leave the quay at Kilronan and sail out a
short distance to where the lifeboat is moored. The local
priest is on board and as the boats pass by, he blesses them

and their crews with holy water and prays for their safety at sea. Once a boat is blessed it circles around the lifeboat, sounds its hooter and makes its way back to the harbour where a quayside Mass is celebrated and awards are presented to the different boats. It's a very colourful occasion, the boats range in size from tiny currachs to big trawlers and they're all festooned with flags and bunting, many of them sporting the Galway colours. It's a lovely custom that I witnessed for the first time on that weekend visiting Tom, a part of our culture and heritage and an acknowledgement of the power of the sea and the respect that it commands. We went out on one of those festooned boats for the blessing and there's no doubt that our spirits were lifted by that evening of celebration.

I don't think it's coincidental that the things that lift my spirits are gardening, friendships, a bit of housework (not too much now), mountain walks and island tours. There's something about all of those things that provides a real antidote to the stresses and strains of modern living. It's nice to be able to forget the routines and deadlines and demands but more importantly it's essential to be able to pull back from time to time and just take the time to smell the roses.

Snapshots of My Parents

When I slow down and take the time to smell the roses, to take stock of things, contentment follows and I can begin the next undertaking with the batteries recharged and a positive outlook. I've discovered that the same is also true of taking the time to allow sadness to register. Blocking it out doesn't make it go away. Acknowledging it and coming to terms with the feelings makes it more manageable and easier to move on. Summer 2002 taught me that lesson. I felt weird and I tried to fight it. Then I realised the sadness would only subside in its own time and when I had acknowledged it. It was such a strange summer. Understandable maybe, when you consider it was the first the children and I had spent without mother and grandmother. Looking back over that summer, I felt I moped around, rudderless and without focus. I felt quite low, as if I'd achieved nothing. This, in spite of the fact that I'd cleared out mother's house; steered Eva and Tom through the Junior and Leaving Cert exams; organised fundraising events for Eritrea; sold my old house and bought Brendan and Viv's around the corner; taken the children to Antibes for a week, followed by Rosslare for a week. I also spent two weeks in that lovely little village on the Côte d'Azur, where I read all 800 pages of Nelson Mandela's autobiography, *Long Walk to Freedom*, which was uplifting and inspirational. But I certainly didn't feel either uplifted or inspired.

In the first six months after Mam died, I had a sense of her being there, just beyond the physical realm as it were, but not too far away. I could see her face and hear her voice and I took great comfort from that. That changed though towards the end of June and instead of feeling her presence, I became very aware of a sense of loss, of her absence from our lives. When I tried to remember her face, all I could see was darkness. I couldn't call up her voice anymore. There was an emptiness and loneliness, where once there was the comforting feeling of her being out there looking after us.

Rosslare was particularly difficult because she always spent time with us when we were there. She'd come down on the train with her bag full of fruitcake and buns that were still warm when we opened them up as soon as she arrived. She'd also have a flask of tea and her mug because she hated the tea that they served on the train in those awful paper cups. And from the moment she'd arrive, she'd enter into the swing of things. She was always first up and I'd know by the sound of the noisy kettle whistling in the kitchen. After breakfast, she'd ramble down to Lambert's shop and buy the paper and the bread for the sandwiches. Then she'd sit at the table and butter endless slices of bread for the picnic in a very businesslike manner that had the effect of making me get myself into gear. After that, while all the stragglers were getting up and having breakfast she'd read the paper in the garden in a deck chair which will never be known as anything other than the 'Nana chair'. Finally, when John and Eileen and their two children would arrive at our house and when my children were at last organised we'd all go down to the beach and set up camp. I know Mam loved those days. She'd sit on the beach in the Nana chair, often with a fleece on and a rug wrapped around her knees, chatting and watching the children swim and play on the sand.

When they and she were younger, she made sandcastles with them, brought them collecting shells and crabs and smooth stones for which she seemed to have a particular affection. In recent years, she used to sit and tell us stories of her summer holidays when she was young. She and her friend Lucy used to cycle from Dublin to places like Arklow, Gorey, Courtown; stay in guesthouses and go for long walks during the day and to dances at night. My children still haven't come to terms with the fact that anyone would cycle such distances. That generation were made of strong stuff.

Part of Mam's routine when she'd join us in Rosslare was to take us all to Kelly's for dinner, as her treat. There was a minimum of 12 that night out, although I never remember it being that small a crowd. We'd all be praying that the smaller ones would behave because children not doing what they're told – first time they're told – is something my mother could never abide and she'd let you know if she was annoyed. So, I'd have my two younger ones under orders and their cousins would have the same instructions. They were only too willing to eat quickly and go to the TV room to watch a video while we all chatted over dinner. Little did I realise in July 2001 that we would never do that again. We've been to Kelly's both this year and last year but it's been different. I cherish the memories and the endless photographs of those ten summers from 1992 to 2001when Mam joined us in Rosslare.

She always stayed with me and I'm really glad now even though there were times when we used to drive each other mad. She felt I was sometimes too lenient with the children. I felt she was old fashioned and they were my children anyway. They were inevitable tensions I suppose between a mother and her eldest daughter. Her standards were very high. She demanded good behaviour always from all of her children and her grandchildren. She could be very strict but even when she had a face on and was obviously 'not amused' you'd never doubt her motives. She did everything, even the giving out, out of love for us and wanting us to be well brought up.

I remember as a very small child coming in after playing in the snow, crying with the pain of frozen hands and sitting on Mam's knee while she cradled my hands between her elbows and her ribs until the feeling came back into them.

In those days, when children were sick they stayed in bed and I have so many memories of her bringing me egg flips and Lucozade and insisting that I stay in bed. Unless the doctor was coming that is. In that case you'd be told to get out of bed while she changed the sheets and tidied everything, Hoovering and dusting in preparation for 'the visit'. Doctors were looked on as gods by my mother's generation.

To my shame, I remember when I was in 1st class and my mother's youngest sister was staying over I asked her to pick me up from school because she was pretty and well dressed and I wanted to pretend to the class that she was my mother. I was seven at the time, which means that Mam also had a five-year-old, an eighteen-month-old and was heavily pregnant with her fourth child. No wonder her sister, ten years younger than her and single, looked more glamorous.

Neither am I proud of the grief I gave my mother when she was making dresses for me and wanted me to try them on. I'd have to stand on a chair while she pinned up the hem. I'd have a face on me that would stop a clock and would be sighing and throwing my eyes up to heaven. I didn't want to be there. Not only that, I never liked the clothes she made for me. I often asked why I couldn't have 'bought' dresses from shops. The fact that my mother was an excellent dressmaker and that this was a cost-cutting exercise in times when there was very little money to spare didn't influence my attitude. And my lack of gratitude as a child didn't influence her either because when Eva was a baby she made beautiful dresses for her out of fabric and old dresses that she had never thrown out.

Mam was a very resourceful woman with a positive outlook on life. She was not one to be hindered by obstacles in her way. When we were all still quite young, fifteen down to six, a friend of hers who had adopted a baby girl became very ill and was faced with having to spend an unspecified amount of time in hospital. She was very worried because the baby had just arrived and there was a real possibility that she would be taken back. My mother offered to help out in any way she could and after a lot of negotiating with the adoption authorities, she was allowed to foster Rosemary until her adoptive mother, Mam's friend, was out of hospital. So this gorgeous, little six-month-old baby girl came to live with us in Brigid's Road, much to the delight of us four children who loved the novelty value of having a playful baby handed to us. My father was delighted too because he loved babies and anyway, he was such an easy-going man, nothing ever rattled him. I remember we were a bit cramped for space; the big pram became a regular feature in the middle of the kitchen floor at mealtimes and we're not talking big kitchen here, but we loved having Rosemary with us. When she smiled her whole face lit up and we had great fun with her. She stayed for ten months and I know I missed her terribly when she left. I can only imagine how heartbroken my mother was to give her back, having cared for her and loved her from the age of six months to sixteen months, through the teething induced sleepless nights, her first birthday party, her first pair of shoes. All the things she had done for us as babies, she did in exactly the same way for Rosemary

Mam was a very good neighbour. Next door to us (on the other side from the cousins) were the McCarthys. Their mother died very young, leaving Con with five children to rear. They had a series of housekeepers, all of whom my mother befriended. I remember them having tea in the kitchen in the afternoons when we'd come home from school. They were all quite young women from the country, much younger than my mother and yet they all seemed to get on well with her. Then Con married Maureen, a lovely gentle woman from Sligo, who still lives next door on Brigid's Road. She told us at Mam's month's mind in our house in January that the day she came back from her honeymoon, my mother called her over the back wall and gave her a sponge cake which she had made to welcome her and said Con's five children were lovely kids and she was sure they'd all be delighted with their second mother and if there was ever anything she wanted a hand with not to hesitate to ask. Maureen said it made all the difference to her starting off and she did call on my mother from time to time. She and Con went on to have five children together and the ten of them have always been such a close and happy bunch of people.

As well as being a good neighbour, Mam was a loyal friend and she valued her friendships greatly. She had a very close relationship with Margaret Doody, a woman much younger than her who moved in across the road when she got married. Margaret would ask my mother's opinion on all sorts of things and Mam was always happy to help out either by going shopping with Margaret or altering some outfit that she might have bought, or suggesting a different way of arranging a piece of furniture in a room. They had long chats together in later years when Mam was living alone and Margaret's two boys were grown up. And when, Mam was in hospital for those seven weeks from Hallowe'en until her death at Christmas, Margaret was in to see her almost every day. She's a minister of the Eucharist in Tallaght Hospital and she'd come into Mam's room while she was on her rounds as well.

I took my mother totally for granted. I suppose I thought everybody's mother was the same. It wasn't until I was in 6th class that I realised that wasn't the case. I was friendly, still am, with Pauline, a girl in my class who lived two doors up from us. Pauline's mother's health had been failing. She had great difficulty walking without support. We didn't know it but she had MS. It was Ascension Thursday and we had a day off school. Pauline, Babs, my other friend from the road (you'll remember she and I taught together in Colaiste Bride and she's the person who keeps us all in touch with each other), and I were in Pauline's bedroom chatting, not realising that the kitchen where Pauline's mother was sitting reading had gone on fire. Her mother died in that fire. We were told she had a heart attack while smoking a cigarette so she was dead before the fire started. When Pauline came running back upstairs, shouting that the kitchen was on fire we ran out into the street in total shock and alerted the neighbours. As twelve-year-olds, we didn't have very good coping skills and my reaction to the tragedy was two-fold.

Every winter night for years afterwards, I stayed awake until both my parents had gone to bed and then went downstairs to check that they had put the fireguard in front of the fire. They obviously knew I was doing this but neither of them ever said a word. They allowed me work through this fear of fire in my own way. These were days when nobody had heard of counselling, not to mention post-traumatic stress.

The other reaction to the death of Pauline's mother, I'm ashamed to say, was that Pauline being around reminded me of the awfulness of what had happened. This was a young girl who had lost her mother in a horrible fire and who obviously needed to talk about it but I just couldn't cope with the memory of the whole thing. My mother saw what was going on and after a very short while I was aware of her steering me out of that frame of mind. There was no way she was going to allow me to turn my back on my friend and she just made sure that when Pauline called I didn't make any excuses. In fact, my mother took Pauline under her wing when her mother died and she and Mam were very close from then right up to the time of my mother's death.

There was nothing they didn't discuss quite openly and candidly, which is more than I can say for myself. It's funny. I never felt I could discuss certain things with my mother. She was very strict and I had some weird notion that if I had a problem it was a reflection on me, not on the other person. I know it saddened my mother that I didn't confide in her about serious matters because she said it to me on a beautiful summer's day in August 2001, while we were driving out of Dublin on a trip that I'm so glad I persuaded her to make. I'd just picked her up from the hairdresser's and convinced her that the alternative to taking a drive was that we go back to her house and do a Shirley Valentine on it – sit and look at the four walls.

Anyway, we were driving along and she told me about a much younger woman that she knew who had confided in her about her relationship problems with her partner. She was thinking of ending the relationship and this saddened

Mam because she liked both of them and thought it was a mistake. As we were discussing this situation in the car that day, Mam said, out of the blue, 'How is it that so many people will come to me with their problems and my own children won't?' I didn't have an answer for her at the time but I do feel that she was more understanding of other people's weaknesses than of ours. I also always felt that if I unburdened myself to her I was adding to her worries, because she was always a champion worrier. I have a theory that anxiety may have contributed to her being struck down by cancer so late in life, because until her eighty-first year, she was a strong and healthy woman who never smoked or drank and who'd only been in hospital to have her babies.

After my mother died, Auntie Eilish next door told me that Mam was deeply saddened by the breakdown of my marriage and Deirdre's, wondering where she went wrong in the rearing of us. I hate the fact that she blamed herself for that sadness. We are, of course, the product of our upbringing but that includes many influences outside the home and I know that my schooldays played a huge part in shaping my personality. Not once, in all the years I spent in school with the Presentation Sisters, did I have any teaching that would encourage self-confidence or empowerment. We were constantly told that we should be ladylike and respectful – nothing wrong with that – but we were never taught to be our own person and to stand up for what we felt was right in our lives, or to take a stand against what we felt was wrong. 'Shameful' was a word that was often used by the nuns when I was at school and of course 'empty vessels make most noise'.

My mother was a tower of strength and support to me when I finally, after 15 years of marriage, confided in her. Maybe things might have been different if I'd confided in her earlier. As I said, she gave me every support from that moment on.

Her support was practical and emotional and it must have been very difficult for her because she was a very conservative, traditional Catholic, for whom marriage most definitely was something that lasted till 'death us do part'. She objected strongly to my removing my wedding rings after my separation. We had words about this. Her belief was that although separated, I was still married and should wear them. I felt that because I was separated it was hypocritical to wear them. I tried to explain to her that if people saw me on TV wearing wedding rings even though my marriage was over, they'd think I was trying to hide the fact and maintain a pretext of being 'normal' – whatever that is. I've kept my rings though as a reminder of a stage in my life that was hugely significant, for which I had such hopes and dreams and which, most importantly, gave me the beautiful gift of four children who mean everything to me and without whom I couldn't survive.

On a practical level she helped me paint my house, she made curtains and cushions and got great enjoyment out of all that homemaking.

She loved helping me in the garden too. In fact, she had this electric hedge cutter that I used to borrow but she would only lend it to me on condition that she operated it. The logic behind that was that if I cut my hand off there were four children who would suffer – she could afford to lose a hand apparently. The children and I laughed at the absurdity of the whole thing but there was no way you'd convince her to change her mind. The scenario therefore was that of an old woman cutting a high hedge with a heavy piece of machinery and her fit and healthy daughter raking up the cuttings.

She would have been really excited about me buying Brendan and Viv's house and would have told me not to worry about repayments. As I've already said, her mantra where money was concerned was 'Sure, we'll find the money somewhere'. She had very little but she never let that stand it her way.

That trip that I made with her the August before she died was a very special journey for her and I am so glad I persuaded her on that sunny afternoon to come with me, even though she wasn't all that well and didn't like to go too far away from home in case she'd be ill. As it happened she was fine and talked about the trip from then until she went into hospital at Hallowe'en. We drove all around Newtown and Fenagh in Carlow. She showed me the house on the main street in Newtown where her mother was born – a couple of doors up from Smyth's pub and across the road from the church. We went into the grave-yard behind the church and found the Hogan grave, where her grandmother, her uncles and aunts were buried. Hogan was her mother's maiden name. I took her photo-graph and it turned out really well. The headstone is a tall Celtic cross and Mam stood beside it looking at the inscriptions. She was wearing a pink and white summer dress and she looked really pleased to be there. I found that photo in her wallet after she died.

Then we drove past the Fighting Cocks pub and called to the farm close by where her mother's friend, Kate, lived till she died and which is still in the same family. There was no one at home so she wrote a note to put in the letterbox explaining that I had taken her on this trip down memory lane. I was quite surprised at how much it meant to her to revisit these parts of Carlow. She was so excited and delighted and was in great form altogether. I am really glad I persuaded her to make the trip. I honestly didn't realise the significance of it when I suggested it.

It was like the old days, before she became unwell and frightened about what was wrong with her. We reminisced about the Sunday visits we used to make to that farm. For us children, Kennedys and Whites next door, it was our exposure to country life. We were city born and bred and we looked forward to those Sunday afternoons in the summer when the two families were invited down to Kate and Mick Esmonde's farm. They were brother and sister, both single and I'm sure it was like a blunderbuss hitting their land when we came for the day. Seven youngsters, beside themselves with excitement at being let loose in hay barns and lofts, chasing chickens and searching for eggs and 'helping' with the milking and the herding of the sheep! Both Kate and Mick were the epitome of patience and good humour and so was their nephew Seán who helped them on the farm and who lives there now with his wife Lilly. They were always smiling and loved company. Well, they enjoyed having my parents and Tom and Eilish visit for the day. I'm sure they could have lived without the collateral damage their offspring were capable of inflicting. Those were happy times and Mam and I relived them that day when we took that drive which rolled back the years for my mother and gave her another chance, a last chance as it turned out, to consider and enjoy her Carlow background. I relived those happy times again during the summer when I was a guest at Seán and Lilly's daughter's wedding. It was funny to hear the account of those Sunday visits from the other perspective. Seán told me that he and Mick would spend the week before putting away all the sharp implements and dangerous machinery because they knew we city kids got very excited on the farm and were

liable to lose the run of ourselves! Kate used to spend that
week in the kitchen because she always laid on a feast
when we were there and she insisted on sending us back to
Dublin laden with fruitcakes, jams, apple tarts and boxes
of fruit and vegetables. Seán also reminded me of a great
laugh they all had one Sunday when they looked out the
kitchen window and saw me taking a hen for a walk. I had
tied a length of string around the poor animals neck and
was parading her around the farmyard!

Before her illness, Mam was well-known for her joie de
vivre. She loved people: chatting to them, hearing their
stories, telling her stories. She was a great person for get-
togethers and games of poker and going to concerts and
shows. People seemed to gravitate towards her. Neighbours
of mine whose children were in the same class as my
children ended up as friends of my mother. She'd get to
know them at the school. She joked that at weddings and
other state occasions, she was always put sitting beside the
person who was quiet, shy or difficult to engage in conversation. She didn't mind that at all though. She was very
kind hearted and would hate anybody to feel unwanted or
a nuisance.

She was also very strict and had a very highly developed
sense of right and wrong. Both my parents left school after
the Inter Cert and got jobs and maybe because of that,
they had great regard for education and great respect for
the teachers we had in primary and in secondary school. I
remember when I was in 1st year, coming home and
complaining about my Latin teacher who said I wasn't
doing a whole lot and that my summer report was going to
be bad. I reckoned forewarned is forearmed so I told Mam
what to expect. She came down very heavily on the side of
the teacher and said that what the teacher had to say

would be nothing compared to what would be said at home if I got a bad report. The dice was cast for that year but I didn't let it happen again. It was easier to keep my head down and stay out of trouble in school and also at home. Later, when I became serious about studying and worried about the results I might get in exams, she always said, 'Just do your best. That's all anyone can expect.' She was happy with any marks if you did your best but if the behaviour part of the report was bad you were in serious trouble.

Mam took her parenting responsibilities very, very seriously and when Dad died of a heart attack at the age of fifty-nine, there was still a good bit of parenting left to be done. I had just finished college and was spending a year teaching English in Brittany, John had started working in the bank and Deirdre and Tony were still at school. In fact, Dad died at the end of March, two months before Deirdre sat her Leaving Cert and Tony, his Inter Cert. When I think of how I ministered to my own two children in the run up to the state exams last year, minding them, keeping them calm and on track, I realise that as well as my mother being devastated by the death of her husband, it must have broken her heart to see two of her children trying to sit those exams two months after the sudden death of their father. It's only now I can fully appreciate how she must have felt then. I would have been so sad if anything untoward had happened in Eva or Tom's lives so close to the exams.

Dad's death really knocked the stuffing out of my mother for a long time. There was a sadness about her that was difficult to penetrate and those were not times when people talked openly about such things. She put on a brave face and got on with life. She was lucky to have great friends who were always about the place and she of course had her sister and brother-in-law next door, which was an enormous blessing for all of us. I would have liked if things had been different and she and I had sat down and talked about the feelings of loss we both had but it didn't happen.

It took me a long time to get over Dad's death. I was the eldest and he and I always got on really well. There was never a cross word between us. He was much more easy-going than my mother and being the eldest I had nowhere else to go to get someone to intercede for me if I wanted to do something that my mother mightn't approve of. He'd always persuade her to trust me and let me off. She didn't want me to go to France for a year; after I graduated – she thought I should do the H.Dip. and get a job straight away but Dad convinced her that it was a great opportunity and that if I was going to be a half way decent French teacher, sure I'd have to spend time in the country, for God's sake.

It was a great year and changed my perspective on life and people and lots of other things as well. I was very homesick in the beginning though and Dad started writing me letters to keep my spirits up. He was a great letter writer with a very funny turn of phrase and our relationship blossomed further during that year of correspondence. One of my major regrets in life is that I was away when he died. I'd been home for Christmas and then went back to France in early January. I remember the morning I left. I'd been out with friends the night before and was still in bed when Dad was leaving for work. He came into my bedroom to say goodbye, kissed me, gave me a few bob, which I wasn't expecting and said as he always did 'Mind yourself'. That was the last time I ever saw my father. On Saturday, 26th of March, I was just about to leave Brittany to spend the Easter holidays in Spain with a group of friends when I got a phone call from Uncle Tom to say that Dad had 'taken a turn' and would I come home to see him. He didn't say he had died and the thought never entered my head. Maybe the belief that he was still alive kept me going because I had to organise train, bus and airline tickets to get from Rennes to Paris and then to Dublin and if I had known that Dad was already dead I mightn't have been so focused about the whole thing.

People around me seemed to know instinctively though. I was walking to the train station carrying a heavy rucksack really early in the morning and an English couple stopped and offered me a lift. I told them why I was going home and they insisted on staying with me until the train arrived. I'd never met these people before in my life. As I was sitting on the train waiting for it to leave the station, a friend I was supposed to be going to Spain with arrived on board. I'd left a note under his apartment door explaining why I wouldn't be part of the group and as soon as he woke up and saw it he dashed to the train station. I asked him afterwards and he knew. When I got to the airport, I explained my situation to a woman at the Aer Lingus desk. I needed to buy a ticket. The flight was full and she said she was putting me on standby. But when it came to boarding, I was called forward first. She must have known.

I spent the flight willing it to go faster. I just wanted to get home quickly to go to the hospital to see my Dad. When I came through the glass doors though, I saw Uncle Tom and my father's brother Seán, my friend Pauline and my brother John. I was very confused for a couple of seconds and then the penny dropped. I went cold and I couldn't stay standing. They tell me I screamed and sobbed. I don't remember much more except arriving home to Brigid's Road to scenes of awful sadness and raw grief. Untimely, sudden death is a sickening experience.

Another regret I have from that time is that I didn't go into the hospital mortuary and see Dad before they put the lid on his coffin. People advised me that it would be better for me to remember him as I had last seen him on that January morning before I returned to France. I didn't know any better and that was that. Those were different times. It was a mistake though. I wish now I could have said my goodbyes and touched his face and I'm glad my children chose to kiss their granny goodbye in the chapel of rest in Tallaght before her coffin was closed. There's a lovely sense of leave taking and saying goodbye and of being there for the person who's departing this life. I suppose when I think about it I didn't have leave taking at all with my Dad. I had no idea when he came into my room on that January morning to say farewell that we would never see each other again. If I had known that I would have taken the time to chat to him over breakfast. I would have kissed and hugged him goodbye properly not that quick peck on the cheek as he was leaving for work and I was still in bed. I'd give anything to be able to turn back the clock and have a second chance. Sadly, life's not like that. I loved my Dad dearly but I never really told him so. I'm sure he knew I loved him but I never said the words 'Dad, I love you. You're a kind, gentle man and I'm lucky to have a father like you who always puts his family first, who has a wonderful sense of humour and a really laid back approach to life'. This really bothered me for a long time after his passing, but it was too late then. However, time heals the broken heart. We pick up the pieces and life goes on and becomes good again. The years pass by and we get on with things. We have good times and bad times.

We fall back into the same habits and when I think about it I don't ever remember actually saying those words 'I love you' to my mother either. Until the last seven weeks of her life, that is. Then the sadness and frustration, and sense of unfinished business I felt when my Dad died so unexpectedly, came flooding back to me, and I dropped my guard and inhibitions and just loved her all the time. This special time of saying goodbye that I had with my mother was very precious and I will treasure the memory of it always.

Mam will be two years dead at Christmas and I've already said that 18 months have passed and I still miss her terribly. Sometimes when I'm least expecting it, a wave of sadness and loss sweeps over me and I just cry for no reason. Except, it's not for no reason – it's because that wonderful being, my mother, is gone from me. For all of these reasons, I am so glad that I had those seven weeks of saying goodbye with her where I left my inhibitions and awkwardness behind and just opened my heart. It was a real gift, a privilege, and I know deep down that I made the most of it, because I already knew how awful it feels when that opportunity is not afforded us and it's quite simply too late. I was lucky. It wasn't too late second time around.

Our loved ones are just that – loved ones. I hope that my memories of two different experiences when my parents died will encourage others to drop the guard with parents and say those 'I love you' words. Once the words are uttered, they enhance the moment for the person who says them and the person who hears. We tell our children we love them all the time. We reassure them when they're insecure; we convince them that no matter what happens we will never stop loving them. Why then do we find it so difficult to do the same for our parents? Maybe we need to remind ourselves that the all consuming love that we feel for our children, our parents have felt for us, their children, since the time of our birth.

After my father died, I returned to France to finish out the four months of my contract and the first thing I noticed when I got back to the apartment in Rennes was a letter from my Dad that he had posted just after St Patrick's Day telling me all about the parade and the family news, like how Deirdre's and Tony's studies were going. He'd written it eight days before he died and I needn't tell you that it and those other letters he wrote to me in Brittany are among my most treasured possessions. I came home from France for good in July after Dad died and the grief hit me again like a ton of bricks. It was so hard to be back home and not have him coming in from work and reading the paper and chatting out the back with Uncle Tom. But if I found it hard, what must it have been like for my mother who had lost her husband and her life partner and who was faced with such responsibility on her own? I wish we had spoken about those things. It would have eased things maybe for her, but she probably didn't want to worry us. I talk to my children about their granny and the relationship they had with her, how special it was and how lucky they are to have had her in their lives for so long. I also tell them when I'm feeling low and lonely and we had a good chat about how different it was to be in Rosslare without her last year.

I feel privileged to have had the parents I had. The values I have I got from them. I know I swore when I had my children, I'd rear them differently. I wouldn't do things the way my mother did. They would be allowed make up their own minds about things and I suppose they can do that but the basic value systems that I am trying to pass on to them are very firmly rooted in the upbringing I had with its emphasis on love, kindness, education, spirituality, community and friendships.

I sincerely hope that one of the ways my relationship with my children will be different from mine with my mother is that when Eva, Tom, Eoin and Lucy have problems they will come to me with them. If they don't, it won't be for want of encouragement. I constantly tell them there is nothing they can tell me that will shock me or that I won't want to hear. I may be saddened, angered, devastated by something, but tell me about it and we can deal with it. I also tell them that the contemplation of a problem is a lonely and futile pursuit. When you share it with someone it never seems so bad. I wish I had that kind of a relationship with my mother and I have no doubt she would have liked it that way. It's too late now.

Maybe the way we repay our parents for their dedication to us is in the way we relate to the next generation. I'd like that to be the case. It would point to an open, deeply communicative relationship between my children and me as they become adults and it would be a fitting tribute to their wonderful grandmother, who loved and watched over them and all of her family every day of her life.

The Dark Continent

I sometimes wonder what my mother would have thought of me going to Eritrea last year. One thing's for sure, she would have worried for my safety. She would probably have felt it was too risky to travel to a place that had known such recent unrest and that necessitated a lot of inoculation before travelling. She would also have worried about Eva travelling. That was her disposition. She loved us all so deeply that she wanted to keep us safe no matter what and being of her generation, that meant keeping us close to home. Having made the trip though and having brought Eva with me, I can say it was a wonderful experience and marked a new level of communication between my young adult daughter and me. As I said, maybe it's by nurturing those relationships with our children that we repay our parents for their dedication to us.

The adventure began the moment the plane landed and we emerged from the terminal building to a scene that was more reminiscent of a country airstrip than the airport of a capital city. On either side of the pathway were long grasses blowing in the hot night air, UN vehicles parked in front of us and rows of buses with roof racks ready to take all our gear. We'd gone through passport control and passed by the duty free section which amounted to a series of wrought iron booths where spirits and perfumes were arranged alongside shampoos and household products on packed shelves. We'd landed in total darkness, so it was hard to make our way as we carried our bags along the pathway to the buses, breathing in the hot night air and realising that finally, after two days travelling, we were in Eritrea.

I had mixed emotions as I walked towards the buses. At long last I'd made it to Africa. From the time I decided in secondary school that I wanted to go to university and study to become a teacher, I toyed with the idea that when I qualified I'd go to Africa and teach there for a while. It was a secret ambition of mine all along but it didn't happen for a number of reasons, one of them being the untimely death of my father the year after I graduated. I was in France at the time and when I came home and was offered a full-time job in my old school in Clondalkin, I didn't hesitate. I was the eldest of four after all and my mother was a widow now. I put any thoughts of Africa to the back of my mind. I remember though feeling great admiration for a girl from Clondalkin who went to Cameroon to teach after she graduated. A part of me was a little envious. Many years later when a teaching colleague, a Presentation Sister with whom I was friendly, decided to leave the school in Clondalkin and go to South America, the itchy feeling and longing returned. Going abroad was out of the question at that time because I was married with small children. The moment had passed and I never thought I'd get to Africa. But there I was last October, getting my introduction to the Dark Continent as I walked out of the terminal building at Asmara airport. I was delighted to be there. I was also a bit nervous; apprehensive about little things like having the various injections before travelling, avoiding the water . . . even when brushing your teeth. The need for vigilance was hammered home by anybody I met who'd already been to Africa. I wondered if I'd be able for the heat. While we were there it reached 40 degrees at times. And most of all

I wondered if I'd be a good trek leader for this Self Help trip to Eritrea.

I'd admired the work of Self Help in Africa since I'd first heard of them. It's the Irish charity founded in response to the awful famine in Ethiopia in 1984. Because members of the Irish Farmers' Association set up Self Help the focus is agricultural. In fact a lot of our cargo when we were travelling to Eritrea was made up of parts for farm machinery that had been donated by farmers and suppliers back home. That and boxes and boxes of Tayto crisps for the Irish defence forces who made up part of the UN peace keeping force in Eritrea.

Every year as part of their fundraising activities and also so that Irish people can see at first hand how useful the Self Help money is, the charity organise a trek to one of the countries they're involved with. There are five in all: Ethiopia, Malawi, Uganda, Kenya and Eritrea. Each year they ask somebody working in the public eye to lead that trek and last year I was pleased to be asked but a bit apprehensive about what it entailed and also about following in the footsteps of the previous four trek leaders: Mícheál Ó Muircheartaigh, John Creedon, Joe O'Brien and Ronan Collins. The fact that they were all men won't be lost on you and it wasn't on me either. I wondered would this be a bit tough? Would it be up to me to see that everybody arrived in places on schedule and would the trekkers tell me where to go if I did? I needn't have worried. It wasn't too tough. It was Seamus Hayes's headache to get us all out of the beds and onto the buses on time. He's the assistant director of Self Help and a master of gentle persuasion. And the people I travelled with were good fun, very supportive and terrible slaggers.

One of my duties as trek leader was to say a few words when we visited different project areas, words of thanks for the wonderful hospitality we received in all the villages, words of appreciation for the good use to which the local people had put the Selp Help money and a few words too about the fact that although Ireland and Eritrea are so different in some ways there are similarities, in terms of population for instance. Eritrea has a population of 3.5 million people. Their character has been formed by hundreds of years of domination and a 30-year struggle for independence from their next door neighbour, Ethiopia. Another thing that struck me was the number of donkeys in the rural areas and the way they're used to carry water in plastic drums. It reminds you of the donkeys in our country bringing the turf from the bog. We visited one village where the stonewalls were very similar to those in the west of Ireland. I mentioned some of these facts in the speeches I made and thought nothing of it until our last night. At the end of the farewell ceremony, the door at the back of the room opened and in walked one of the male trekkers dressed in a tinsel wig and a sarong who proceeded to take me off and make a mock speech. He had all my mannerisms and all my turns of phrase and he mentioned the donkeys and the struggle and the other similarities between the two countries. It was hilarious. Like I said, they were great fun and awful slaggers.

The trek was a challenge certainly, an adventure and a life-changing experience and I'm so glad I was part of it. It made me realise how important it is to push the boat out a little and do things that neither you nor others will expect of you. I suppose you could say I took the advice of one Johann Wolfgang von Goethe.

Whatever you can do,
or dream, you can
begin it.
Boldness has genius, power
And magic in it
Begin it now.

Begin it I did, along with my fellow trekkers, 54 of us from
various walks of life, most from farming backgrounds
admittedly and from all parts of the country.

Our first visit to a project area outside Mendefera was
enjoyable and uplifting. I'd been told that the local people
would welcome us in to their village but I wasn't prepared
for the sights and sounds that met us in that first village
and which were repeated everywhere we went. The whole
village turned out, waving huge tricolours alongside the
Eritrean flags. There were welcome signs posted to trees.
The schoolchildren, hundreds of boys and girls in some
places lined the track leading into the village, clapping
their hands and chanting 'Wel-come, wel-come' over and
over. They were dressed in their school uniform, a brown
sweater with a blue stripe around the V-neck and the cuffs.
Some of the children didn't have the uniform and it was
obvious their clothes had been donated from other parts of
the world. One little boy was wearing a tracksuit with a
McDonald's logo on the front. Beside him stood a little girl
in what looked like a Communion dress. You wouldn't
notice their shabby clothes though because their beaming
smiles lit up their faces and they were as excited to see us
arrive as we were humbled by the enormity of the
welcome. The women sang an energetic guttural welcome
chant and threw popcorn like confetti over us as we
walked along. Their heads were covered in snow-white

cheesecloth shawls and for the life of me I cannot make out how they kept them so white, given the primitive conditions in which they live. Their hospitality was boundless, with trays of coffee and sweet tea and local breads and pancakes. The children were delighted with the lollipops and sweets, the pens and tennis balls that some of the trekkers had in their rucksacks for them. And they were all so proud of the improvements they had managed in their lives with the support of Self Help.

In Adi Mongeti, we saw the water pump which services three villages, 130 households. Before its installation the people were faced with a three-hour round trip to get water. The pump was installed by Self Help: five local men dug the well first – a task that took three months to complete because of the depth they had to dig to find water. I stood on the side of that well and looked down and down. These men had to dig with shovels to a depth of ten metres before they struck water. It was worth it though. Five years ago they were working as labourers for other farmers but with this pump they've been able to irrigate 20 acres of land and grow vegetables for themselves and their community. Any excess is sold in the markets. The rains have been poor in Eritrea for a few years now and there was only a small amount of water at the bottom of the hole. We were told they were preparing to dig deeper. The Eritreans are not afraid of hard work, and they take great pride in their abilities and their achievements. One of that group of five men took us to visit the brick house that he built for his family and which is right beside the mud hut they lived in previously. It's a rectangular room with bright blue walls decorated with pictures of all kinds, from Chinese young men in military uniform to a picture of the Sacred Heart. He outlined the difference Self Help had made to the lives of his family and the others in the community in five short years and he finished by admitting that their next requirement was a tractor for the village because it costs six euro a day to rent one.

They're enterprising and energetic people and it was a pleasure to share their hospitality and see the confidence and the hope in their eyes and their demeanour. Two things struck me on the return journey to Asmara that evening. One was the catchy billboards on the side of the roads at regular intervals showing a young couple in silhouette against a pleasantly coloured background of pinks and purples merging into lilac. Alongside them on the poster was a dolphin in flight. I was told they're advertising condoms in an effort to promote safe sex. HIV/AIDS is a serious problem in this country as in the rest of Africa and Self Help is involved in that area of public health as well as others. Another striking sight was that of cattle being herded from the market in Asmara. There's nothing unusual about that except for the comment made by Michael, an Eritrean, the Self Help manager for the whole country. As we passed by the cattle, he turned to me and said, 'You can tell by the cattle that the drought is coming.' The cattle were slow and scrawny, their bones sticking out through their skin. A shiver ran down my spine. It was my first proper realisation that water is gold in Africa and it's in short supply.

The following day we visited the town of Newih Zeban and I was honoured, as trek leader to be asked to cut the ribbon as part of the official opening ceremony for their water harvesting system. It's on the roof of the school and it consists of a series of gutters and pipes that are linked to 30 large tanks which store the water when it rains. They were last filled during the scant rainfall during the summer of 2002. The tanks hold enough water for the needs of the six teachers and the 300 pupils and have transformed their lives. Before their installation, water had to be carried to the school. Children were travelling up to ten kilometres to fetch water in plastic drums before going to school. The result was that many of them were exhausted from the journey and the weight of the water and stayed away. Attendance figures have increased since the installation of the water harvesting tanks and so too have the children's confidence and aspirations. Self Help provided the €10,000 for the materials, the Ministry of Agriculture provided the engineers and the local community provided free labour.

The Eritrean people are happy to work hard to improve their living conditions. One of the problems though is that there is a huge shortage of young men between the ages of eighteen and forty. Some of these young men are doing military service on the border with Ethiopia, some were killed in the conflict between the two countries and others were stuck in Ethiopia when the borders closed. Eritrea has had a difficult history and has only been independent since the beginning of the 90s.

The country has been colonised by Italy and Britain and was engaged in a 30-year struggle for independence with Ethiopia from 1961. The legacy of the Italian colonisation is evident in the capital Asmara, which has a lot of ornate architecture including some lovely art deco cafes where you can buy coffee and a pastry for two nakfas, that's about ten cent. The Italians were responsible for developing transport and communications in the country making them the best in Africa during the period they were in Eritrea. The country was colonised from 1880 to 1941 providing Italy with access to the Red Sea and a lot of agricultural potential. In the twilight years of that colonisation, there were 70,000 Italians in the country. Their agricultural policy was designed to primarily benefit the settlers who viewed the local population as cheap labour. Now where have you heard a story like that before?

The British followed the Italians but at the same time Ethiopia had designs on the country, being landlocked itself and taking a shine to Eritrea's access to the Red Sea. During all of this time, however, feelings of national identity were growing among the Eritrean people. A substantial working class population was developing alongside an urban intelligentsia. In fact in the early '50s, when the UN passed a resolution federating Eritrea to Ethiopia, 75% of Eritreans favoured independence. The first act of armed resistance took place on 1 September 1961 and the Eritrean Liberation Front (ELF) was formed. By 1965, they numbered 1,000 fighters but when you consider that the total population of Eritrea is 3.5 million and they were taking on the might of 60 million Ethiopians, you'd wonder how they ever thought they had a chance of defeating the enemy and winning their independence. They did though, in 1991, after lots of ups and downs along the way.

A second military force, the Eritrean People's Liberation Front took over from the ELF and the resistance fighters started making significant advances. Their policy was one of strategic retreats and lightning counter attacks. And they knew the terrain. A trip from Asmara, which is nine thousand feet above sea level, down to the coast at Massawa yields many examples of the war. Around every corner and over every ditch you'll see abandoned rusting tanks, guns and jeeps. And in the capital itself, there's a sort of military graveyard which is piled high with rusting artillery and military vehicles. The Eritreans are very proud of their success in turning back the Ethiopians who were by far the superior power in terms of numbers. Remember we're talking 3.5 million against 60 million. Understandably, the Eritrean fighters were renowned for their military skill and bravery, but they also had huge support among their own people because they set up a network of hospitals, factories and schools in the liberated zones. Literacy and public health were high on the agenda in these areas and they developed an innovative system of civil administration. That innovative mind is in evidence today in the enterprising ways in which they've taken on this new struggle against the lack of water. They're resilient, hard working and optimistic people and it was a joy to spend time with them and sample their way of life and their culture.

Eritrea has a very rich musical tradition and on one of the evenings in Asmara, we were treated to a cultural evening which gave us an insight into their dance, their songs and their customs. There were lots of rebel songs which included sword dances. Also flirtatious song and dance in brightly coloured flowing costumes, and working songs. I chatted to some of the artists about those different songs and customs. Dignity and diversity summed it up for me. One of the ways the Eritrean people adorn their faces is by cutting the cheek and when the wound has healed they put black kohl into it. Sometimes, in Christian cases, instead of cutting a straight line, they cut the sign of the cross. Personally, nothing would tempt me to inflict that kind of pain on myself although when I think about it, I've sat while somebody shot a hole into my earlobes for the same purpose of adornment. That was a great evening of cultural exchange and we ended up learning how to perform some Eritrean dances. It's all in the way you shrug your shoulders. We taught them some céilí dances too.

There is evidence of the pride the Eritreans take in their country wherever you go. I've already mentioned the art deco cafes and bars in Asmara. Everywhere is clean and well kept, although some of the roads leading in to the main thoroughfare are crumbling and pot-holed and the pavements are falling away. I was fascinated to see a huge poinsettia tree growing wild on the walk in to the city centre and bemoaned the struggle I have every year to try to get a tiny plant to last until the end of Christmas. There's an impressive Catholic cathedral in the centre that was finished in 1923 and of which the people are extremely proud. It's a beautiful Italianate building. In another part of the city is the mosque: Eritrea is 50% Christian and 50% Muslim. This was my first time to hear the call to prayer and seeing the two traditions celebrated side-by-side made me realise that we have quite a narrow view of what cultural diversity exists in other parts of the world. It's when we open our hearts to the fact that we don't have the blue print on sophistication and the right ways of doing things that we can truly welcome other nationalities into our country and accept their differences and embrace the ways in which our lives can be enhanced by their presence among us.

Eritrean independence is marked every day in Asmara by the raising in the morning and the lowering, at sunset, of the national flag. A whistle blows and everything stops and everyone stands to attention. There's total silence in the streets as the ceremony is performed. Drivers even get out of their cars and stand to attention. It's reminiscent of the effect of the bells of the Angelus in former times in our country.

As a woman I was particularly impressed and encouraged by the success of the women's programmes around

Mendefera: the beekeeping and the honey that they harvest and sell, the poultry programme whereby the women buy hens with a grant that they repay when they've sold enough produce in the markets and on the city streets. The women also have a credit union that they operate themselves. I met one particularly enterprising woman, who at forty-four is a widow with seven children. Before becoming part of the Self Help poultry rearing scheme, she was dependent on aid. Later she became involved in the beekeeping. With the profits she made from selling eggs and honey, she bought a black and white battery operated television that she has positioned in a shed alongside her house and which she allows her neighbours to watch for a fee. And you thought pay-per-view was something associated with Premier League matches and the like. This is just one example of the energy and initiative of the women that I met in Mendefera. It was a joy to share the hospitality offered by these women, to witness their contentment, to meet their poorly dressed but happy, healthy children, who go to school and have ambition. At 16 the children have to leave their rural communities and go to high school in Asmara, which seems a shame.

The other project area we visited, around Keren, is mostly Muslim and the contrast between these women and the Mendefera women was stark. When we arrived the women stood to one side against a wall, watching us and saying nothing. I will never forget the moment when I went over to this group of Muslim women who were covered, head to toe in vibrantly coloured and stunningly beautiful saris and gold jewellery. Two older women in the group clasped my hand in their gnarled and deeply tanned ones, which were adorned with many gold rings. They squeezed and shook my hand vigorously in a deeply affectionate way and they spoke to me in their language. I didn't understand the words but it didn't matter. You could say that culturally there was a chasm between us. Our lifestyles, our mores, our expectations were totally different but for me there was no barrier, no difference at that time. It was a joyous and deep moment of empathy and connection beyond words which I will treasure always. I hope they felt the same way.

The welcome ceremonies in this project area were very spectacular with village elders on camels leading us in and others dancing, singing and jumping over swords. The society is as patriarchal here as it is matriarchal around Mendefera. The women were in evidence all right, bent over working in the fields in those beautiful saris while the men were visible drinking coffee in the town. I think the elders were a bit surprised to see a woman leading the trek. They presented me with a gift of a hundred-year-old ceremonial sword and a traditional outfit . . . for a man! They were delighted to welcome us all. The governor of the area came out to meet us. He had lost an eye and a leg in the war. It's hard to go anywhere in Eritrea without seeing men who have been injured during the 30-year conflict and more recently the two-year border conflict that began in 1998, and which resulted in the international border commission being set up to decide the issue. In March 2003, the UN Security Council urged both countries to cooperate fully with the border commission in the implementation of the demarcation between Ethiopia and Eritrea and also extended the duration of the peacekeeping mission. The two hundred members of the Irish defence forces that were serving in Asmara have come home now. They were very helpful and hospitable to us during our trip. They also raised money within their camp, called Camp de hÍde for Self Help. The prospect of eventual UN withdrawal is a worrying one for many Eritreans who feel that the hostilities will resume as soon as the peacekeepers leave. I hope not. These people have suffered enough.

We visited the military cemetery which is maintained by the Italian embassy and where Italian and Eritrean soldiers are buried. Sadly, most of the headstones in the Eritrean section bear the simple inscription 'Agnosto' (unknown). I got chatting to a Franciscan priest in that cemetery. He told me he was from the area, had studied in Rome and was now back working in the school and the Catholic church. He was a very gentle, friendly man who was really interested in hearing about our trip and our lives in Ireland. Before I left a friend here had given me money for the children and I decided there and then that this was the person to give it to. He was so pleased to get it and later that afternoon, he pulled up alongside me in a clapped out jeep, while I was walking in the town to say thanks again because the money would make a huge difference to the lives of the children. He gave me a relic of Padre Pio and a prayer to Saint Anthony. I was touched and it wasn't even my money. A reminder though that we never know when we're going to connect with somebody in a way that will change lives. Since I returned, I've had letters from this Franciscan letting me know how the children are getting on. He also enclosed photographs of their Communion Day, about ten boys and girls sitting on the steps of the altar in the church in Keren.

It was around Keren that I saw at first hand the Self Help sprinkler system at work. In fact I was posing for a photo when they came on behind me and drenched me, which gave everybody a good laugh. The contrast between two fields of corn was shocking. They were side-by-side, one inside, the other outside the project area. The one was dead for lack of water, the other had a thriving crop because of the Self Help sprinkler system. The drought has taken its toll. It was here also that we walked along the bed of the Anseba river. It's as wide as the Shannon in places and it was like walking on a beach, except there was no water whatsoever on the shore. It's a humbling experience to walk across a dry river bed and to try to understand how a community suffers when this commodity is withdrawn – this commodity that we take so much for granted, that we curse sometimes for its overabundance.

We also visited Massawa on the Red Sea where the heat was unreal. The day-long drive from Asmara at nine thousand feet above sea level brought us through spectacular mountain scenery. The buses were a bit rickety and there was a scramble for the one with the air conditioning but either way, whenever we stopped and got out of the buses it was like stepping into an oven. The approach to Massawa was a bit shocking. It was the first time we'd come across shanty towns and they were pretty grim. There were lots of mud hut settlements in the various places we visited but there was a wholesome, traditional feel to them and certainly the people living in them seemed very content. The shanty towns were awful though; deprivation and squalor were written all over them. Massawa itself has some very beautiful buildings; unfortunately, many of them are full of bullet holes. The ruins of Emperor Haile Selassie's palace gave us a good idea of two extremes. Even though the gold leaf is flaking and the blue dome looks like a giant ostrich egg whose shell has been broken, there's no doubting its former opulence. A very far cry from the shanty towns on the outskirts of Massawa and from the mud huts in the interior and in Selassie's native Ethiopia. We were brought to visit an enormous airstrip; the United States provided its funding. Let me remind you that Massawa is on the Red Sea and across that narrow stretch of water is Yemen and behind that is Iraq!

When I reflect on that trip to Eritrea there are so many ways in which it was extremely valuable. It opened my eyes to the resilience and strength of character of a whole community of people, especially the women. I remember one day hiking through the mountains. It was a tough enough climb, in intense heat even though we were all well equipped with walking boots and water and sun protection. I was surprised to see little clusters of huts almost at the summit. I wondered how did people get up and down to those heights over those tracks? As we began our descent, exhausted but exhilarated by the achievement and the breathtaking views from the top (I've spoken already about the uplifting effect that mountains have on me). I got the answer to that question about how people got up and down. I turned a corner and coming towards me was a woman covered in one of those snow-white cheesecloth shawls. She had a toddler strapped to her back, she was carrying a plastic bag with shopping in either hand, and she was wearing flip-flops. This was very rough terrain and she was walking at a fair pace. She was also the first of many women who were making their way back up the mountain. It was a holy day and they had gone down to the church in the village and bought provisions while they were there. I felt like a wimp, picking my way along the track in a pair of sturdy walking boots. But I also felt very proud of my gender. These women were the essence of resilience and strength, dignity and good humour. They chatted to each other all the way up the mountain and stopped and shook hands with us and made welcoming gestures. There may have been a language barrier but there was a good sense of communication between people of different cultures.

As well as meeting the people of Eritrea and enjoying their hospitality and culture, the trek provided an opportunity for me to travel with Irish people from different parts of the country and from different walks of life. We had a lot of laughs and we learned a lot about the things we take for granted in our part of the world and we've also continued to support the work of Self Help since we returned. We've had a lot of help in that regard. I've been amazed by the number of people who are willing to organise fundraisers or to support charity events.

It was fun to be able to travel with my sister Deirdre and also a great thrill for me to introduce Eva, to this wonderful continent at the age of eighteen. I have no doubt that her view of the world will be coloured in a humanitarian sense by her time in Eritrea. In fact she was so impressed by what she saw that she signed up for this year's Self Help trek to Uganda. She's also persuaded a friend to go with her and they've raised the necessary €4,500 each through the summer. That bit of it can be hard work but it's important work and I'm glad they took the trouble. They had a lot of support from family and friends which helped fill the coffers. I've said it before and I don't mind repeating that we in the affluent parts of this planet have a moral obligation to help those who are less well off materially than we are. My heart aches at the thought of people starving, actually dying because of a lack of food – another commodity we take totally for granted. We, in the developed world have a duty to relieve their hunger and support famine relief. But it's heartening to witness the work of groups like Self Help in famine prevention so that in the future the people of Africa won't have to rely on outside aid.

They say that Africa gets into your blood. I think they're right. I'm very grateful for the chance I got to get to know the country and the people of Eritrea, to enjoy their hospitality, to witness their positive outlook, their cheerful disposition and their strength of character. They have achieved a lot in ten years of nationhood. In April 1993 the Secretary General of the provisional government, Issaias Afrewerki referred to the country's referendum as 'a delightful and sacrosanct historical conclusion to the choice of the Eritrean people'. They're nice adjectives and they sit very well with the Eritrean people I met. They celebrate their independence on the 24th of May each year. I thought of them on that date this year and I believe that given the character of its people, the country will develop and prosper, provided the border doesn't become a conflict point again. The biggest lesson I learnt is that appearances can be deceptive. For instance, Asmara airport, which as I said at the beginning, struck me on arrival as being more reminiscent of a country airstrip than the airport of a capital city, it is the gateway to a country that has a rich and ancient heritage; a past of struggle and dominance; an independence that is greatly prized, major development and climatic difficulties, but most importantly, a country that is home to a proud, dignified and delightful people, who are prepared to work hard for a bright future for themselves and their families. They're an example to the world.

À La Mode

The time I spent in Eritrea was inspirational in so many ways. There's no doubt that a trip like that changes the way you view life. It took me a while to be comfortable again with the way we live our lives in this part of the world. We have so much material wealth by comparison with the people I met but they have a dignity and serenity that is captivating, particularly the women. I mentioned that I was amazed at how white their shawls and wraps were, considering they live in very primitive mud houses and have a very short supply of water not to mention things like washing machines that are just plain non-existent. They have a sense of style which has nothing to do with designer labels but which has the effect of eliciting 'admiration in the eye of the beholder'. . . the desired effect of designer labels, too after all. On the subject of style and returning, for the purposes of this to our affluent western world, I was chuffed earlier this year, when I was voted Most Stylish Woman in Ireland by the readers of *VIP* magazine. I can admit to that now that I've got my head around the whole concept. To be honest I would never beforehand have considered myself as having any knowledge of style. Other members of my family maybe, but not me. My fifteen-year-old niece, Clare, for instance is the epitome of style as far as I'm concerned. She just loves it. She knows what's in fashion; mixes and matches and always looks great. Her nails are French manicured regularly. If she decides that straight hair is called for, she has the tools. The ESB would be rubbing their hands in glee if Clare's appliances were all plugged in at the same time. And if a crimped style is the order of the day, the time it takes to put in all those tiny plaits is not a problem. Extensive is the adjective I would use to describe Clare's wardrobe. She went to the Gaeltacht for the first time this summer and we were joking that they'd need an extra boat to ferry all her clothes and accessories over to Inis Mor. Besides her flare for fashion, Clare is also a very talented pianist, a super basketball player and a great student. She's got style and both her parents admit readily that she certainly didn't get it from them. As they say in the song 'You either got or you haven't got style'.

My own twelve-year-old daughter is showing signs of heading in the same direction. I've noticed Lucy paying a lot of attention to what Clare is wearing and the colours that go together and those that don't. One Sunday during the summer when Lucy and I were walking out of Mass together she pointed out to me that there was a woman behind us who was wearing Burberry runners and carrying a Burberry bag and it looked really 'cool'. I was flabber-gasted that she would have noticed such a thing. Not only that. She started asking questions about the whole Burberry label and the fact that she saw men wearing it in magazines. Her style antennae are obviously up and she'll be learning from the expert when she spends time with Clare.

I wouldn't even be in the ha'penny place compared to the two of them and their knowledge and awareness of style and what's out there. However a friend told me I was nominated for this year's *VIP* Style awards along with 23 fashion heavyweights. I'm talking about women who have poise, pedigree and deep pockets when it comes to investing in style. Women with hour glass figures, flawless complexions and shiny hair. Women who put the hours into grooming and it shows. I can remember Cindy Crawford referring to the amount of time she spends on her appearance so that she has that golden girl look in public always. She quipped 'Even I don't look like Cindy Crawford when I wake up'. This is heartening news for the rest of us mere mortals. I was certainly not in that league of having hours to spend on my appearance. Nor would I want to be. I'd been brought up to believe that it was pure vanity to spend too much time looking at yourself or thinking about how you look. I have the nuns to thank for that and my mother, but sure she was a product of an earlier generation of nuns. I also had this notion that the kind of women who would be 'stylish' would be too into themselves. They'd be selfish creatures, and clothes horses. A perusal of the list of nominees shows that nothing could be further from the truth. These were women who were doers, doctors, actors, lawyers, carers, campaigners, mothers, broadcasters, fundraisers. Women for whom there just aren't enough hours in the day, who love life and give a huge amount back to the community by way of the causes they espouse. Once I got used to the idea that it was okay to be considered stylish, that it wasn't a reflection on your brainpower, I was flattered to be included in that group of women. That, I thought, was the end of that.

To say that I was surprised a couple of months later to be declared the people's choice is a huge understatement. I felt like a bit of an impostor in a way, because obviously I was being judged by people on how I look on television and so much of that is the result of the creative input of a number of people, myself only barely included. The *Open House* production team decided on a certain style for the programme at the beginning of the season and they then had a meeting with RTÉ's wardrobe department, to let them know the look that would suit *Open House*. Eileen Chalmers has a great eye. She can go into a shop and immediately see what will look well. I bow to her superior knowledge. She arrives back from the city, laden with bags of clothes from different shops and as soon as I try them on, she'll know straight away what will work and what won't. There are times, of course, when something looks nice on the hanger and when I put it on, I look like Mary Hick, or mutton dressed as lamb or some point in between. In those cases, we have a laugh and put the outfit swiftly back in the bag. Nine times out of ten, though, Eileen's eye will hit the target and I'll have another outfit for TV that's stylish, comfortable and a little bit different.

When it comes to clothes colour is a major consideration. There are some colours that make me look like death warmed up and there are others that lift me out of the doldrums. That's true of everybody I think. I remember years ago being given a birthday present by my mother of a *Colour Me Beautiful* consultation. I was sceptical to say the least as I sat down in the chair looking into a mirror without a screed of make-up on. The consultant put lengths of different colours around my neck and the difference was amazing. At one point I looked so pale that I was of the opinion that 'another clean shirt will do ye' as my grandmother used to say if somebody was feeling sorry for themselves because they were feeling poorly. The contrast was incredible when other colours were put close to my face. They gave my skin tone a huge lift. The bottom line is if a colour brightens up your face when you're wearing no make-up, it suits you and you'll look better again when you have the war paint on. If however, a colour makes you look deathly pale or has you fading into insignificance, it's no good saying that the make-up will improve things. It won't. There are colours that suit our skin tones and there are ones that don't and the acid test is to look at yourself honestly and coldly in the mirror without any make-up.

It's great for me not to have to actually go to the shops. I don't know where I'd find the time and anyway I'm not a good shopper. I'm indecisive, and rails and rails of clothes just add to my dilemma. It's great when something is chosen for you and it's just right and I know that a lot of women will understand exactly what I mean by that because every time I appear on *Open House* wearing something new, we get tons of phone calls to the office wanting the details of the outfit. Women will call who are going to a party or a wedding or Communion perhaps, or who just like the colour or the cut maybe and think it would look well on them. And if we can save them precious time going from shop to shop we're happy to oblige. There are some outfits that strike a chord with viewers every time I wear them and we joke in the office that it's going to be a busy day on the phones. There's one trouser suit in particular that's about three years old and every single time I wear it, the phone hops.

The other great perk that goes with the job and must have played a major part in the style awards is having my hair and make-up done. Gary Kavanagh is the artistic director with Peter Mark and he's been looking after my hair since the time of the Eurovision in 1995. Like Eileen, he knows far better than I do what needs doing and I'm happy to let the experts at it. He's adventurous with colour and will put in light and dark streaks, which I used to be apprehensive about but now I say why not. We paint the walls of our houses, don't we? Why not put lots of colour into our lives, starting with our heads. It's not that long since we were shy about the whole notion of lightening and darkening our hair, afraid people might say 'oh she colours her hair'. You're damn right she does and loves to ring the changes from time to time. And another thing, you don't need me to tell you how relaxing it is to go to the hairdresser's knowing that you are going to be there for a couple of hours and can read magazines and drink coffee without interruption and will emerge feeling so much better about yourself. There's nothing like a visit to the hairdresser's to put a spring in your step. It's funny but when your hair looks well, you feel you can take on the world. Maybe it's got something to do with the fact that you've had a bit of time to yourself and a bit of pampering. What's seldom is wonderful after all and most women lead such busy lives that a visit to the hairdressers is often the only opportunity they get to have that precious head space, if you'll pardon the pun.

Few women have the privilege of having their make-up done on a daily basis. Believe me, I'm very aware of how lucky I am and I don't for a minute take it for granted. The *Open House* production team put a lot of thought in to the make-up look at the beginning of the season in consultation with Antoinette Forbes Curham, the head of Make-up in RTÉ. Different colours, styles and amounts of make-up were tried until we decided what worked and what didn't. I often hear people who are about to be appear on TV for the first time telling the make-up artist that they don't wear much make-up normally, and a little will do. I know it's because they're nervous and not used to having their make-up done. Once they relax into it, they enjoy the interlude and then when it's all over they are thrilled at how good they look and tend to say something like 'Can I come here everyday' or 'I wish I had you at home.' Isn't it great to be doing a job that makes people feel better about themselves after your intervention, because as with the visit to the hairdresser's, when you've had your make-up done, there's a spring in your step and life is more manageable. So far, talking about style and the accolade I received I've mentioned the *Open House* team, the wardrobe department, the make-up department and my hairdresser. You're probably wondering at this stage where I fit into all of this and maybe now you'll understand my feelings of being an impostor when my name was read out. I did mention all those people and my misgivings when I was accepting the award and I also mentioned my mother and I suppose whatever style I have innately, I got from her.

I've already mentioned the fact that when she and my Dad were rearing their family of four, there wasn't a penny to spare and she didn't have a huge amount of money even before she was married. She did the Civil Service exam and left school when she got a job in the College of Science, which she loved. She had a lot of good female friends and they were always going to dances and they'd go on holidays together. Money was tight for most people in the '40s and '50s and my mother was giving up a good portion of her wages to help out at home, but as I've said before, she had a great pair of hands. She was a gifted seamstress and she could go along to a fancy shop, stand outside the window and look at a dress or a coat that she liked, study it, then go off and buy material and make an exact copy of it. Speaking as someone who couldn't sew a straight line, I find that pretty impressive. As a child I enjoyed going through her evening dresses, feeling the fabric and dressing up in them. They were gorgeous and all home-made. Mam also made our clothes as children.

There's no doubt she had style. Or maybe a better way of describing it would be to say she had a sense of occasion. If we were going visiting or if people were coming to our house, we dressed up. The same rules applied to going into town or to Mass or even to the doctor. When there might be dissention in the ranks, with one of the boys perhaps complaining about having to wear a tie, she explained that it was a mark of respect to the person you'd be meeting, to make an effort and dress well. So we'd be scrubbed and polished. Now that's not to say that she was going around in high heels and jewellery all the time. She loved gardening and clearing out cupboards and painting and decorating. Those pursuits gave her great satisfaction and I can relate to that because I get hours of enjoyment out of that kind of dirty work myself. This work would be carried out in what she always referred to as 'old clothes'. But when she was going out somewhere, she looked a million dollars. Right up to the time she became ill, she'd have her hair and make-up done; her nails varnished, wear jewellery and perfume and a stylish, smart unfussy outfit with matching shoes and handbag. And she walked tall. She had good carriage and deportment always and was forever on to us to 'stand up straight'.

When I think about it, the apples don't fall far from the tree, because I would be like my mother in that regard. I'm very conscious of what my children wear when we're going out and I do feel that courtesy demands that we make an effort and show we care. On the other hand, I do not feel the need to get dressed up or have make-up on when I'm going to the supermarket. I know some people do and more power to them. Each to his own. I would have no inclination to spend time choosing an outfit and putting on make-up when I've been pottering around in jeans or maybe a tracksuit in the house and garden. I don't care if people see me and say 'Gosh she's not very stylish now, is she?' I'm definitely of my mother's school of thought where style is about having a sense of occasion, not about being dressed up and made up all the time.

Style is also about confidence and self-esteem; for me those two linked qualities are tied up in health and fitness. So maybe that's part of my style as well. When I'm fit I feel good about myself. If I've not been running for a good while and am not toned and have gained pounds, the most beautiful gown in the world won't make me feel good and if you don't feel good, what's the point in looking good? I drink a lot of water, which is good for the system and the skin. I use moisturisers and body lotions because I developed the habit when I was about twelve years of age and started getting gift sets as Christmas presents. They do work though because after four pregnancies, during which I put on enormous amounts of weight, I ended up with no stretch marks. I deserve to resemble an ogham stone but so much cream had been applied to my body for so many years it must have paid off. We're not talking expensive lotions and potions, here which of course are lovely, but any moisturiser I firmly believe is worth its weight in gold.

Sometimes I'm asked for my fashion style or beauty tips. Generally speaking, once I've taken a deep breath and gotten over the shock of being asked, I come back to the old moisturisers again. Once you're in the habit of using them regularly, the benefits will follow. I also think it's very important to cleanse tone and moisturise twice a day, even if you're in a rush to get out in the morning, even if you're exhausted and just want to fall into bed at night. I'm a recent convert to the benefits of exfoliation and face masks. I learnt about them from Bronwyn Conroy who gives great skin care advice on *Open House*. You're supposed to do both about twice a week. The difference exfoliation and a face mask makes to your skin is incredible. The grittiness of the exfoliant deeply cleans and when the mask comes off, the skin is really soft. This is well worth the effort.

My bathroom cabinet is packed with moisturisers and toners and body lotions. I could open a chemist's shop with all those accoutrements. I have far more of that kind of thing than I have make-up. They're not necessarily expensive creams, but they're to hand which is important. You won't use them regularly if they're tucked away and difficult to get at. Another commodity that I have in abundance is perfume. It's my weakness. I just love the stuff and I cannot pass through the airport without buying some. I've recently gotten into the habit of buying the body lotion to match any perfume I'm buying which makes the purchase much more expensive but I convince myself that it's an economy in the long run because if I use both together I'm getting extra value out of the scent. Please, tell me that makes sense. I have different perfumes that I use at different times of the year, the heavier musky ones, like Opium for the winter, I like Dune in the springtime and Issey Miyake anytime really. If I never bought another bottle of perfume, I wouldn't run out this side of the next decade, but it's my one indulgence. I can go out without make-up but I cannot be without perfume. I'm often reminded of events in the past that happened while I was wearing a certain perfume and the memory can take me by surprise. Last winter I sprayed a certain perfume that I hadn't used in a while and as soon as I put it on, I realised why. It was obviously the perfume I was using while my mother was sick because no sooner had I sprayed it than the memory of those visits to the hospital came flooding back. There's another perfume I bought recently and I couldn't remember how long it was since I'd had it before. Until I opened the bottle and sprayed it. I got a lovely feeling then and was transported back to the time my first baby was born. That was obviously the perfume I was using at the time. There's no doubt that smells can be very evocative and that's one of the things I like about perfume. I also like the bottles and the packaging and the luxury of the smells. Like I said it's an indulgence.

Whatever about perfume and smelling nice, the importance of diet and exercise for our physical and mental well-being cannot be overestimated. I know from my own experience. When I'm fit and healthy I can cope with problems much better. If I've neglected one or other, or, horror of horrors, both of those over a period of time, I start to feel low and depressed. Now I know there are people who will think it's fine for me because the most I'd have gained in a period of neglect would be about half a stone, but that's because after a half stone I say enough is enough. Got to take action here. The more there is to lose, the harder it is. But be assured that it's well worth it and the rewards are enormous. Once you get started and break the old habits, new good ones start to form. I find the words of Amelia Earhart inspirational when I have to face up to reality and tackle the eating habits and lifestyle that put on the pounds. She was the first woman to fly solo across the Atlantic, taking off from Newfoundland and landing in 'Gallagher's pasture' in Derry. She was a great champion of women and when she was voted Outstanding Woman of the Year in 1932, she accepted on behalf of 'all women'. She was honoured many times that year and on one occasion, the French press closed an article about her achievements by asking the question, 'but can she bake a cake?' She replied by saying publicly that she accepted 'these awards on behalf of the cake bakers and all of those other women who can do some things quite as important, if not more important than flying as well as in the name of women flying today'. She uttered many other words of wisdom and my particular favourites give me the motivation necessary to tackle any difficult situation (and gave me the title of this book):

> The most difficult thing is the decision to act, the rest is merely tenacity. The fears are paper tigers. You can do anything you decide to do. You can act to change and control your life; and the procedure, the process is its own reward.

I know she was talking about flying planes in the first half of the last century when women were more likely to be sitting knitting or doing embroidery by the fire, but her mind set can be applied to any situation that needs tackling.

No amount of lotions and potions and diet and exercise will actually stop the clock from ticking though. There is one certainty in this life and that is the fact of ageing. We move from childhood through teens, to twenties, thirties, forties and so on through the decades for as long as we are lucky enough to live. Each stage has its advantages and its disadvantages. How often have you heard somebody say they'd love to be thin and wrinkle free like they were in their teens and early twenties but would hate to be back at that stage of awkwardness in relationships? Sorry but that's the way life tends to be. Confidence in dealing with others comes with age and maturity. So too do the lines that denote the cares and concerns and anxieties that we encounter through life, which build our character and improve our levels of confidence in relationships. You can't have one without the other. Unless you go seriously and constantly down the route of cosmetic surgery and how many of us have the means to do that? How many of us want to do that is another question?

I've often wondered why people go for it. Is it so others will think they're younger than they are? People are not stupid, they can generally tell. All you've got to do is look at the person's hands or neck or middle perhaps. The longer people act out of that viewpoint, the longer ageist mentalities and policies will persist. I'm fully convinced that ageing gracefully is far preferable to pulling and tugging and making one's face different to the rest of one's body. I know people in their seventies who are young in their minds and their hearts and equally I know people in their thirties and forties who are old in their outlook on life.

One of the advantages of living in this twenty-first century is the fact that health and nutrition are substantially better than in earlier centuries. We can be healthy and strong and live long and energetic lives if we take care of ourselves. There was a time when women, once their children were reared, were expected to 'sit by the fire and spin'. Not any more. There's so much living out there to be done, so much fun to be had. The time when the children are reared is a time of opportunity, exploration, and discovery. And if the mindset is right the rest will fall into place. Because if I want to be able to go off on adventures, I'll also want to have a fairly healthy lifestyle, with lots of exercise and fresh air, good food and lots of water and just as important, social interaction that's stimulating and gives opportunity for laughter.

The way I look on ageing now is: it's inevitable. I value hugely the life experiences I've had and the people I've met along the way and I look forward to many more adventures and experiences and encounters. Life can be hard at times, it can also be a lot of fun at times but the important thing is that it's vital. I've changed as I've gone through life, I've no doubt I'll continue to evolve while still holding close the values and the friendships that are important to me. I will continue to exercise and to eat healthily and to have a laugh. My wish is for the people around me to also live long and stimulating and healthy lives and for my children to grow up in the same way. If that's ageing, bring it on.

I know I started off this chapter talking about style in terms of beautiful African women, French manicures and Burberry runners but really, for me, while I love to wear nice clothes and I certainly feel good when I'm dressed up and I will always dress to suit an occasion, if the other elements that I've finished this chapter with, like health and fitness are out of kilter, the style won't ring true. If I don't feel good on the inside, what I look like on the outside won't matter. Style is about looking good because you feel good and when the two come together it's great because you send out happy, bright and positive vibes and people are happy to be with you. And the bottom line through all of this writing is, as I've said often before, the connection between people which makes life a real joy.

Ambassadors of Greatness

I met some people during the summer who send out happy, positive vibes to the extent that it's uplifting to be in their company. Connecting with others and welcoming them with open arms seems to give them great pleasure and their motto when it comes to numbers is undoubtedly 'the more the merrier'.

On the first day of July, I was invited to a party in their house. This was a very special party to celebrate a very special occasion and the achievements of a very special person. It was a welcome home party for a member of Team Ireland, that amazing group of people who did us proud at the Special Olympics and who made us rethink our attitudes to a whole sector of our society. This young lad, Stephen, is a hero and received a hero's welcome home with his two medals, one gold and one silver from his feats in the equestrian events which took place at Kill in County Kildare. I'd never met him but I know his sister and she phoned me when he won his first medal; she was beside herself with excitement and pride and said that if they were having a do for him, would I come. I was delighted to be invited and it was a great celebration.

It was a lovely balmy evening. The house was in the country, just outside a tiny village in the midlands and there was no mistaking what was going on. There were cars parked all along the narrow country road up to the house. The tricolour was flying proudly on a huge flagpole in the garden. One each of every colour of those flags that had been made by the prisoners in Mountjoy and distributed to everyone at the opening ceremony in Croke Park were attached to the railings outside the garden. And there was a big welcome home banner on the roof of the house. There was a bouncy castle for the little ones, beer on tap for the older ones, wine and soft drinks and lovely food and loud music. But most of all, there was an amazing atmosphere of celebration and achievement, of love and warmth.

The place was packed and all ages were represented from tiny babies to grannies and all points in between. Everybody in the area had been invited and they must have all turned up to be a part of this great occasion. Relatives travelled from all over the country. One woman told me it took her two hours to get out of Galway city because the rain had been so heavy during the afternoon. No matter how far the distance, it was well worth the journey to share the moment with this fourteen-year-old athlete and his family. I referred to him earlier as a hero. He won a gold and a silver medal and he wore them with pride. The people in his life, his family and friends who love and care for him have nurtured his equestrian skills. They were justifiably proud of their son's achievements. And that was where the focus was: 'achievement'. They know it's the result of hard work on his part and dedication, love and support on theirs. I learnt a lot from the example of that family throwing the party. There's richness about their lives. They're open, warm and welcoming to all. I got the impression they wouldn't get into a tizzy about silly little things. They laugh and joke a lot. They love life. And people. All people.

There was no talk of disability and not being able to do things. We were there to celebrate what had been done. I was very conscious that for a lot of us in this country, this summer marked the beginning of recognition of a sector of our community who quite simply achieve differently. In a way, I suppose, we loosened our beliefs about how life is meant to be and no matter what the situation, the sky will always grow bigger when we do that. Nothing can be more life changing than escape from our preconceptions. There can be no doubt that the Special Olympics gave us an opportunity for just such an escape. I was out of the country on the 21st of June so I missed the opening ceremony in Croke Park. My daughter Eva was there though and she phoned me to let me listen to Nelson Mandela on her mobile. I got texts right through the ceremony from a friend who was there letting me know who was coming on stage. And a long phone call after it was over filled in the gaps for me. I could sense the awe, the colour, the euphoria. I heard about the teams and their escorts, the Macnas balloons, Riverdance, those coloured flags, Shaun Davey's Special Olympics anthem, *May We Never Have to Say Goodbye* sung by Ronan Tynan and Rita Connolly, the amazing cross community pageant of song and dance called Solstice, performed by people with special needs from Northern Ireland, Bono bringing Nelson Mandela onstage to the strains of Pride, Eunice Shriver's speech and the little girl with Down Syndrome who said to the crowd and the television audience, 'Look at our ability, not our disability'. And for the first time ever, we did.

The week of competition provided a further awakening for the general public. The host towns had already welcomed the athletes from all over the world; opened their homes and their hearts to these visitors and were rewarded with a lot of love, pleasure and gratitude in return. The rest of us got an insight into this new way of viewing life as we watched and read about the various achievements in the Games. For me, the most moving story came from a friend who was a volunteer in Santry. He was watching a race and with about 50 metres to go to the finish, the athlete who was way out in front stumbled and fell. An opportunity presented itself for the guy in second place, who, when he realised what had happened, went for the win with renewed vigour, passing out the athlete who had stumbled and was still lying on the track. Just as he was approaching the finishing tape and with his supporters' cheers ringing in his ears, he stopped, turned around, went back to the fallen athlete, helped him to his feet and the two of them proceeded and crossed the line together. It was a spontaneous gesture filled with love and humility that could teach us a lot about what's important in life.

I was really moved by the many photos in the newspapers, during the week of the Special Olympics, of the bear hugs enjoyed by the athletes and their coaches and volunteers. You could almost feel the squeeze in some of those pictures and the joy in the achievement. And that pure joy seemed to be shared in equal measure by the athletes and their coaches. I was reading about a swimming coach from County Mayo who said he felt privileged to be a part of the whole Special Needs swimming programme. He says it's his passion and the most rewarding, enriching thing he will ever do in his life. He reckons that whatever you put into the coaching you get ten times as much out of it. It would put you in mind once again of the words of Saint Francis of Assisi: 'It is in giving that we receive'.

Ask any of the 30,000 volunteers who gave of their time training and being briefed before the Games and performing many and varied tasks during that week and they'll tell you that they got at least as much out of the whole experience as they put into it. Ask the people in the host towns who went to no end of trouble to make the delegations' first few days in the country memorable and comfortable and who, as I said earlier, opened their hearts and their homes to the visitors. They all seemed to feel the time went too quickly. They were sorry to see the athletes and their coaches leave. They also found the experience a very enriching one.

The bottom line is that these Special Olympians have opened the eyes of the community at large to a different way of viewing life and the world we live in. I was chatting with a friend about the difference the Special Olympics made. The main thing she gained was an ease about interacting with people with special needs. She admitted that she used to feel a bit awkward; not sure what to say, not wanting to put the person under pressure to respond or to make them feel anxious. The events of June have made her see that they are not under pressure in company, that they have a powerfully positive outlook on life and that they enrich the lives of the people they come in contact with because their good humour is infectious. To put it simply, people with special needs may have different gifts and qualities to us but gifts and qualities they are none the less. Their own families were already aware of this but they had a hard job convincing the rest of us that it's wrong to focus on disability where there is so much ability in evidence. It's a pity that we can't all be so full of joy and take such pleasure out of life and be so spontaneous and guileless in our dealings with others.

It really is a question of recognising that there are many different ways of achieving which are worthy of celebration. It's also a question of making sure the momentum generated by the Games is harnessed so that the State recognises the rights of this sector of our society and makes funding available so that people with special needs and their families can have basic civil rights. Eunice Shriver pulled no punches during her speech at the opening ceremony when she said it just wasn't good enough for the government to plead lack of available funds. You could just imagine what her response to that excuse might be; 'Well go find them!' She's some woman; she's a doer, full of energy and commitment. The same can be said of the people of Ireland who pulled out all the stops to make these Games the phenomenal success they were: the organisers, the host town committees and the volunteers.

To be fair to the government, everybody acknowledges that the personal efforts of the Taoiseach were highly instrumental in bringing the Special Olympics to Ireland. Ask any of the host town committees though and they'll tell you that the follow through was sadly lacking. Many of them felt let down by the agencies of the State and had to plug unforeseen gaps themselves. They put their frustrations and grievances on hold though and they fundraised some more, they volunteered some more because they were determined that the Games would be perfect. And they were. These people have all seen first hand the qualities and the achievements of people with special needs. They've also seen first hand the short-comings of the State in providing for them. They've got votes and they have to use them now to put pressure on the powers that be, to face up to their responsibilities with regard to this very special sector of society. It was very heartening to read at the end of July that the government has earmarked 50 million euro for people with disabilities.

During that spectacular and uplifting opening ceremony, Nelson Mandela referred to the athletes as 'ambassadors of the greatness of humankind'. He said: 'You inspire us to know that all obstacles to human achievement are surmountable. Your achievements remind us of the potential for greatness that resides in every one of us. May the world learn from your example'.

There can be no doubt, after the Special Olympics, that the obstacles to human achievement are very definitely surmountable. The Games were a major learning experience for all of us and it was a mark of the 'potential for greatness' that resides in those athletes that so many well-known and well respected people from the worlds of sport and entertainment and politics gave their time to make that Midsummer's Night in Croke Park, such a memorable occasion. Another person who springs to mind when I think of surmounting obstacles and achieving a huge amount against all odds, while adding to and improving the lives of many children is Christina Noble. I'll talk more about Christina in the following chapter.

The Fame Game

I've been fascinated by Christina Noble since the time many years ago that her autobiography was about to be published and I read parts of it which were serialised in the *Sunday Independent*. I couldn't wait for *Bridge Across My Sorrows* to hit the bookshelves and I read it with a mixture of admiration for this woman and all she achieved, and shock at the horrific circumstances of her early life. She was one of four children and grew up in poverty in the Liberties in Dublin. Her mother died when she was ten. I'll never forget Christina's account of standing on tiptoe outside the hospital window to have a last look at her mother in her hospital bed. It was heartbreaking. So too was the fact that after her mother's death, the children were taken into care and Christina spent four years in an institution in Clifden convinced that her siblings were dead. She escaped by jumping out a first floor window and made her way to Dublin where she dug a hole for herself under trees in the Phoenix Park and lived there for a number of months. She was raped during this time, became pregnant and was forced to give her baby son up for adoption. My heart was aching for this young girl as I was reading this account of her life and realising once again that I had a charmed upbringing. We were happy and secure and so well loved and looked after. I never thought while I was reading *Bridge Across My Sorrows* that I would one day meet Christina Noble and be able to tell her how much I admired her then and still do. She went on to have three other children with her first husband whom she married in England. That was a violent marriage and ended in divorce. Her second marriage ended amicably as she and her husband outgrew each other. That this woman not only survived all that tragedy and trauma but went on to found the Christina Noble Foundation which has so far improved the lives of 140 thousand needy children in Vietnam and Mongolia puts her in a class of her own. She had a hard life, she suffered ill health but when it comes to speaking up for the children that need help, she's confident, forthright and determined. She was a guest on *Open House* when her second book, *Mama Tina*, a sequel to *Bridge Across My Sorrows* was published and I was delighted to meet her, having followed her story from the beginning. She's a warm, friendly person who talks at length about the children. She asked me all about my children and she signed a copy of *Mama Tina* for me. She drew a smiley face and wrote: 'Every child has the right to sleep on their pillow with peace and security around them'. I met Christina again a couple of years later when I was presenting The People of The Year Awards and she was a recipient. She's been honoured with 22 national and international awards, the latest being an OBE presented to her by Prince Charles last February. An amazing woman.

One of the by products of working in television is the number of well-known people you meet. I could have said one of the 'perks', but I deliberately chose not to, because I have a horror of people being categorised by the fact that they are in the public eye. The job they do gives them a profile and the profile increases the public awareness of them and what they do but that doesn't make anyone a better or worse person. There are great people in every walk of life, from the inconspicuous to the world famous and all are equally important. What I like about *Open*

House is the opportunity it gives us to celebrate both extremes. There is no doubt though that people are fascinated with the big names. I'm constantly asked, 'What's so and so really like' about people I come across through my work and I can honestly say that the bigger the star, the easier they are to work with. There's no evidence of a giant ego wanting a bit of extra exposure. They tend to approach the task professionally, arrive on time, deliver and realise that everyone around is there to do a job too, less high profile perhaps but equally valuable. A good example of this professionalism involves Terry Wogan. When he was at the height of his fame in the UK, an Irish film crew went over to him to do an interview for Irish TV. When it was finished, Terry went off to a production meeting for his TV show which was on five nights a week at that time. Meanwhile, the Irish crew discovered when they were checking the tape that they had pictures but no sound. This was obviously a big problem. There was nothing for it but to go back to Terry and explain the situation in the hope that he'd be able to repeat the interview before going on air because they had a flight back to Dublin that evening. Now you'd be forgiven for thinking that Terry Wogan needed to redo that interview like he needed a hole in the head. He didn't have much time, because he was preparing for his TV show in a couple of hours. He couldn't have been nicer though. He agreed to do it again after his production meeting and when he arrived into the room not only was he pleasant and smiling but he quipped; 'Don't know what it is about me guys, electronic equipment and me don't seem to sit easily together. Now, where were we?' You can imagine how relieved the sound engineer was to hear him talk like that. The people skills and the sense of humour he displays on air are also there when he's not broadcasting. I think that's the key to why people like Terry Wogan achieve such public recognition. They're talented, they have a genuine interest and concern for people and they are therefore not pretending to be something they're not. They respect the contribution of every member of the broadcasting team and therefore they're not wrapped up in their own self-importance. Let's face it, no matter how big the star, if the camera, sound, lighting and other team members are not onside, that big star can fail to shine brightly.

Over the years, I have certainly met some big names as they say and I can safely say that in most cases, the bigger the name the less pretentious the person. Daniel O'Donnell is a good example. We celebrated his fortieth birthday on *Open House* with a special programme in his honour. There was a studio audience and the numbers of applications for tickets astounded us. We could have filled the Point Theatre, not to mention studio one in Montrose. In the weeks prior to the programme, there were phone calls backwards and forwards from the office to Daniel and he was helpful, good humoured and obliging always; nothing was too much trouble. And on the day of the programme, there was no doubt as to why he's such a huge star. First of all, he's got the talent, but as well as that he's got an amazing rapport with his fans. We've all heard the stories of him staying back after concerts, talking to the fans and remembering all their names. Well it's true. I was amazed at the way he could recall so many names. During the commercial breaks, he was up off the couch and down in the audience, chatting to people he'd spotted, genuinely interested in how they were. Another important aspect of Daniel's life is the support he has given to the Romanian orphanage he took under his wing. He has fundraised tirelessly and as well as improving the conditions in the original building which were appalling when he first visited, he has built a house so that teenaged orphans can experience some independent living before leaving the confines of the orphanage and moving out into the world. The house is called Kincasslagh . . . a little bit of Donegal in Romania. We had a surprise for Daniel for his fortieth. The cake was wheeled into studio by three of the children from that Romanian orphanage. We flew them in for the occasion and Daniel knew nothing about it. He was bowled over and thrilled to see them. That tribute pro-gramme was a fundraising opportunity as well because we put the number of the bank account for Daniel's Romanian appeal onscreen and people phoned in their contributions and you couldn't but be generous if you saw the way he hugged those three children. Also in the audience that day, along with Daniel's mother Julia and his sister Margo, was a woman called Majella, a friend who was very relaxed and obviously got on very well with the family. Little did we realise that romance was in the air. She was a lovely friendly person and is now the envy of many thousands of women since she's become Mrs Daniel O'Donnell.

That generosity of spirit, epitomised by Daniel, is a feature of many well-known people who give a lot of time and energy to helping others. Bill Cullen, Renault boss comes to mind immediately. We're all familiar with his rags to riches story. I love the bit about selling oranges outside Croke Park on All Ireland Sundays when he was a young lad. When the fruit was all sold, he'd hire out the orange boxes to people without tickets so they could look over the wall. Then, after the match, he'd chop up the boxes and sell them as firewood. The future entrepreneur was clearly visible from a young age. We also all know that he bought Renault for £1 and that the company came with £18,000,000 worth of debts, which he successfully turned to profit and has become a very wealthy and well-known man. He's been a guest on *Open House* and once again, it was an enjoyable, hassle free experience. He's obliging, agreeable and patient and appreciative of other people's concerns and requirements. So much so that he gives a huge amount of time and energy working on behalf of less fortunate people. Remembering his humble beginnings, he works tirelessly on behalf of the Irish Youth Foundation, raising massive amounts of money to give young people a bit of a start. I see the work he does at first hand every Christmas when the Renault Sports Awards take place. He and Cecil Whelan and the golfer Des Smyth, are all involved in the Links Golf Society and they put great effort into organising the night which honours sports people and raises money for the Irish Youth Foundation. And then there's the Celebrity Bowling night he organises and lots of other functions throughout the year, all with a view to giving something back. I admire him greatly for that and my goodness, I'm not alone, because if there's one person who can fill a room with 'celebs' to raise money for his charity, it's Bill Cullen. It's a measure of the high regard that he and Cecil and Des are held in, that the sports awards are such a huge success every year.

The more I think about it; it's those kind of people that stand out in my mind. They're famous certainly but the answer to the question 'what are they like?' is invariably 'Grand. Nice people. No nonsense.' They don't trade on their celebrity status. They're not looking for special treatment because of who they are. They're comfortable with who and what they are. Because they're talented, well balanced people who haven't lost the run of themselves.

Look at Ronan Keating. He had fame thrust upon him from a young impressionable age and it's to his credit that it didn't go to his head. In fact he seems to get more and more laid back all the time. I remember presenting him with a Rehab Person of the Year award a couple of years ago and he was calm, cool and delighted to be honoured. He turned up for his rehearsal like everybody else, although the purpose of the rehearsal is to give people who wouldn't be used to television a run through beforehand. He's a huge pop star but he's not showy. I can't imagine him sending in a long list of requirements for his dressing room as a lot of pop stars do. There are, of course, essentials that have to be provided but I've seen visiting celebs listing industrial quantities of things like goat's milk and passion fruit and all sorts for their dressing room. There's a funny story about a rock band from abroad, visiting Dublin. It must have been their first time in Ireland because they requested, among other things, cases of best vintage local wine. The concert organisers thought long and hard and left some six packs of Guinness in their dressing rooms! Ronan Keating uses his fame to help others too. There was great excitement in villages and towns throughout the country last summer when he walked from Malin Head to Mizen Head raising money for the breast cancer programme he founded in memory of his mother, who died a few years ago. I was in a hotel in Tipperary a few days after he'd gone through and everybody was talking about how unaffected he was, how obliging he was when it came to photographs and autographs. They described him as ordinary and there's no doubt that it was said as a compliment.

D.J. Carey is another one. A huge star, as good a hurler as we've ever seen. People falling over themselves to share his airspace, sought after for sporting and other functions and once again, no 'notions of upperosisty', to quote Sean O'Casey. I've never interviewed him on *Up for the Match* for the simple reason that Kilkenny have been All Ireland finalists every year but one that I've presented the programme. He has however, been a guest on *Open House* on more than one occasion and there's always great excitement among the other guests when they hear he'll be in. He has time for everybody, a word, a smile, an autograph, a photo. He likes to give a bit back as well and was in Calcutta early this year on a Goal fact-finding mission. He was happy to oblige when John O'Shea collared him and asked him to come on board. He went over and was so impressed with the work Goal is doing to educate the street children that he's been highlighting it since his return. This is a man who has a career, a family, and a training schedule that would make you wilt at the thought of it. If you want something done, ask a busy person to do it for you.

For further examples of the truth of that adage, we need look no further than Adi Roche and Ali Hewson who, since the horrific nuclear accident in Chernobyl in 1986, have dedicated so much of their lives to improving the lot of the children of Belarus who were born into a contaminated world. Adi is like a dynamo running on a long-life battery. She has an energising effect on people around her and is always grateful for the aid given by the Irish public. She's good fun too. Always ready for a laugh. I remember being onstage with her at the end of the Trilogy fashion show in the RDS just before last Christmas and no sooner had she begun her speech thanking everybody for their support than she swallowed a fly. It kind of took her breath away! We'd seen it buzzing around the stage and both of us knew instantly what had happened but she soldiered on with the odd cough and splutter. She laughed about it afterwards though and when we've met since, she'll be the one to bring it up joking about the fact that she's a vegetarian and that the fly was therefore alien to her system in more ways than one. She doesn't take herself too seriously; enjoys a good laugh and at the same time is working in a harrowing environment a lot of the time and giving hope to a whole generation of Russian children. Adi's dynamism and Ali's serenity complement each other very well. Ali too has given a lot of time and energy to the Chernobyl Children's Project. That alongside rearing four children, taking a University degree and being married to one of the world's biggest rock stars, which has to involve a lot of travelling and meeting people. Ali is a quiet, gentle, extremely friendly woman who never makes a fuss, never seeks to be treated differently because of who she is. Quite the opposite in fact. She strikes me as somebody who feels a sense of responsibility, because of her privileged position, to look to the needs of others who need help. Aren't we lucky to have people like that in our world?

John Hume has dedicated his life to the people of Northern Ireland. He's been prominent in Northern politics since the civil rights campaigns of 1969 and has never tired of working on behalf of his fellow man. He was born to it in a way. I remember him telling me in an interview for a radio programme called *Words and Music* about his father being the person on the street who would write letters for the neighbours who couldn't read or write. There'd be people in the house always having some document or other deciphered and replied to. John obviously followed in his father's footsteps and felt the urge to speak up for the disadvantaged. It was during that radio programme many years ago that I realised John Hume has a great love of singing and also has a lovely singing voice himself. I've heard him sing *The Town I loved so well* with its composer Phil Coulter accompanying him at the piano and the passion for Derry is palpable. In his political life, his work for peace and justice in Northern Ireland, John Hume has known a lot of frustration, disappointment and heartbreak and yet he's never lost his sense of fun and love of a good singsong and a bit of craic.

Rolf Harris was a guest during the first season of *Open House* and he entertained everybody at home and in studio with his incredible sense of fun and his energy. He drew a caricature of me while he was chatting and he laughed and joked and sang at the same time. His warmth is infectious. It's hard not to feel the clouds lift when someone like that is around. The warmth of their personalities passes a positive vibe to the people they meet.

That's certainly true of President McAleese. She oozes warmth and it's amazing to watch the smiles on everyone's face when she walks into a room. She was a guest on *Open House* also. We did a special programme for Saint Patrick's Day one year and we were delighted when President McAleese accepted our invitation to be a guest. It was funny really because when she walked into studio she was wearing a lilac suit. And so was I. It wasn't a problem at all though. She just said 'Snap' and joked that we were obviously both up to the minute with that season's colours. It really is nice to meet these people who have such a high profile, who work hard and achieve well and who don't give the impression that they should be treated as better than others because of their position.

It was a great thrill for me to meet Meryl Streep when she was over for the premiere of the film version of *Dancing at Lughnasa* at the Savoy. There was a party afterwards in Dublin Castle at which Marty and I were guests of Tyrone

Productions. I was struck by her serenity, the delicacy of her features and those amazing cheekbones. She was chatty and warm and has a lovely giggly laugh.

Gabriel Byrne was the guest speaker one year when I was presenting the Press Photographer of the Year Awards and we had a great chat about teaching Irish. He's one of the few people I've met who, like myself, actually enjoyed Peig Sayers's autobiography, *Peig*. We exchanged anecdotes about the different reactions of students to her memoirs. We were both teaching in Dublin secondary schools, he in Crumlin and I in Clondalkin and this woman's adventures in the first half of the twentieth century on the Dingle peninsula and the Great Blasket held very little attraction for those city teenagers. He's a very down-to-earth man and good company.

Maybe that's the key to the success of these well-known people. They don't lose sight of the important things in life. They realise that connecting with others is what gives us a sense of belonging. As Mitch Albom says in his book *Tuesdays with Morrie*: 'The most important thing in life is to learn how to give out love, and to let it come in . . . Love is the only rational act'. In this country it's hard to find anybody better known than Gay Byrne and a gentler man you would be hard pressed to find. For many years, when I was working part-time in RTÉ I'd pass him by on the corridor and I knew he wouldn't have a clue who I was but he would always, always smile and say 'Hello'. When I was chosen to present the Eurovision, he stopped me outside the studio building one evening and wished me well and told me to make sure I enjoyed every minute of it. I hadn't been really thinking 'enjoyment' up to that point. More 'challenge' and 'nerve wracking experience' really. That encounter gave me a new perspective and great encouragement. Gay Byrne has always been encouraging of other presenters and a most gracious co-presenter. As recently as last summer he and I were filming together and the opening sequence involved the pair of us walking and talking to camera. The script was divided between the two of us. I left out a piece of my script and once Gay realised his immediate reaction was to dig me out. He turned to me in a conversational manner and just said 'And wasn't there something else we wanted to tell folk about that?' which immediately jogged my memory and came across as the most natural interchange imaginable. He didn't try to score a point. He doesn't have to. He's extremely professional and secure in himself. What you see is what you get.

That's another key aspect of those well-known people. They're not trying to be something they're not. As I say, what you see is what you get. They do their job and want to make life easy for those working around them. It's great to be able to say with my hand on my heart that such is the case with the vast majority of people that I meet through this job that I do. And there is no good reason why it should be otherwise. They're famous, they're sought after, but their focus is outward not inwards towards themselves. Great people like Brendan O'Carroll who has a huge heart, is extremely kind and always helping others out. Brian Kennedy who is always obliging and if he can do something for you, he will, without any hesitation. Niall Quinn, who was the Rehab Person of the Year last year and who couldn't have been more open and honest during our interview, saying that he deeply regretted not volunteering to take a penalty against Spain during the World Cup. He said he should have and had sleepless nights thinking about the younger guys who did and about his responsibility to step forward as the pater familias among them. And there are many more. Those that I have spoken of are an example of what I mean when I say that my answer to that question 'What's so and so REALLY like?' is, for the most part, 'Grand. No nonsense.' There are so many other people who are also like that. I think it's a nice quality in this country that our famous people are well grounded and haven't as they say 'lost the run of themselves'.

Taming the Tigers

It's ten o'clock in the morning. I'm sitting in front of the computer at home. It's not a pretty sight. I'm dressed in a sweatshirt, old tracksuit bottoms and flip-flops and I haven't even 'run a comb through my hair' as my mother used to say. I hope the style police don't call to my door. If they do they'll be looking for the award back. Like I said earlier, I dress to suit the occasion and to be perfectly honest, this is not a stylish occasion or setting. I was at the computer till late last night and my first task when I came downstairs this morning was to clear away the cups and water glasses that I'd accumulated during yesterday's session. And to clear a path through the books and papers that are littering the floor around the computer. I was just too tired to do that before I went to bed. I slept well and I feel refreshed but I know that in a while the stiffness on the left side of my neck and lower back will return and my arms will feel heavy just above the elbows. When this is all over, I'll be on to my friend who's doing her final assessment in aromatherapy massage. We've buoyed each other up these past few months. You see both of us would be used to having our summers free. She's a secondary teacher and for me the *Open House* season finishes around Easter, so when we were feeling miserable about having to sacrifice the summer to our projects, we'd convince each other that it would be worth it in the end. I think we'll have a joint celebration after all of this. Not before she's eased out my aching back though.

The house is very quiet, because it's the end of the summer and the children are still asleep. They seem to sleep later and later in the mornings as the summer holidays progress. Not much evidence of summer though as I look out the window to the back garden. It's raining again and the shed door is blowing open. That reminds me, I have to put a wash on and I have to take meat out of the freezer for tomorrow's dinner. I'll look forward to those two chores when it's time for my first coffee break. Yes, you heard right. I'm actually looking forward to putting on a wash and taking meat out of the freezer. In fact, when I go out to the shed, I'll be itching to start clearing it out because it hasn't been sorted since the children and I moved into this house almost a year ago now. But that's a treat I'm reserving for when this book is all finished. All those normal domestic pursuits that I do automatically most of the time but which have been done in a rush and fitted in around my writing this past while, are beckoning and I'm really looking forward to indulging myself in some good scrubbin'! They may be mundane and it may not be fashionable to admit this but, as I said in an earlier chapter, they're therapeutic and physical and give a great sense of satisfaction when they're accomplished.

At least I'm not missing out on good weather. It's pretty grey and dismal out there but when I need a bit of lift, I just look at the wall above the computer at a super enlarged and nicely framed photograph that was taken by one of my fellow trekkers, Donal Powers, while we were in Eritrea last year. He gave it to me as a gift for leading the trek and I was really touched by his generosity and the beautiful job he made of enlarging and framing it. It's got such a positive vibe, that photo. In the background are the high mountains reaching into a clear blue sky and you know my thoughts about the uplifting effect that mountains can have on the old psyche. In the foreground, there's a local farmer and me with his donkey whose load shows again the benefits of the water systems installed with the help of Irish aid. In the wooden box on the donkey's back are big ripe lemons and on top, the green leaves of a healthy crop. You can almost feel the heat just by looking at the photo. I love the fact that when I look up from the computer I'm transported back to that time in Eritrea.

I've already said how special that trip was for me and I truly feel that our lives are enriched when we bite the bullet and take on new challenges. It took effort to get to Africa last year, a lot of juggling and a lot of organising, not to mention having those injections that I had nightmares about for weeks beforehand. I've had a mental block about needles since I was brought to the dispensary as a very young child for the usual booster shots and the woman doctor dismissed my tears by reassuring me, in what I remember as a shrill and posh tone, that it would be 'just like the sting of a nettle!' I could have fallen into and rolled around in a bed of nettles and it wouldn't have been as painful as her administration of that injection into my arm. So you can understand why the series of shots necessary for travel to Eritrea was a bit off putting. There were times, in the run up to the trip, that I felt it would be easier not to go but I'm glad I did and my wish in writing this book is that there may be people reading these accounts of various episodes in my life, who will say to themselves, 'Well if she can do it so can I' or 'It wasn't a doddle for her either. I'll give it a go'. These are my stories and I believe that by sharing stories we give each other courage and a better understanding of hope and also of the human spirit. It's obvious at this stage that Amelia

Earhart is a woman I admire greatly and I find her thoughts about courage a great inspiration to face those paper tigers, those fears, and to strive for the heart's desire in spite of them.

> Courage is the price that Life exacts for granting peace,
> The soul that knows it not, knows no release
> From little things.

We all underestimate our abilities and our resilience and we all need a boost and a leg up from time to time, somebody to say quite simply 'Go for it'.

She goes on:

> Each time we make a choice, we pay
> With courage to behold the restless day,
> And count it fair.

If someone told me six months ago that I would be sitting at this computer, writing the final chapter to a book, I'd have told them to get off the stage. Me? Write a book? Not a chance. For goodness sake, I only learned how to use this machine after Easter last year, when I decided to record my thoughts and feelings about my mother's death and my memories of my childhood. This was an exercise undertaken for my children. I wanted them to have a record of what my childhood had been like. We'd spoken about bits and pieces of it over the years but in a haphazard way. Then I was telling the story to a friend and he asked if I'd ever thought of writing it down. The answer to that was an emphatic 'No!' 'Who me?' I came up with all the excuses that we use when something that we're not used to presents itself. Where would I start? Where would I find the time? What would I say? Then one evening, I was cutting the grass and I started thinking about the whole thing again. I decided to sit at the computer, tell nobody what I was doing and see what happened. It happened. The memories and the feelings were there and I just put them down on paper. I started to enjoy myself and for the next four days I added a bit whenever I had some spare time. When it was finished I printed off several copies, tied them with ribbon and gave them to the children with all my love. And that was that. Until I came back from Rosslare that year, the first without my mother being with us and felt the urge to record my memories of other years. And that was that. Until I came home from a Mass in Clondalkin church that November in memory of the people of the parish who had died during the year and felt the urge to write about it. And that very definitely was that. Christmas was coming and life was very busy and writing was the last thing on my mind.

I had enjoyed those three bouts though and what strikes me now as I remember them is that they were all sparked by a desire to hold onto the memory of my mother and her place in my life. I've already said, in the first months after she died, I had a real sense of her closeness, her presence around me. That was replaced after about six months by a sense of loss, of emptiness. I used to be able to remember exactly how Mam sounded, for instance, when she answered the phone. That voice was fading. So was the smell of her Aran cardigan that I had retrieved from the clothes recycling bin. That loss made me feel a bit panicky for a while and I did everything I could to keep those memories alive in my head. I didn't want to lose that contact, that sense of her presence. This summer has given way to a whole new phase in this grieving process. A realisation that she is gone from this life and that she is not coming back. Even writing that down is difficult. There have been many moments during this summer when I just wanted to ask my mother's advice, to tell her my problems, to cry on her shoulder, but the bottom line is that's no longer an option. The realisation of that is horrible and led to awful bouts of sadness in the early part of the summer. I couldn't put my finger on the reasons why I was feeling such cold miserable lethargy. I found it very hard to summon up enthusiasm for anything and wondered when this black cloud would lift. I remember drinking coffee in the conservatory with a good friend and feeling very close to tears. The weather didn't help mind you. It was a dull, drizzly, chilly day in May, in the middle of a run of similar days. My friend's mother died several years ago and she related to that feeling of finality that hit her after about two years, that yearning to be able to confide, to ask advice, to be mothered again. We talked for ages about that, we compared experiences and as I said earlier, it's by sharing stories that we give each other courage and hope. I wasn't jumping for joy after she left but I felt better for her visit and I know many people will relate to that feeling. I felt I could cope. It's such a shame when we hold our worries and our grief inside because the human condition is one that responds well to sharing with others. I hope that people will feel a bit better for reading this book in the same way that I felt better after that visit from my friend last May.

It's been an interesting experience, writing a book. Some days I sat at the computer and it rattled along. Other times, it was like looking into a ditch where there was nothing happening. On those days, I bemoaned the fact that I'd ever accepted the invitation. Having the summer to get it done seemed like an age at the time, but the time passes very quickly and there's a certain amount of discipline involved. I brought the computer down to Rosslare this summer and began each day with four hours writing from 6.00 to 10.00 a.m. The conversation at the breakfast table invariably revolved around what I'd written that morning. Everybody threw in their tuppence worth and my brother John is convinced that *War and Peace* didn't take this long. Yeah right! Even if that were true, Tolstoy didn't have to make sandwiches for picnics and cook meals and wash and iron clothes at the same time. For me, life went on and I cursed that alarm clock when it went off at 5.30 each morning in Rosslare.

I used a laptop in the south of France. That was hard for two reasons. For a start, the keys are very close together and I made so many typing errors which frustrated me and that I felt the need to correct. Once a teacher, always a teacher. The other hard part about spending three hours at a computer while the sun is beaming is evident I would have thought. I was sitting in the shade, looking at the sun and wishing I was out there enjoying it. Still, I'm glad I wrote that week because the thoughts that struck me while I was there and which I wrote about might not have seen the light of day otherwise.

What's between the covers of this book are stories about some of the things in my life that I hope will trigger memories for people who read them. Some of them are about ordinary, everyday occurrences, others are about more unusual events, but I believe the benefit of stories is that they touch our soul and make us feel human. They make us realise that we share so much in common. The ways in which we react to events in our lives can differ and that's the ultimate human freedom. I was very touched by a story I read about a man in a Nazi concentration camp during the Second World War. No matter what cruelty was meted out to him, he continued to smile. He always shared his food with others and when his captors noticed this, they reduced his rations to dissuade him. Yet he continued to share, no matter how meagre the amount. When asked why he persisted, he pointed out that, although he was in captivity, he still had a very important freedom; the freedom to chose his attitude to that set of circumstances. He chose his own way and it was a way of love, kindness and forgiveness.

For me, this summer of writing has been a chance to celebrate, through stories, the way we live our lives, the fact that we do our best for ourselves and for others, to make this world a good place. The writer, Jean Houston summed it up well when she said 'Storying is living and dynamic. Stories exist to be exchanged. They are the currency of human growth'. That's certainly true in my case anyway because at the beginning of the summer I felt very unsure, shy and embarrassed almost at the thought of writing a book. I was afraid people would think it very pretentious of me; that there'd be a 'who does she think she is' reaction. I was so self-conscious of the whole thing that during a magazine interview at the end of the *Open House* season, when I was asked if I had any projects lined up for the summer, I muttered something about doing the garden. I just couldn't bring myself to utter the words, 'I'm writing a book'. As I began putting words down I kept thinking about other people who I felt would have more interesting stories to tell. They should be writing a book. Then I came to terms with the fact that we all have interesting stories because we are all living different lives and that since I was asked to write, why not enjoy it. From that moment on I've felt comfortable with the whole idea. It's been hard work and I'm looking forward to writing 'The End' and having a break from this computer but it's been worth it. For me, it's definitely been a time of reflection and acceptance. I sincerely hope that people who read these stories will get enjoyment from them, consolation sometimes and maybe even inspiration to try something different in their lives.

When I think back to the beginning of the book and the photograph of that eight-year-old girl with her grand-mother, the things that were in store for her in her future years, the good, the bad, the happy, the sad, I realise that the important thing is to embrace life, to do our best and to try to have a positive outlook. That doesn't mean we're going to be happy all the time but it does mean that we recognise sadness as part of our lives because we have known joy. And joy tends to have a knock on effect.